L. L. Bean, Inc.
Spring 1971

L. L. B...
Spring...

L. L. Bean, Inc.
Fall 1973

L.L.Bean™
Spring 1976

L.L.Bean
Spring 1978

L.L.Bean®
Fall 1979

L.L.Bean

L.L.Bean

The Making of an American Icon

Leon Gorman

Harvard Business School Press

Boston, Massachusetts

Thanks to jacket designer David Ekizian, sketch artist Lauren Rudy, and company photographer Alan Boutot.

Printed in the United States of America

10 09 08 07 06   5 4 3 2 1

978-1-57851-183-9 (ISBN 13)

Library of Congress Cataloging-in-Publication Data

Gorman, Leon A.
    L.L. Bean : the making of an American icon / Leon Gorman.
      p. cm.
    ISBN 1-57851-183-6
  1. L.L. Bean, Inc. 2. Camping equipment industry — United States. 3. Mail-order business — United States. I. Title.
    HD9993.C354L1828 2006
    381'.4579654 — dc22

                                                        2006011142

The paper used in this publication meets the minimum requirements of the American National Standard for Information Sciences — Permanence of Paper for Printed Library Materials, ANSI Z39.48-1992.

To all the great L.L.Bean people,

past and present,

who helped make the icon.

Contents

Contents

Part Four: 1991–2000

Acknowledgments

HEARTFELT THANKS to my wife, Lisa, for her steady support and forthright advice throughout the tenure of this project. Grateful recognition to Kent Lineback for his exceptional storytelling skills and great insight into the evolving story of L.L.Bean. And special thanks to L.L.Bean's Brenda Markee and Beth LeBlanc for their heroic administrative efforts that kept the train on the track.

All of these people were critical to whatever success the book enjoys, as were the voices of our interviewees. Their participation was representative of the many substantial contributions they have made to the success of L.L.Bean over the years.

Thanks also to the folks at Harvard Business School Press, who came up with the idea in the first place and patiently awaited its completion.

The list goes on. So many have participated in the L.L. story: customers, employees, family, vendors, friends, and neighbors in our various communities. Thanks to you all.

Preface

LEON L. BEAN was my grandfather. Back in the early 1900s he had a hunting camp in the Haynesville Woods in northern Maine, one of many such camps he'd had in various parts of the state during his lifetime. He and his cronies had some tongue-in-cheek rules of conduct posted in the camp. The last rule, number 7, admonished, "If you get lost, come straight back to camp."

I've always seen the values of the L.L.Bean company and the L.L. story as our camp and our place to go back to whenever we seemed to be going astray.

L.L. was born in the Oxford Hills country of western Maine in 1872. His father was a horse trader. Orphaned at the age of twelve, L.L. grew up working on the farms of various family friends and relatives. He managed to complete the eighth grade. His main enjoyment in growing up and in his adult years was hunting, fishing, and life in Maine's great outdoors. But his first forty years, as he himself once said, were "otherwise uneventful."

All of a sudden the light went on. In 1912 his latent Yankee ingenuity combined with his many years' experience in tramping the Maine woods. L.L. came up with a new and improved design for a hunting boot with a leather top and a rubber bottom. He successfully tested his design in the field and immediately decided that every other hunter should have a pair. He founded our company, and the foundation was his new Maine Hunting Shoe. He borrowed some money from his brother Otho and offered the shoe in a three-page catalog of his own creation, which he mailed to a list of nonresident hunters he had acquired from Maine's Fish and Game Department.

According to corporate lore, 90 of the first 100 pair sold came back as defective. The uppers tore away from the bottoms. L.L. refunded his customers' money, perfected his boot design, borrowed another $400 from his brother, and started all over again. This time with complete success.

L.L. learned four lessons from this experience (in addition to staying out of debt in the future) that enabled his growth over the years and form the core values and brand attributes of L.L.Bean today.

- To sell fully tested, high-quality products of the best functional value

- To provide superior and personal customer service backed by a 100 percent satisfaction guarantee

- To write honest, straightforward catalog and advertising copy that builds trust and mutual respect with customers

- To sell through the catalog channel that can reach a national market from Maine and its outdoors heritage

L.L. died in 1967 at the ripe old age of ninety-four and he'd enjoyed every minute of his life. Business and pleasure in the Maine outdoors had all been the same for him. He was a legend in his own time, and he'd established a reputation for integrity and reliability as broad in its appeal and as enduring in its acceptance as any in marketing history.

This is the "L.L. story" that I refer to throughout this book. It's a story about trust and reliability and perseverance, about a genuine American hero, hard work, and a happy ending. There is, of course, a lot more depth and richness and humanity to L.L.'s complete story. But this is the nub of it.

The L.L. story is also a parable from which we've drawn various lessons or values throughout my years running L.L.'s company, and it's a story that's proven ever relevant to millions and millions of people over these years. You won't understand L.L.Bean or what we're about if you don't understand the story. It's what sets us apart from all the others. Not just that we have a story, but that we live by it.

Preface

I wrote the book at the request of the Harvard Business School Press. They felt the L.L. story and its evolution had iconic merit for the business reader as well as the general reader. I agreed. Kent Lineback was a critical help in pulling it all together. He also interviewed the off-stage voices you hear throughout the book. Information on each is in the section titled "Voices." They kept us honest in our reflections, and this is a lot of what it's all about.

PART ONE

1960–1967

Bean Boot

1

L.L. Gives Me a Job

I WAS HONORABLY DISCHARGED from active duty in the U.S. Navy on 3 May 1960. I'd served as a line officer on destroyers for three years, the last one being spent on a destroyer escort training ship for Naval reservists home-ported out of Portland, Maine. My years in the service had been a wonderful experience in seeing the world and in learning to lead a division of sailors. Now it was time to do something else.

My discharge process took place at the Brunswick Naval Air Station in Brunswick, Maine. Brunswick is also home to Bowdoin College, where I had graduated four years earlier. I stopped at the college on the way home after my discharge. I was hoping the placement director, Sam Ladd, might have some ideas about where I could get a job. Sam suggested I stop in Freeport on my way home and talk to my grandfather. He was Leon L. Bean, and he ran a small but well-known catalog company and retail store located there. Sam saw a lot more opportunity there than I did and perked up my interest. Maybe L.L. had something for me to do.

Freeport in 1960 was a shoe factory town of about five thousand people. Big arching elm trees still lined Main Street, which was also Route 1—and, until a few years before my arrival, the only way into

Maine. During the tourist season it was bumper-to-bumper traffic all summer long. By 1960 they'd built a turnpike as well as a Route 1 bypass around Freeport. Worried about losing store traffic, L.L. had put a map in his catalog showing Freeport, the bypass, and the turnpike, saying you could save $1.05, without spending any more time, by not taking either and still coming directly through Freeport.

I had worked two summers at "Bean's" when I was going to school. The first summer I helped a fellow named Delet Moody doing odd jobs around the company. This included attending to parking in our small lot, receiving freight, and picking high-bush blueberries on L.L.'s farm outside of town.

The second summer I worked in the retail store. Most people new to the store in those days started by selling shoes because it was a "gofer" job. You kept going for more and more pairs until you found a fit. If somebody asked you a question about the shoes or boots, there was usually a seasoned clerk handy to answer the question. Eventually you learned the footwear line. If you started waiting on a customer for shoes and they wanted some clothing, you went with them to the clothing department. Then if they wanted some camping gear, you went with them over there. It turned out to be a very personal shopping experience for the customer, even though we weren't very well trained.

When there was nothing going on in footwear, you just hung out in a corner away from the fishing department. The scariest part was to get asked for help in fishing tackle, because all sorts of special knowledge and experience were required. At the time I didn't fish, nor did most of the salesclerks. We were ignorant of the product line and didn't want to be embarrassed with a customer. Unfortunately, the store wasn't very big and it was hard to hide. We were constantly going out back for Wid Griffin, the tackle buyer, to answer customers' questions.

What was I thinking that day in 1960 when I walked in? Was this a job to tide me over until something better showed up? Was it a career? Was it just something to do and a modest paycheck while I applied to graduate school? I didn't know.

I'd always had something of a one-track mind, preoccupied with whatever I was doing at any particular time and not looking ahead. So whenever the present thing ended, it was, "What do I do now?" For instance, I'd never planned beyond Bowdoin. All of a sudden I was graduating and wondering, "What am I going to do now?" I started scrambling to get in a law school application and take the foreign service exam, and I was doing job interviews. But all the time I knew there was universal military training, and if I didn't go to graduate school I was going to be drafted. A friend of mine had just graduated from Naval Officer Candidate School, and that seemed like a good idea. Then I just focused on the Navy. When I was discharged in May 1960 there it was again: "What do I do now?"

I remember hearing Earl Nightingale, a popular radio commentator at the time, say that most men spend more time picking out a necktie than they do a career. I was part of that. L.L.Bean was a job. I didn't think of it as an opportunity. When I started to work there, I still had thoughts of going to graduate school.

I can remember how the interview went. I still had my uniform on and thought L.L. would be impressed. After walking up the stairs to the third-floor retail store and going out back to his office, I sat down in the wooden armchair he had for visitors. He was at his best—hearty, genial, and grandfatherly. I can't remember details of the conversation, but L.L. seemed genuinely pleased to see me. I asked for a job. Although he didn't have anything for me to do, he put me on the payroll at $80 a week. My Navy experience may have convinced him I could be of some use. Or my college education. Also, he'd never turned down a family member looking for a job.

On the job in those first days I had a lot of time on my hands and wandered around the place trying to find out what was going on. Everyone who worked there referred to it as "the factory." It was an ark of a wood-frame building, 63,000 square feet in size, and made up of many additions over the years. Depending on where you stood, it was a two-, three-, or four-story building, with lots of ramps connecting the sections. Nothing was level or square, and it rambled and sagged all over the place.

The original three-story building had been known as the Warren Block and was part of the town square. L.L. had moved into the third floor in 1917. The post office was on the first floor, along with a print-ing shop and a barber shop. Prior to L.L., the third floor had been a movie theatre. There was an outside stairway to the upper floors.

In 1919, L.L. took over the second floor for his enlarged factory and added a storage room. Other additions followed, and in 1934 he dou-bled the space with an addition in the back.

> JOHN GOULD: Now, there wasn't, in those times, any good way to get into the Bean plant. The building hadn't been built for him, and he had grown into it deviously. The outside stairway went up three floors from the sidewalk, and having mounted it you would arrive all a-pant in a little room that smelled of oil-tanned leather and rubber cement, and you had to look around to see where to go. If you persisted, you'd startle various employees hidden away in random cubicles pursuing some manufacturing task like a dedicated neophyte. Whoever it was, he'd look up surprised that you found him, as if only the initiated could gain admittance. He would gladly direct you to Mr. Bean's office, usually through the mailing room, stitching department, and fly-tying department. You would per-haps arrive to find a spirited discussion going on between Mr. Bean and assorted Freeporters, as to the relative merits of the .30-30 and the .32 special. All such conferences were pitched above the whir of the stitching machines. After you had been greeted by L.L. and the others, there was the absorbing problem of getting back to the street again. The L.L.Bean factory, in those days, was about as efficient as a wet sponge at opening a beer bottle.[1]

The original building fronted on Freeport's Main Street. The post office, in 1960, was still on the Main Street level of L.L.'s building. His brother had been postmaster for many years. Guy Bean was reputed to be the only Democrat in Freeport during the Roosevelt years, which was why he got the appointment. Outgoing mail, catalogs, and parcels were all chuted directly to the post office for immediate processing. The brothers had a good partnership.

Our printer, Dingley Press, was located on the first floor of the three-story warehouse and shipping building in the rear across the alleyway. Catalogs moved on pallets to our crew of "stuffers" in the middle building, who tucked them into envelopes, and thence to the post office out front. The old fly-tying shop (no longer in operation) was out back among the cartons of merchandise in storage.

L.L.'s leather and fabric cutting room was over the post office. Raw materials and rolls of leather hides were stored in the basement. The rich, agreeable smell of tanned leather permeated the place. There were two stitching rooms on the third floor of the original building, one on either side of the salesroom. Our stitchers, pushing carts of work in progress from one room to the other, regularly dodged store customers.

RUSS DYER, JR.: The sewing machines . . . were in the front of the building and Winny Given always repaired the machines where they set in the window. The bank was across the street, and you could line up the needles with some of the lettering on the bank window, and that would adjust the machines so they would stitch properly . . . Years later, they moved the machines, so I don't know how they ever adjusted them after that.

Everything was made of wood—buildings, shelving, workbenches, and most of the desks—all of it quite old and dusty and broken in. Everything creaked. A lot of people still smoked in those days, and I found more than one cigarette butt that had burned itself out on a wooden shelf in the stockroom. The main building was so old and settled that L.L. had to add an external wood frame truss, a U-shaped contraption that arched over the building like a suspension bridge.

In 1960, to reach the salesroom, customers had to negotiate that two-story flight of stairs off the alleyway where the parking was. The stairwell was narrow and fully enclosed, and it had one short landing halfway up. We kept a settee at the top for people to rest on and regain their breath. Our freight elevator was available on request for the faint of heart, but most customers seemed to feel the climb was an essential part of the L.L.Bean experience.

The store was open twenty-four hours a day, seven days a week. It had been since 1951. Hunters and fishermen stopped by at all hours and got the night watchman to let them in to buy something. L.L. decided to hire a second person, "threw the key away," and let them both serve customers. The store, being the only place that was open all the time, maintained the twenty-four-hour fire alarm system for the town.

As you entered the store, at the top of the stairs, there was a whole row of windows on the far wall. You got a sense of light and the outdoors, with lots of gear hanging on the wall and over the windows. Snowshoes were prominent year-round. There was no organization at all to the salesroom, and it was fun for people to browse around. There was only one sample of each clothing item in the store, and so if customers wanted to try something on, they had to get someone to fetch it from the stockroom. Quite often they would wander into the stockrooms themselves and dig into the cartons, trying on clothing in the aisles.

> TOM MAHONEY: One mailing-room employee is also a member of the volunteer fire department. "I've got to change levels four times and go through five corridors, five doors and two flights of stairs when the siren blows," he says . . . Customers aren't always so agile. In the small hours of the morning, a sportsman somewhat under the influence lost his way. He was found the next day peacefully asleep under an overturned stack of hunting pants.[2]

Our salesclerks were extraordinarily friendly and accommodating, although they did not know a lot about the products. Customers liked the personal attention and the natural quirkiness of L.L.Bean and felt a particular warmth and even a proprietary relationship with the company.

We had a part-time cashier then who, when asked how far it was to Bangor or Millinocket or wherever, would invariably respond by asking the customer what kind of car were they driving. When the store got busy—and it did in the summer and in hunting season (at one time more than half the nonresident hunting licenses in Maine were sold in the L.L.Bean store)—the lines would be very long and slow-moving. As customers waited to check out, they could look on the wall behind the cashier at a moose head with a relatively small rack shot by L.L., alongside a stuffed sailfish his second wife, Claire, had caught in Florida.

> TOM MAHONEY: Sportsmen who climb the stairs to Bean's factory salesroom are exposed to the same temptations and organized

chaos the catalog reader undergoes. In spite of the sales staff, it's often necessary in a rush season for customers to wait on themselves. They're encouraged to prowl around, write out their own sales slips, and bring the load to one of the girl cashiers. When a cashier checked over one sportsman's order, she noted that the red hunting cap for which he'd written a sales slip was missing. The man pointed to his head. The girl glanced up and said: "That one's soiled. Let me find another one for you." "No," replied the customer. "I got this one here last year and somehow forgot to pay for it so I just included it in this batch."[3]

If you wanted to see L.L., you'd climb the two flights of stairs and you'd stop at the cash register and ask Carlene Griffin, our regular cashier (she's still with the company). She'd direct you through the women's area ("Ladies' Department") to the front office.

In the front office there were probably twelve women working at desks typing either shipping order forms or the catalog mailing list. Offices, including L.L.'s, were tucked into whatever space was left over. His office was in the front of the building. Its inside wall was lined with clapboards. It had been the outside of the original building, which he had extended to enclose the former outside stairway. In extending the wall, he simply left the exterior (now interior) wall just as it was—clapboards, yellow paint, outside windows, and all. He talked to his secretary, Ethel Williams, through one of the windows.

SAM CONNOR: In his shirtsleeves with his coat hanging from a nail in the corner of the office, whistling softly, L.L.Bean was giving the fish reel in his hands the works. He was finding out what sort of construction and material entered into its making and how.

It wasn't at all the kind of picture one conjures up of the head of a business which has an annual postage bill of about $80,000, but it was true to life of "L.L."

Husky—he's a bit over 6 foot and works the scales in the 200 class—a voice that booms all over the place, a smile that is good natured and twinkling eyes which always go with a fine appreciation of humor, L.L. is a typical out-of-doors man, the kind of a chap you'd know loved the woods and the fields, the mountains, a sportsman.[4]

The mail was opened at the far end of L.L.'s office, so he wasn't cut off from anybody. All those women in the front office listened to everything he said. Of course, L.L. always talked as loudly as he could. Being partially deaf, he seemed to assume everyone else was similarly impaired. The windows were always open, and so every presentation or discussion with L.L. was conducted with an audience of ten to twenty people listening to every word. Nothing was confidential. You had to get used to it. I'm sure my first conversation with L.L. was broadcast company-wide in a matter of minutes.

ETHEL WILLIAMS: He was really a charming person. I think he enjoyed having a nice looking woman come in and talk to him, try to sell him something. He'd be real charming. It's very possible he felt [more comfortable with women than men] . . . I thought he was a very attractive man. The wavy hair and the hearty laugh, the whole bit. A lot of charisma.

Carl Bean, L.L.'s son and for many years the general manager, was hidden away on the second floor near our cutting room. Access to Carl's office was through a secret door off the stairwell to the salesroom. It didn't look like a door. At the first landing, underneath the railing, there was a buzzer you pushed, and a panel—part of the wall on the right—popped open. You pushed the panel all the way open and walked through to Carl's office, on the right.

BARBARA BEAN GORMAN: Carl was quiet, you know, reserved . . . He was trying to go up quietly and tell my father [L.L.] that [Eleanor Roosevelt] was there. Gosh, she was standing right behind Carl. He went in and here's my father looking at the stock report. His nose right in the paper. When he was concentrating on anything, the place could burn down and he wouldn't know it. And Carl says, "Mrs. Roosevelt is here to see you." "Who! What! Which Mrs. Roosevelt!" And there she is, standing right there. Carl says, "Mrs. President Roosevelt." "What did you do then?"

L.L. Gives Me a Job

[I asked my father, and he said,] "I stood up and shook hands with her and said, 'This is indeed an honor, Mrs. Roosevelt.'" ... Then he gave her a trout knife to take back to Franklin ... When she went to leave he hollered out the window ... from the third floor to the policeman leaning up against Curtis's Grocery Store ... "Clear the road! Mrs. President Roosevelt is coming down to leave for Campobello! I want the highway cleared from here to Brunswick and an escort!" And, my gosh, she had it! She went off in a cloud of dust, all right. I'll bet she never forgot that.

That first day after I talked to L.L., I checked in with Carl. There was Carl and his wife, Hazel, along with Jessie Beal, Carl's secretary, and an assistant, Fran Stilkey, who all worked in Carl's pine-paneled office. Carl had a desk in the corner. Like L.L.'s office, Carl's always had an audience of three listening to every word. It made it difficult to talk with Carl.

I spent a lot of time that first summer working in the salesroom, since I didn't have much else I was supposed to do. The salesroom was always busy in the tourist season, with no end of customers to wait on. Working there gave me a chance to learn about L.L.Bean, our products and service, our personality and our customers.

I rarely heard a bad word about L.L. or Carl. Despite any managerial shortcomings they might have had, L.L. was regarded with respect, even awe, and Carl shared in that aura. Their words were not challenged. The atmosphere was like a family, comfortable, with everyone knowing everyone else for better or worse. Many were related to each other. L.L. was the head of the family. He could be enthusiastic or stubborn or arbitrary at times, but he always had his down-home charisma.

WID GRIFFIN: Well, the first raise that I got, I got by asking for it. L.L. had a boat down at South Freeport and he used to go out tuna fishing and he would have George [Soule] or [me] go out with him sometimes, more or less to do chores and do some fishing ... He came to me one day and said, "We're going out fishing tomorrow and I'd like to have you come along." Great. So being a good little boy, I went to my boss, Jim Cushing, and I told him that L.L. wanted me to go, and Jim said, "No, I guess I can't spare you." So I stewed all day long and I could see L.L. over in his corner desk . . . Finally it came five o'clock. I went in to see him and I told him, "I can't go fishing. Jim told me he can't spare me." And by that time I'd worked up my courage and told him, "If I'm so geedee important around here that I can't be spared to go fishing, I think that I ought to have more money." I can hear L.L. now saying, "Well, ha-ha-ha, so do I, and you can go fishing." Well, I went fishing and I got a raise from thirty cents to thirty-one and a half cents an hour.

I remember trolling with L.L. when he had a place on one of the Belgrade lakes in Maine. He'd take us fishing up there when we were little, but he didn't have a lot of tolerance for kids not catching fish. They weren't fun times. He just couldn't sit back and see us foul up the landing of a trout or bass or whatever. After a lot of yelling he'd eventually take the rod away and land the fish himself. We were either letting slack in the line or reeling too fast. I know that makes him sound mean, but he really was a good guy. He just couldn't contain himself. L.L. was almost always good natured and affable. I can't imagine anybody not liking him. Even when he was upset about something, he was upset in kind of a humorous and likable way.

MEL COLLINS: He never kept his voice low at all, you could hear him comin' down the factory. If we were behind one of the racks and heard him come in, we'd get right busy. Course, way back, no question about it, there was a lot of slack time. There was a lot of conversation went on amongst the help. Quite a lot of delays. Things didn't get done quite as fast as they do today. But it was family, more or less.

L.L. assumed that everyone was as interested in his business and what was happening to it as he was. To a great extent, his assumption was correct. He'd developed a loyal following. His small catalog company had grown and prospered through the Depression. The following comes from his Fall 1934 catalog, the year I was born.

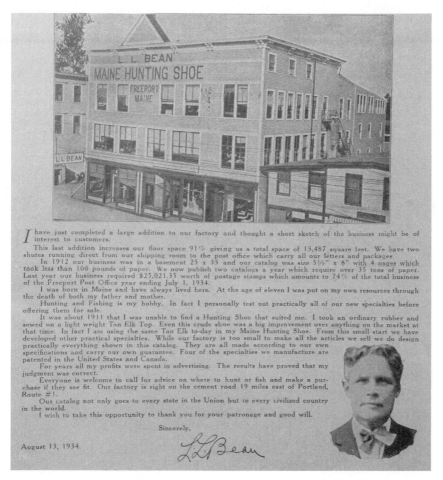

I have just completed a large addition to our factory and thought a short sketch of the business might be of interest to customers.

This last addition increases our floor space 91% giving us a total space of 13,487 square feet. We have two shutes running direct from our shipping room to the post office which carry all our letters and packages.

In 1912 our business was in a basement 25 x 35 and our catalog was size 5½" x 8" with 4 pages which took less than 100 pounds of paper. We now publish two catalogs a year which require over 35 tons of paper. Last year our business required $25,021.35 worth of postage stamps which amounts to 74% of the total business of the Freeport Post Office year ending July 1, 1934.

I was born in Maine and have always lived here. At the age of eleven I was put on my own resources through the death of both my father and mother.

Hunting and Fishing is my hobby. In fact I personally test out practically all of our new specialties before offering them for sale.

It was about 1911 that I was unable to find a Hunting Shoe that suited me. I took an ordinary rubber and sewed on a light weight Tan Elk Top. Even this crude shoe was a big improvement over anything on the market at that time. In fact I am using the same Tan Elk to-day in my Maine Hunting Shoe. From this small start we have developed other practical specialties. While our factory is too small to make all the articles we sell we do design practically everything shown in this catalog. They are all made according to our own specifications and carry our own guarantee. Four of the specialties we manufacture are patented in the United States and Canada.

For years all my profits were spent in advertising. The results have proved that my judgment was correct.

Everyone is welcome to call for advice on where to hunt or fish and make a purchase if they see fit. Our factory is right on the cement road 19 miles east of Portland, Route #1.

Our catalog not only goes to every state in the Union but to every civilized country in the world.

I wish to take this opportunity to thank you for your patronage and good will.

Sincerely,

August 13, 1934.

L.L. Bean

L.L. Bean, Hunting, Fishing and Camping, *5th ed., 1944.*

There was more to L.L. and his business than enthusiasm, pride, and a domineering personality. In the introduction to his book, *Hunting Fishing and Camping*, he wrote, "To my mind, hunting and fishing is the big lure that takes us into the great open spaces and teaches us to forget the mean and petty things of life." He attributed his long life to the healthful benefits of his outdoor recreational pursuits. He saw a greater good in the outdoors business than simply selling products by mail. L.L. was not one to philosophize a lot or pontificate, but he had a personal relationship with the great outdoors. It was there that people were at their best, he believed, and his quintessential products, like the Maine Hunting Shoe, helped their users go outdoors and reap the benefits of being there. His catalogs and his book reflected his vision of readers enjoying the outdoor life. L.L.'s visionary business concept was contained in his saying, *"Sell good merchandise at a reasonable profit, treat your customers like human beings, and they'll always come back for more."* He fully subscribed to this concept throughout his business life. We refer to it as L.L.'s Golden Rule.

L.L.'s company reached its peak in the 1930s. He wrote every word in his catalogs, including tips on outdoor living as well as buying by mail. "It is no longer necessary for you to experiment with dozens of flies to determine the few that will catch fish," he wrote. "We have done that experimenting for you." He showed his employees at the company picnic and himself discovering the joys of sportfishing for tuna. In 1935 he devoted an "editorial page" to showing pictures of his factory to "bring us in closer touch with our customers." George Soule and L.L. invented cork decoys while duck hunting on Lane's Island. Everything came together in a grand perfection.

Despite the Depression, L.L. quadrupled his sales in the 1930s. His factory was a lively place to work. He'd send exhibits to the Boston sportsmen's shows and half the town of Freeport would go. He was actively involved in town affairs and served on the school board and the town budget committee, and he led a group that attracted three new businesses to town. His employees were all friends and neighbors. Talk of hunting and fishing experiences was common. He set up one of the first skeet fields in the state so everyone could practice shooting. The offices, manufacturing spaces, and shipping areas were all mixed together. Orders received in the morning were mailed out within the promised thirty-six hours. Sales passed $1,000,000 in 1937.

ARTHUR BARTLETT: It is the catalogue . . . through which most of Bean's customers discover him and become addicted to him. It is a remarkably graphic and accurate extension of his small-town, down-East personality . . . He often does considerable violence to academic English, but he becomes personally and unmistakably present on almost every page. "I am very anxious," he writes, "that all my customers who do both duck hunting and stream fishing try a pair of these boots." Or: "This is the shirt I personally use on all my hunting and fishing trips." Or, in the equally identifiably plural: "We do not know of a warmer, more nearly waterproof fabric."[5]

In spite of his limited education, L.L. wrote compelling prose that brought into focus both the essence of the product and the essence of the writer. L.L. was a natural, one-of-a-kind communicator. When you bought from L.L.Bean he made you believe you were buying not just a product but, more importantly, his judgment and experience.

JOHN GOULD: People wanted something different. It identified them. They were an L.L.Bean customer. "I got the L.L.Bean gum shoe." And L.L. was smart in that respect. He knew what that meant. I think he knew from the very start, perhaps intuitively. Certainly he had no advice from a business counselor of any sort in those days. But I think he just recognized that he was creating a personality that was going to stand behind his business and that was it. You take those early catalogs and how many things in it "Mr. Bean personally . . ." until the word "personally" almost got to be a little obnoxious. He overworked it, of course. But it was important and it sold goods for him. And people could walk off in the woods carrying the same hatchet that Mr. Bean personally carried into the woods.

Along the way L.L. became something of a celebrity. Many articles were written about him in the 1940s and 1950s. Ethel Williams kept copies of all the magazines, including *Life, Yankee, Forbes, Reader's Digest, The Great Merchants* (a book by Tom Mahoney), *Sports Illustrated*, the *New Yorker, Sports Afield, Alaska Sportsman,* and *Down East.*

In 1946, one of the most widely read magazines in America, the *Saturday Evening Post,* did a major story, with full color illustrations, titled, "The Discovery of L.L. Bean."[6] The writer, Arthur Bartlett, deeply understood the L.L. story and did a thorough and very readable job in capturing everything that was human and American and outdoors and inspirational about L.L. and his company. The publication of this article may well have been the proudest moment of L.L.'s life. He never ceased to refer to it and to his high regard for Arthur Bartlett. It was a definitive work and not only established the L.L. legend for all time but substantially expanded and enriched it.

> IDALYN CUMMINGS: I remember the *Saturday Evening Post.* Oh! Every day, we'd keep track. Every day he'd want to know how many [letters] he got.

One of the article's clearest insights on L.L. captured the essence of his business concept: "L.L. sells only what he likes, and likes everything he sells, and wants everyone to know it." This thought pretty well explained the eclectic and idiosyncratic but generally outdoors product line that L.L. had put together over the years.

> L.L. BEAN: No doubt a chief reason for the success of the business is the fact that I tried on the trail, practically every article I handle. If I tell you that a knife is good for cleaning trout, it is because I found it so. If I tell you a wading boot is worth having, very likely you might have seen me testing it out at Merrymeeting Bay.

Who else but L.L. could assemble a coherent and compelling line of outdoors products that included "Bean's Business Man Shirt" (a broadcloth cotton dress shirt), "Bean's Mallard Blanket," and "Bean's Brief Case," along with a "Double-L Fly Rod," "Bean's Pack Basket," and a "Maine Duck Hunting Coat" among myriad other indoors and outdoors products, in one comprehensible catalog? And all described in honest, straightforward, unique language that only a smart, self-confident, self-taught Maine country boy could write. This text from his Fall 1937 catalog for "Bean's Maine Woods Compass" (found on the following page) is one example.

L.L. enjoyed his life to the fullest and wanted everybody else to do the same, and he knew just how they should do it. His enthusiasm in wanting to share his good life experiences found him a lot of kindred spirits in the marketplace. At his company's peak, what made his product line come together in a sensible whole was its reflection of L.L. and the way he lived his life. It wasn't just hunting and fishing but everyday

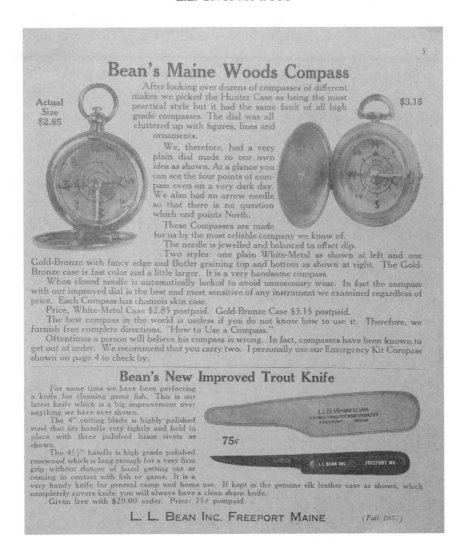

living as well. The products expressed L.L.'s way of life centered on the outdoors—his lifestyle, in today's language. And he wanted to share it.

ARTHUR BARTLETT: It seems to be an almost universal illusion among his customers . . . that Bean is a personal discovery, to be cherished as a rare and rich curiosity. Bean, as a shrewd businessman, does his best to foster this impression, but it doesn't take much effort. All he really has to do is be himself.[7]

The *Saturday Evening Post* article also suggested the tremendous credibility and charismatic appeal L.L. brought to bear in merchandising and marketing his products through the catalog medium. L.L. seemed to talk personally to each of his customers. He attracted a fanatic and dedicated following. They were more than customers. They were fans and believers. L.L. was a true Maine Guide, a competent and trustworthy leader. He had personally used all of his products in the outdoors. He was a friend, outgoing, with boundless energy. His enthusiasm was contagious and he had a vision, which was the value of the outdoor experience and a profound respect for people. L.L. wanted to share with his customers the way he lived.

Unfortunately, all that was in the past when I joined the company in 1960. I reread the catalogs, old and new. Things had changed since L.L.'s heyday. The current editions no longer had the charm and exuberance of L.L.'s 1930s catalogs. The Fall 1959 catalog was a hodgepodge of apparel and footwear and bags and outdated fishing tackle and World War II surplus spread throughout. The products were of uneven quality, and there was little relevance to the assortment. It included a nurse's shoe at the request of Claire, L.L.'s second wife, a former nurse (his first wife— my grandmother, Bertha Bean—had died in 1939), a "Moisture Proof Pipe" because L.L. determined that most fishermen and hunters smoked (although he did not), and a "Freezer De-Icer" tool for the home freezers of the day.

During World War II, L.L.'s business, like many others, had been placed on the back burner. A lot of his manufacturing went to supporting the war effort with boots and bags for the armed forces. He spent time in Washington as a consultant to the War Department (and a lot of time watching the old Washington Senators play baseball, he once told me). His customers were out fighting a war, not hunting and fishing.

With the exception of Arthur Bartlett and the *Saturday Evening Post* article in 1946 and the subsequent 42 percent increase in business, most of the postwar years through 1960 had been years of stagnation and deterioration. Besides the problems with the product line, the quality of the catalog's printing and graphics had declined. L.L. had become increasingly frugal with age and wanted the lowest-cost coated paper and catalog printing he could get. L.L. was no longer writing the copy, only editing it. The result was bland and even silly on occasion. His point of view, which used to tie his catalogs together, was no longer there.

L.L. attempted to rationalize the disarray of his catalog in an article for *Sales & Marketing Management* magazine in September 1955. He said, "You see, there are so many new items coming along, we've found it advantageous to print the catalogs right in our own factory. To keep our printers working the year round, we give them from four to eight pages a week, filling each page with whatever pictures and copy we have ready. At the last minute, we fix up an index."[8] But he never did include an index. His theory—that people would buy on impulse because they had to thumb through every page in order to find the few good core products they wanted—seemed more rationalization for the poorly organized catalogs.

> IDALYN CUMMINGS: So many people would write in and want to know why we didn't have an index. You know, he wanted people to look through that catalog. He didn't want people to go to one page. Oh, there must have been thousands of letters over the years asking about an index.

The catalogs of the 1950s showed a pronounced shift to humdrum streetwear. But the Maine Hunting Shoe, Chamois Cloth Shirt, Zipper Duffel Bag, Coastal Decoys, Hudson's Bay Blankets, Camp Moccasins, and a few other core products continued to carry the business. Sales had fluctuated around $2 million in the 1950s and were $2.2 million in 1960 when I joined the company.

By this time, service standards had deteriorated significantly. Customer inquiries and complaints were handled slowly and inconsistently. There was no guarantee of satisfaction printed in the catalog or supported in practice. Our product buyers got in senseless debates with customers by mail about the validity of their claims and refunds. Internal fulfillment times went well beyond the thirty-six-hour standard L.L. had set in the 1930s. In fact, during the Christmas rush it took more than two weeks to process orders. In-stock service levels were not even measured because there was no inventory management system to measure them. We were back-ordering or canceling 25 percent or more of our customers' orders.

All of the systems for order entry, fulfillment, and mailing-list management were 100 percent manual. Electric typewriters were the only concession to current technology. Any changes in any of the order processes or fulfillment systems were simply not considered. If a new desk or filing cabinet was needed, Carl Bean personally negotiated for it from a secondhand business equipment dealer in Portland. A new pickup truck required a board vote. The only copier was at our lawyer's office across the street. Overall, operations of the company were pretty much as they had been since the end of World War II.

Financially, in 1960 L.L.Bean was essentially a cash business. L.L. bought goods for cash and sold goods for cash. There was no debt on the balance sheet. Fixed assets were minimal because little was reinvested in the business. The current ratio (current assets to current liabilities) was a healthy 4:1 and had been for quite a few years. Credit rating agencies and the banks liked L.L.'s financial condition, but they had some qualms.

The problem was that profit was marginal (less than 2 percent of sales) and his return on equity was less than 4 percent. (I would later joke that if I'd known how to read a financial statement at the time, I'd have gone to work for the phone company.) The buildings were of poor construction and design and had limited future usefulness. Nothing had been invested in new distribution systems or manufacturing equipment for many years. A friend in the shoe industry once told me in all sincerity that L.L.'s manufacturing area looked like a Singer sewing machine museum.

Since there was no budget or even the simplest of operation plans, last year's income statement was the de facto plan for this year. Everything had to be done more or less as it had been the year before, or the company would lose its equilibrium.

Almost everyone at L.L.Bean was paid a minimum wage of $1.00 per hour. Exceptional performers received $1.05. These levels were surely below whatever the poverty level might have been if there was such a calculation in 1960. But to L.L. and Carl's credit, they were willing to share profits with their employees. In 1960 the cash bonus to all employees was 20 percent of base compensation, and it enabled our people to get their household budgets back in balance.

The average age of Bean employees in 1960 was in the mid-sixties. There was no pension program. Although a profit-sharing program had been started in 1953, individual accounts were not sufficient to retire on. As a result people continued working into their seventies and eighties. L.L. was in his late eighties at the time and did not find it unusual that these younger people were still working.

Another troublesome aspect of the aging workforce was in the area of quality. For example, the man who "vamped" our Maine Hunting Shoes (he stitched the three single rows of cotton thread that attached the leather uppers to the rubber bottoms) could no longer stitch a straight line. Vamping is a difficult freehand stitching operation (there are no guides or supports for the operator's arms), and it requires exceptional steadiness and a skilled eye. We had some poor-looking boots as a result of our aging vamper.

Still, for those who chose to stay, job satisfaction at L.L.Bean was OK. It was a comfortable environment. Workers spent the first hour of the day in manufacturing reading the paper, eating doughnuts, and drinking coffee. Nobody worked very hard, nor were they expected to.

IDALYN CUMMINGS: I think [people in Freeport] felt it was just an old ladies' home. You heard it called that. I used to get so mad. "You still up at the old ladies' home?" After a while I'd say, "Oh, yeah." . . . I think it was because, well, if you worked at Bean's, you really didn't have to work too hard, you know, and they didn't pay too much.

But there was concern about the future, at least on my part. The business was slowly running down, though it still had some year-to-year momentum. It's hard to kill a good brand, and L.L.'s prime years had created an enormous reserve of strength. That first summer I began to learn about the company and its ways of doing things, its strong points and its weak ones. And the latter were gaining.

2

Learning the Business

THE FIRST SUMMER I worked for L.L., he gave me my first assignment: to put together and mail a summer camping circular. It was June, late in the selling season for a camping mailing. Wid and the other buyers helped me select an assortment of tents and camping gear from the Spring catalog. It was all equipment such as our Zipper Duffle Bag, Cottagaire Wall Tent, and Hudson Bay Cruising Axe. Actually our catalog assortment was so small that I included all of the gear that could be useful on a tent camping trip. There was no apparel or footwear in the circular.

Ethel Williams, L.L.'s secretary, helped me put the pages together using clippings from the Spring catalog. I worked in Carl's office, and making up the pages, cutting and pasting, made a mess of my desk. (This bothered Carl sufficiently for him to ask Jessie Beal, his secretary, to relocate me.) Carl limited the size of the mailing to a small part of our list, but it was enough to expect measurable results. Jessie picked the names from our mailing list.

We inserted a coded order form, and after a couple of weeks I began checking the mail room for orders. We didn't get any, or no more than a handful. I couldn't believe it. Being new I hadn't expected a big response. But the lack of almost any was a revelation and a shocking one at that. The catalog business was a lot more than putting something in the mail and sitting back while the orders came rushing in. I had a lot to learn. I also gained a lot of respect for L.L.'s early success in the catalog business. I wrote a brief report for him and Carl, but I heard nothing back from them.

Jessie relocated me to my father's old desk because it was the only one available in the back office. My father, Jack Gorman, had been the clothing buyer. He had come to work for the company at L.L.'s insistence in 1938, a few years after marrying my mother, Barbara Bean Gorman. I think he'd gotten along with L.L. all right, but I don't believe he'd liked being there. He'd always advised us boys—my brothers, Tom and Jim, and me—to become "professional" men (doctors, lawyers, etc.).

My father had died the previous winter and had not been replaced. It was a little strange sitting at his desk as I sorted through his notes and papers and talked with Mel Collins, his longtime assistant. Mel was carrying on the clothing buying function and serving as photographer for our catalog. He was a most agreeable old-timer. He had recently given up smoking cigars and spent a lot of time talking about his former habit.

Ethel and Jessie helped me the most in learning about L.L.'s and Carl's parts of the business. At this point, L.L. oversaw the makeup of the catalogs, approved new products, and managed the advertising program; Carl oversaw order writing, shipping, manufacturing, and employment. Ethel and Jessie served as go-betweens (and buffers, in more serious situations) between L.L. and Carl and the rest of the organization. Neither L.L. nor Carl communicated with each other or me on a regular basis.

In fact, L.L. was not in the office much. He was not in at all from midfall to late spring, when he was in Florida. The rest of the year, he would come to his office for just a few hours each morning. That's where Ethel was the gatekeeper. If she knew we needed approval on something, she'd tip us off that he was in, and in a good humor or not.

L.L. was eighty-seven, and Carl was sixty. I was twenty-five. So we didn't have a lot of interests in common (none, in fact) or common aspirations for the business. Neither of them had any inclination to act as my mentor or show an obvious interest in my business education, so I was left pretty much on my own. This arrangement was fine with me as

I'd always been used to figuring things out for myself. I'd never had a favorite teacher or bosses to take problems to, and I hadn't received much in the way of coaching while I was growing up. Nor did my early experience in business provide much in the way of management role models. I learned by observing things and studying a lot and listening to whoever seemed to know something I was interested in.

For me to understand L.L.Bean, it seemed that the first thing I needed to do was to learn about the outdoors. Working in the retail store, in particular, I ran into active hikers and fly fishermen and outdoors people looking not only for products but also for advice and expertise. Our customers saw us as an outdoors company and expected us to know something about the outdoors and the activities we catered to. I was certainly deficient in expertise, but so was the company as a whole.

When customers came in and asked questions, you had to find whoever in the organization would have an answer and could help you out. The only one, other than Wid Griffin, who seemed to know anything about where the fish were biting was the fellow running the postage meter at the end of the packing line. If somebody asked me where they could go on a canoe trip, Maurice Hilton, our manufacturing supervisor, was the one to see. It bothered me that the L.L.Bean people in the store or the ones answering customer letters knew so little about the outdoors. There was something a little hollow about the company's reputation.

Before I joined L.L.Bean my outdoor experience was limited mainly to my years as a Boy Scout. I had been active in Scouting from ages eleven to fifteen and had a fair amount of exposure to camping, canoeing, and woodcraft skills. When I left Scouting, the outdoor experiences stayed with me, along with such Boy Scout values as trustworthiness, service to others, and respect for the outdoors environment.

I didn't get into the outdoors much during my college and Navy years, but the interest had been planted in my Scouting years. Now I needed to get outdoors for business purposes, as well as personal recreation.

A manufacturer's representative who sold us paper products invited me to go fly-fishing that first summer. He expected I knew how to fly-cast and so I needed to learn in a hurry. Wid Griffin took me to the roof of our warehouse. It was flat enough to cast, and there weren't any trees to worry about. Wid was a patient teacher and eventually I got the knack of it, at least to get enough line out to catch fish. Learning how to cast on the roof gave me enough of a start to make the trip a success. I wasn't embarrassed, and I actually caught some trout.

In the fall, Wid introduced me to upland bird hunting. Almost every Saturday several of us visited the local covers and scared a few woodcock or partridge. Each season brought new opportunities to experience the outdoors, and eventually I got into all of the outdoor activities L.L.Bean catered to. Initially it was L.L.'s hunting, fishing, and camping and later hiking, backpacking, canoeing, cycling, cross-country skiing, and so on as we expanded our product lines. I was convinced you could not understand any of these businesses without participating in them.

Wid Griffin was the classic Maine outdoorsman and a critical part of the L.L.Bean tradition. Proficient in fly-fishing, bird hunting, canoeing, and the outdoors in general, he did everything with ease and a Down East style. If you were making a movie about the north Maine woods and you needed a game warden or a real Maine Guide, you would have picked Wid Griffin. He was the kind of guy you wanted to have along on a trip, and, to a great extent, he personified for me the outdoors tradition of L.L.Bean.

Wid was in his forties when I joined the company. He had worked for L.L. since graduating from Freeport High School. Thoughtful, hardworking, modest, and honest as the day is long, Wid was committed to L.L. and the L.L.Bean customer. He believed in practical, well-made products and in keeping our customers happy with our service. His job was difficult, given our lack of systems and any investment in modernization. Yet his strongest language might include a "golly" or a "gee willickers." He was highly regarded by all, including Carl and L.L., who put him on the company's board of directors about the time I arrived.

WID GRIFFIN: L.L. came down and sat on the corner of my desk and he shouted, "Keep this under your hat, but we're going to appoint you to the Board of Directors." I kept it under my hat, but so did everyone else in the front of the office.

My formal education in business subjects was minimal. I'd been a liberal arts major at Bowdoin and was exposed to a broad range of knowledge, including Platonic philosophy, English literature, biology, and comparative government as well as good writing and critical thinking skills. A capacity to be curious and to want to learn more were the practical applications of my studies when I graduated in 1956.

Prior to going to Navy OCS in January 1957, I had spent the interim six months at Filene's department store in Boston. It was an intense and memorable experience as I worked for Henry Allen, one of Filene's most legendary and successful buyers. He educated us daily in crisis management as well as in keeping good inventory records and floor salesmanship. Trainees typically worked in the office, but he wanted us on the floor talking to customers as much as possible. Whenever I did something that displeased him, he'd tell me that I'd be "left at the railroad station when the train pulled out." Not wanting to hear it again, I stayed late one evening to get a report ready for him the next morning. Unfortunately, I had forgotten to tell the store security people and found myself cornered in the stockroom by a large Doberman, one of several they set loose in the store at night to ferret out intruders.

At L.L.Bean I began studying our modest clothing sales records. Mel had a Kardex binder, with a card for each item in the catalog. He recorded the beginning inventory for each season (spring or fall), added the receipts, and subtracted the ending inventory to calculate sales. Not hard to understand. We had a lot of products showing very little activity.

I took on the customer correspondence, which forced me to do research in order to answer questions. Many concerned the fit of garments—how you measured the inseam on trousers, or the sleeve length on a shirt, or the height of stockings—or the meaning of such terms as "virgin" wool or "worsted" wool. Some customers challenged our use of certain tartan names, and I'd have to check their claims against a reference book we had on Scottish tartans. Sometimes we hadn't sent what they ordered. I'd have to track down the order and in the process learn the filing system and details of inventory management.

Traveling salesmen stopped by regularly, and they were a great source of market information. The ones who had been selling to L.L.Bean for many years had good insights into the company and could narrow down their lines to the few relevant new products we should consider. Don Wallace represented Woolrich at the time, which had a broad line of rugged outerwear, shirts, and trousers we sold under the Bean label. Don knew which of his products, maybe 20 percent, would interest us, because he knew Bean so well. He and I had a good relationship for many years.

Many of the salesmen suggested I get out of the building more often and learn what was going on in the retail world. So I was the first person from L.L.Bean to travel to various apparel, footwear, and sporting goods trade shows in Boston, New York, and Chicago. Over the years I saw many new products, met a lot of smart people, discovered new vendor companies, and learned the industry. Most of the show exhibitors, I discovered, had never heard of L.L.Bean, nor were many quite sure where Maine was. I used to be offered exclusive distribution rights for Freeport.

I was also reading the three major outdoors magazines every month as well as a variety of special interest magazines. There was a lot of material on outdoors equipment and manufacturers' advertisements. There was also a lot of competitors' catalog advertising—more than I'd realized. I was increasingly dismayed by how little was known at L.L.Bean about business in general as well as the business we were in. The company was insulated from the rest of the world. When L.L. and Carl came into the office, all they did was handle their personal mail, pay their bills, and chat with whoever was handy. There was very little business work being done. We were in a highly competitive business, and no one was competing.

I began taking correspondence courses on business finance and began attending business seminars. I spent time talking to our banker and to sellers of business services and supplies who called on us. I discovered the Small Business Administration and the dozens and dozens of publications it offered on all aspects of business. When my first order arrived, they made a tall stack on my desk. L.L., in one of his few visits to the back office, spotted the stack and reacted with great good humor. I wasn't sure whether he appreciated my ambitious reading program or considered it a bit ridiculous. I didn't ask.

In the Navy, I'd developed the habit of carrying with me a pocket-sized "black book" to note important bits of information or things to do. I started keeping a similar black book at L.L.Bean to record the thoughts and ideas I was picking up from all these parts of my "business education." However, keeping the notebook was more than a habit from my Navy days. I knew there probably wasn't much I could do with most of my ideas at the time, given L.L.'s and Carl's strong feelings about not changing anything. So I'd put them in the book to keep track of them for possible implementation later.

The list of to-do's grew to more than four hundred notations during that first year at L.L.Bean. It included ideas to improve the retail store, facilitate order picking, add new products (especially up-to-date camping equipment), buy a mail-opening machine, include inserts in packages, devise faster ways of handling returns, change office layouts, and rent canoes, as well as notes on the importance of the "uniqueness of L.L.Bean products" and of "quality products at reasonable prices."

I'd written notes on holding semiannual sales of discontinued products, collecting customer suggestions, developing employment policies and the importance of good morale, conducting annual pay reviews, writing catalog copy ("keep it simple"), building the mailing list, encouraging our buyers to add new products, using management consultants, adopting inventory control systems, improving customer communications, commissioning original art for catalog covers, improving manufacturing and shipping room layouts, and changing the description of the company on its letterhead from "Manufacturer" to "Hunting, Fishing and Camping Specialties." I wanted to look into order entry systems, an Addressograph system, pension plans, better fit instructions in the catalog, "No gimmicks in catalog," training our salesroom staff, and on and on and on—topics from the strategic to the minute.

Looking back, I think the black book held a pretty good assessment of what the company needed, and most of the ideas were eventually implemented. They would have been obvious to most people, although not to L.L. and Carl. Several years ago I was given the call reports of the loan officer at a Portland bank who was assigned to sell bank services to L.L.Bean during the sixties.

BANK LOAN OFFICER (1960): Called this morning upon
[Shailer] Hayes . . . Hayes handles the personal financial records
of Mr. L.L. Bean as well as performing bookkeeping functions for
the company. In confidence he told me that Mr. Bean has no will,
is in the 52% tax bracket, has made no provision for continuation
of the business upon his passing, in the past has refused to discuss
his personal estate and company plans with Lawyers and Trust
Officer . . . It is believed that Mr. Bean would like his son, L. Carl
Bean, now Vice President, to assume head of the company . . .
Two young grandsons of L.L. Bean, Leon and Tom Gorman, are
now in the organization. Both are in minor positions at the present
time and apparently very little is being done to groom them for
better things.

In 1962, *Time* magazine published an article on L.L.Bean's fiftieth
year as a company:

Bean rules his [company] with a firm hand and brushes aside suggestions from his heir apparent, grandson Leon Gorman, 27, that
the company "automate" by buying an Addressograph. "Why expand when you're 90 years old?" demands Bean. Besides, "I get
three good meals a day, and I can't eat four."[1]

My being the "heir apparent" was apparent only to the writer. Certainly L.L. and Carl had never conferred such status on me, and it was
definitely not the feeling I had. My future with the company was to me
still uncertain. L.L. was ninety and clearly approaching the end of his
tenure, although he refused to formally let go of anything. But Carl was
L.L.'s apparent successor and, in his sixties, might live on like his father,
heading the company for another thirty years.

L.L. had been an achiever and an innovator in his younger days, aggressively pursuing his own ideas or those he borrowed from others,
and he'd taken some risks. He rarely delegated any responsibilities. It
was clear what he wanted done because he made all the decisions. He
fully enjoyed his company and his reputation as a Down East merchant.

Because L.L. was outgoing, energetic, and personable, people enjoyed working for him. But he never was and never pretended to be a

manager in the conventional sense. He had little interest in planning and budgeting, in organizational issues, in training or developing people, or in performance management. Team building was something he left to the manager of his beloved Boston Red Sox.

> MEL COLLINS: I remember one time when these mittens came out with the slot in them, the trigger finger could come out through, for hunting. L.L. came out waving one of those. Jack [Gorman] was there. [L.L.] says, "Whoever put this thing into the catalog? No man is going to use one of these things. If he's going to hunt, he's gonna take that mitten off and throw it on the ground." He says, "That's just a nuisance. Who put those in the line anyhow?" Jack says, "You OK'd 'em yourself, L.L." "I did? Well, guess I didn't know what I was doing. Well, get 'em out of here. Don't want any more of them." That was the end of that one. He had the final word.

L.L. had a strong sense of who he was—or who he had become—and what he had accomplished. I wasn't around at the time of the 1946 *Saturday Evening Post* story mentioned in Chapter 1, but it well could have led L.L. to think of himself as a living legend.

> L.L. BEAN: There is one outstanding date in my business life that I will never forget. That date was December 14, 1946, when *The Saturday Evening Post* came out with a 4 1/2 page story entitled:
> "THE DISCOVERY OF L.L. BEAN"
> Over a page and a half consisted of four color pictures. To have bought this space would have cost us about $53,000.
> Almost without exception the newspapers of the state carried columns of comment and editorials about the POST article. The Selectmen of the town of Freeport passed by unanimous vote a resolution designating Monday, December 16th, 1946, as "L.L. Bean Day."
> On the day the POST appeared I had an interview on one of the Portland radio stations. A testimonial dinner was given to me by the town's business men with the Governor of the state, Horace A.

Hildreth, and a representative of the Maine Development Commission, Harold Schnurle, among those present.

The speeches by both the Governor and Mr. Schnurle contained admission of frank wonder that a business man of Freeport could have made the honor roll of publicity in the top weekly of the nation . . .

The business today exceeds my wildest dream. There are few enterprises that begin so modestly and grow so rapidly.

I hesitate to advertise with names of customers. There is hardly a famous person who hasn't worn my boots, packed my knapsacks, or cast my flies. A Prince in India is a steady customer; Babe Ruth, Jack Dempsey, Commander MacMillan, Mrs. Roosevelt, all the governors of the State of Maine and of many other states.[2]

I was always struck that, near the cashier station in the retail store, L.L. had put up a big formal portrait of himself in a pin-striped suit. It was incongruous among all the snowshoes, fishing and hunting gear, and other outdoors paraphernalia—certainly not the image people had of this country uncle running a little catalog operation up in the woods of Maine.

BARBARA BEAN GORMAN: He'd never compliment anybody on what they could do in the business. No, he was L.L. Bean. He was the one who knew what to do and how to do it. Everybody else could help but not ever take his place. He'd always had to take care of everything himself and he never got over it . . . No, he was L.L. Bean and his word was it. When he'd argue . . . this always made me smile . . . if he knew he was losing an argument, he'd just turn around and walk out of the room. He always had the last word.

How L.L. thought of himself—as a living legend—was probably captured in the words he wrote of himself for the jacket of his autobiography, *My Story,* which he self-published in 1960 at the age of eighty-eight: "the world-famous Yankee hunter and fisherman" who "turned his love of outdoor life into a multi-million dollar success story."

In his old age, when I arrived at the company, L.L. had lost the energy and ability to do much, but he still didn't delegate anything except by default. He didn't believe in retirement, and I think he was going on just to keep himself alive and stimulated. He used to say, "If a man retires he's done for." The problem was that by this time he had become a very old man who was no longer capable of leading the business. Like countless other entrepreneurs, he simply couldn't let go.

> JOHN GOULD: I always used to think in the early days that L.L. wasn't aware that he was becoming a famous person. I don't think in those days, in the 30s, when these people began to come up and call on him, that [he] realized . . . he thought he was being honored to have Eleanor Roosevelt in the office. The truth is that Eleanor Roosevelt came up to meet L.L. Bean . . . I don't think he was publicity conscious in the beginning, and then all at once the *Saturday Evening Post* had a story about him and he realized that he'd achieved something . . . There was a little change came over him because of that.[3]

But by the 1960s, L.L.'s vision for the company was failing. In the six years I worked with him, I never heard him stress the importance of product quality ("good merchandise") or of superior customer service ("treating customers like human beings"). All that would have been expressed before I arrived. I'm sure he still believed in those things, but he certainly never sat me on his knee and said, "Here's what serving customers is all about," or, "Here's why product quality is so important." I can't ever recall his speaking in those terms.

> SHAILER HAYES: He sure kept [pretty tight control], he sure did. He wouldn't give anyone authority. You could make your suggestions to him. If he liked the sound of them, all right. And if he didn't, it was too bad, they didn't go through. Even the buyers couldn't put a new product in without consulting him first.

One of my biggest challenges in working with L.L. came when I tried to update the product line. I would bring in a new flannel shirt, for example, and he always wanted to know what it cost. He had gotten very price conscious. So I'd tell him. He remembered when he'd worked in his brother's dry goods store at the turn of the century and they sold shirts for 50 cents apiece. It could be comical in a way, but it was hard to deal with. He was completely out of touch with product values. Often I couldn't get past the cost question.

Everything had to be related to hunting and fishing, too. I'd stand on my head relating a piece of sportswear to hunting and fishing. Of course he had his sandwich spreaders and canvas sneakers (for Florida), but he didn't have to apply the test to himself.

DON WILLIAMS: A salesman would come in with something in the clothing line, maybe a new coat, jacket of some kind. And Leon would try to push it to L.L. You know, you couldn't push much. Leon would take a coat and go out and say, "I think this coat would make a good thing in the salesroom." L.L.'d say, "How much it cost you?" First thing. Leon would go in with his figures. "This is what it cost me, this is what I want to take for a markup on it, this is how many I want to buy." And so on. Well . . . Leon would get mad and he'd come out and say to me, "How do you get along with that man? I wanted to buy something, he won't let me. I can't sell it to him." I'd say, "Why, what do you mean?" "Well, I just can't sell it to him." I'd say, "Give it to me." And I'd hang on to it three or four days, kinda hopin' L.L. would forget all about the figures. So I'd hang on to it and I'd say, well, guess it's time to attack him. So I'd go out and show L.L. the coat. "What do you think of it?" he'd say. "Well, I don't know," I'd say. "What'd it cost you?" I'd tell him. After you told him what it cost, don't try to tell him what you're going to sell it for . . . He wanted to name the price, see. So you left him right alone, on his own, and he'd say, "All right. Do you think it'll sell?" "I figure it'll go all right." "All right. Buy two dozen. Try 'em out [in the salesroom]. Good enough, go in the catalog." That's the way he worked.

On the other hand, working with L.L. on the advertising program was a good learning experience. He had developed a clever and effective advertising formula for acquiring new customer names for his catalog. Every month we met with Ed Whitmarsh from our agency and set up the next advertising month's program of coupon ads in a wide variety of print media: all the outdoors magazines as well as the *New Yorker, Yankee,* and so on. L.L. listened to Ed a little but made all the insertion decisions himself. When he got tired, he'd just sit back and say, "Well, I guess the clock struck twelve on that one." Whether or not we'd finished the roster of magazines, that was it for that month's program.

You could work with L.L., to a certain extent, if you knew how, because he was predictable in his reactions. New products, for instance, had to be for hunters and fishermen and low in price, or quite similar to something he had sold in the past. You could often anticipate what he would say, so you could be prepared with an answer. There was enough latitude in his criteria to do some upgrading of the product line. When he was in a good mood it was fun to work with him.

What was difficult for me were his hopes for the business, which by now were limited to his personal comfort level. He had a way of expressing this, which everyone who knew him seems to remember.

> BUCKY BUCKLIN: I always remember [L.L.'s] favorite quote. Somebody asked him why he isn't expanding the business. [He said] he eats three good meals a day and can't eat four.

> MEL COLLINS: I think he used to like to keep the company just about so, you know. I don't think he wanted too much growth. He used to say that he got three meals a day and couldn't eat four. That was one of his old statements.

> SANDY FOWLER: I was always anxious for Bean to print more catalogs than the 750,000 runs we had . . . So, I would say to L.L., "How about increasing the run, building things up a little?" And he would say, "Well, Sandy, I can't eat more than three meals a day."

For his part, Carl also was a frustration for me, and an enigma. He had no management or leadership interests or aptitudes and would have been much happier running an antique shop or playing golf full time. These were his two main interests. His third was to frustrate me at every turn by rejecting virtually every recommendation I made that required his approval. It took me an hour once to convince him that our best salesperson and a wonderful individual in the retail store deserved a 5-cent pay increase. I never figured out how to deal with him.

> JESSIE BEAL: There was a time or two [that Carl and Leon] had little set-tos and Carl would have to slap Leon down a little bit. Uneasy times . . . Leon would have some good ideas and Carl would kind of shoot them down. I think it was because of his father shooting him down.

I remember Carl used to talk about doing menial tasks, humiliating tasks, when he had first joined the company. He couldn't understand why I didn't have to do those same things. They used to get barrels of some kind of grease for the boot dressing. Before it could be sold, it had to be heated up, so it would be fluid, and then poured into little cans that had L.L.'s label on them. Carl's first job was to fill all those little cans. And, too, they used to make anchors for the decoys out of melted lead poured into little molds. That was another job I think Carl had done, and he couldn't understand why I wasn't doing that, too.

Because Carl was peevish and unpleasant to work with, I tried to involve myself as little as possible in anything that required his OK. If there was an issue in relation to Carl or our operating areas, I generally dealt with Jessie. Working with Carl, as with L.L. in some cases, meant working *around* Carl. The first spring, 1961, that I was with L.L.Bean, I enlarged the retail store and changed its layout. We had been limited by space to selling our apparel from single floor samples. With the changes, we could get full-size runs on the floor. We also put a little more logic and space into all of our product displays. I never told Carl about the changes, and since he never climbed the stairs to the third floor he never noticed or objected.

> BUCKY BUCKLIN: Carl was really General Manager but L.L. had to put the stamp of approval on anything. I remember once . . . Carl came out of the conference room and I happened to be the first guy he ran into. He says, "How much can you spend without my approval?" I think then it was kind of an unwritten rule, $100 or something. He says, "Now you're down to $50." After all the

facts came out, Carl had tried to spend an amount of money on some project and L.L. got wind of it and says, "Now you can't spend over X amount of dollars without my approval." So Carl in turn put some clamps on me. It was purely a spasmodic thing.

L.L. told me once he wanted me to be the "straw boss." I didn't know what it meant but I had an idea. His wife, Claire, was pretty observant on her trips escorting L.L. to his office. I think she'd convinced him our people weren't working very hard, which was true. L.L. wanted me to walk around the work areas and pick up the pace, but he didn't tell Carl. I felt this assignment trespassed a little into Carl's domain and told him of L.L.'s instructions. "Forget it" was Carl's response. But he didn't tell L.L.

ETHEL WILLIAMS: I can remember [Carl] calling me down to the office after Leon was there and saying, "What has that boy got in mind? What is the limit? How high does he want to go? Five million? Ten million?" and I sat there not saying a word, wondering what—something Leon had wanted to put in the catalog, who knows what it was.

During my first year at L.L.Bean, I naively introduced our local IBM representative to Carl to discuss the feasibility of the IBM 1401 punch card system. I'd seen several applications of the system in local businesses, and it had possibilities for our manual order entry and mailing-list maintenance. The presentation took place in Carl's office. As it progressed Carl got increasingly agitated and ultimately enraged at the thought of changing anything. I got our presenters out of the room as quickly as I could.

SHAILER HAYES: If we got too many orders in, more than we could handle, "Send them back." That would be Carl's opinion. "Send them back. Got too many. Can't handle them. Send them back to them." Course they'd be handled some way, but that would be his thoughts. "Send them back." He'd come right out with it too. "Got too many orders. Send them back to 'em. Got business enough without 'em."

L.L. always had a big laugh and warm welcome for everybody except his two sons. His relationship with Carl and Warren was his only dark side. (Warren, or Warnie, worked in the company, but he played no real role or he refused to play any role of significance.) My mother, L.L.'s one daughter, always said that L.L. treated Carl very harshly growing up, Warren as well, but more Carl than Warnie.

BARBARA BEAN GORMAN: He just expected perfection of his children. They ought to do whatever he told them to. Like me with the swimming. Well, I adored, worshiped the ground my father walked on. To me he was a hero all of my life. If he thought it was a good idea for me to swim, I would swim across the lake and dive off a second-story building, probably, if he was behind me. But with Carl and Warnie he was too critical. He'd bawl them out in front of people, you know, which was a terrible thing to do. Made them even more self-conscious than they were. It isn't too easy to say your father owns the company you're working in. "Well, can't you go out and get a job of your own?" . . . I think [Carl and Warnie] had a hard life. It made me feel bad for them. I think it took away all their initiative. They had the feeling their father was king of the castle and that was it, and they could just come and go when he told them to. Didn't want to have any trouble with him and all that.

During my years with them, Carl and L.L. rarely spoke. Board of directors' meetings were the only opportunity for them to get together to talk. Most of the votes were legal formalities, but the two men nonetheless vehemently disagreed on everything and, after the meetings, again went their separate ways.

JESSIE BEAL: Well, they were father and son that weren't buddy-buddy, let's say. They did a lot of arguing over a lot of things. Mostly about company things. Carl had some marvelous ideas and he would present them to L.L. and L.L. would bomb 'em. And then maybe three weeks later, L.L. would call up and say, "I've got a great idea, Carl." And he would tell him just exactly what it was that he suggested. But it would go through and they would do it and it would actually be Carl's and not L.L.'s, but L.L. took credit for it. He would think it was his own . . . Carl didn't have the desire to go anywhere else, even though his father did put him down. He loved the company and I think most of the good things that the employees got out of it were Carl's doing and not L.L.'s—the profit sharing, the vacations, the bonuses; those were all the things that Carl fought for for the people.

It was a wonder the company functioned at all. In fact, it did because in reality it was being run by Ethel Williams and Jessie Beal, L.L.'s and Carl's secretaries. To say that Ethel and Jessie were secretaries is a gross understatement. If you wanted to get something done, you worked through the two of them. They were both very capable, very committed to the company, and trusted implicitly by L.L. and Carl. In turn, they behaved responsibly and intelligently in keeping company processes moving, and involving L.L. and Carl to the extent they wanted to be involved.

Jessie ran the order entry and mailing-list functions and oversaw all of the personnel issues. She was smart, energetic, and feisty. She knew everyone in the company and everything that was going on. She kept Carl informed. She kept all of us informed. A long-term employee in the 1960s once recalled, "It was Jessie that you approached if you wanted a raise. You saw her first, and then she went on to see Carl on your behalf."

Ethel ran L.L.Bean's catalog production and advertising program. L.L. gave overall approval, but Ethel did all of the preparatory work and follow-up, coaxing and cajoling L.L. and his rubber stamp into making the right decisions. Ethel dealt with the buyers, the ad agency, and the printer. She made sure the catalog merchandising process worked. L.L. also edited catalog descriptions with an overactive blue pencil that cared little for subjects and predicates. He was convinced "people don't read much anymore," probably because he didn't. He cut out the meaning and charm of copy he had written himself. With calm persistence and unfailing respect to L.L., Ethel was able to facilitate the new-product presentations and to restore meaning to the catalog copy.

It all required tricky diplomacy, as shown in a 1965 letter from Ethel to L.L. and his wife in Florida:

ETHEL WILLIAMS: Thank you for returning the last pages of the circular material but I am sorry that they upset Mr. Bean . . . As to the long descriptions . . . Wid Griffin feels that the sleeping bag business is getting very competitive and this new sleeping bag filler material is a major improvement but requires a lot of explanation . . . But I'm sure that if Mr. Bean were here in Freeport he could take Wid Griffin's copy, or Leon's, and put the old red pencil to it . . . just one more reason why we will be glad to have you two back in town soon.

Wid Griffin was the third key employee who kept the company going. Wid and Jessie were especially critical in handling our Christmas peak business. A big percentage (25 percent) of our business came in between Thanksgiving and Christmas. Because we had no automated systems and everything was done by hand, we always fell behind. Everyone from all over the company pitched in, getting the mail orders written up, picked and packed, and shipped to our customers. Wid and Jessie kept track of everything and scheduled us all for evening and weekend work. It was a family affair.

L.L. and Carl did not worry much about the peak or the business itself or catalog competition or any other unpleasant factors in the business environment. Their basic assumption seemed to be that L.L.Bean would simply go on for another fifty years as it had in the past.

I was less confident. I had been reading all the catalogs I'd sent for from the magazine ads. We obviously weren't alone. I received catalogs from Herter's, of Waseca, Minnesota; Gokey Company, St. Paul, Minnesota; Norm Thomson, Portland, Oregon; Corcoran, Inc., Stoughton, Massachusetts; Johnny Appleseed, Beverly, Massachusetts; Carroll Reed, North Conway, New Hampshire; C.C. Filson Co., Seattle; Deerskin Trading Post, Danvers, Massachusetts; Eddie Bauer, Seattle; Charles F. Orvis Co., Manchester, Vermont; and the biggest retailing name of all in the outdoors, Abercrombie & Fitch of New York.

Abercrombie & Fitch was the outdoors company I most admired when I first joined L.L.Bean. This was the original and legendary Abercrombie & Fitch, founded in 1892 by David Abercrombie and Ezra Fitch. Over the years it had acquired the preeminent position in the business and among outdoors people. It had outfitted many major expeditions and had served such notables as Theodore Roosevelt, Ernest Hemingway, Charles Lindbergh, and Admiral Richard Byrd.

Abercrombie & Fitch sold the best and newest of everything in hunting, fishing, and all outdoors equipment, as well as attractive sportswear for its outdoorsy clientele. Salesmen calling at L.L.Bean told me how much of their product Abercrombie & Fitch was selling, as an inducement for us to buy. It was the big name. Its multistory store on Madison Avenue in Manhattan (with a fly-casting pool on the roof) was one of the wonders of the world for people interested in outdoor activities and related lifestyle products. To my knowledge it was the largest sporting goods store in the world.

In the 1910 catalog, Ezra Fitch wrote ("From one sportsman to another"), "Our goods are made up, not merely to sell, but to use, and each individual thing we carry is selected by us, because it is the best thing we can find for the purpose for which we suggest it." This was a worthy commitment and one shared by L.L. in his catalogs.

Abercrombie & Fitch's approach was an elitist one, however, and its prices were correspondingly high. I always felt a bit out of place when I shopped its sales floors. But its comprehensive and quality approach to outfitting its clientele of outdoors sportsmen was an impressive concept, and everything it did in store merchandising, promotions, and catalog creative was first class and reflected its high-quality credentials.

Reading all our competitors' catalogs made me nervous, given how little the people at L.L.Bean knew about the outdoors or about the outdoors business. Judging from their catalogs, the other companies all seemed a lot more proficient and expert than we were—more advanced in their product assortments, the relative sophistication of their catalogs, and their apparent knowledge of the outdoors and outdoor activities. Their products seemed to me more contemporary in styling and more technologically advanced than ours.

I feared for the ability of L.L.Bean, Inc. to compete. No one else in the company seemed to be aware of any danger. There was no leadership. L.L.'s and Carl's purpose was to make sure there was as little change as possible. But I thought that we had a responsibility for the people who depended on the company for their livelihood. If the company failed, given their ages and the lack of any provision for retirement, many of them would have difficulty finding new work or a comfortable retirement. At the same time, I sensed real opportunity at L.L.Bean. There were many obvious ways to improve.

Then abruptly, in the fall of 1961, after almost a year and a half with the company, I was recalled to active duty in the Navy with my Naval Reserve unit. Our reserve destroyer, home-ported in South Portland, was sent to Guantanamo Bay, Cuba. We spent a year patrolling the Windward Passage as the cold war heated up in the Caribbean.

While I was gone from L.L.Bean, L.L. and the board of directors voted that "each new item be approved by all of the Directors before going in the catalog." The vote was a reaction to the few changes in the product line I had been able to make in my first year. Getting *everyone* on the board, especially both L.L. and Carl, to approve every new product meant that there would be virtually no new products. If the directors had taken this step before I was recalled, I would have had to leave the company.

3

Who Will Succeed L.L.?

I N HIS FALL 1962 CATALOG, L.L. celebrated the fiftieth anniversary of his company's founding.

Freeport, Maine
July 30, 1962

For fifty years I have been sending catalogs to sportsmen all over the world. I wish to take this opportunity to express my heartfelt gratitude to the many friends I have made and the many hunters, fishermen, and campers who have seen fit to trade with us over these years.

I have always greatly enjoyed hunting and fishing and can honestly say it has been a pleasure helping others enjoy these wonderful sports.

In 1912 the first 4-page catalog illustrating my Maine Hunting Shoe was mailed out. The shoe is still with us. The catalog has grown to 116 pages. I believe the success of our catalog has been that everything we offer is guaranteed to be practical for its purpose. We never hesitate to return a customer's money, no questions asked, and intend to follow this policy for the next fifty years.

I should like to remind everyone who comes to Maine that the latchstring is always out at L.L.Bean, Inc.

[signed] *L.L. Bean*

It was his valedictory, after half a century in the business he had started at forty. "I'm not sixteen anymore," he joked to a reporter on his ninetieth birthday that year. L.L. was still a charmer, especially when the press was involved.

He could make light of his age, but he was clearly showing it. His energy level had declined noticeably and his attention span was limited. He had remained interested in the outdoors, at least until his late eighties. Until then he could still hunt deer from a stand or troll for salmon on East Grand Lake, but then he pretty much had to give it up.

He began coming up to the office by way of the freight elevator, and usually Claire escorted him. He had to come all the way across the salesroom floor and through the Ladies Department, so it was something of an event when he arrived, particularly for customers. Everybody would stop and watch. He was still fairly erect but he walked with a shuffle. In the early 1960s he began to use a walker. He had started to become feeble, though he still had that booming voice.

L.L. hurt his back in late 1964 and thereafter rarely came to the office or held directors' meetings. The modus vivendi was similar to when L.L. was in Florida, except Ethel commuted daily to his house in Freeport to keep him involved. The rest of us visited periodically to get approvals.

I had returned in 1962 from my year's recall to active duty in the Navy. The board vote taken in my absence—to require full board approval for all new products added to the catalog—was never communicated to me and was never enforced. It would have created an impossible situation for me in trying to update the product lines. I learned about it only in writing this book; it was another example of the lack of communication among Bean family members in the company.

While I was away, merchandising and marketing activity had ground to a halt. It was increasingly difficult for the buyers to meet with L.L., and they had given up trying to introduce new products. The catalog continued to be the same outdated mishmash. L.L. and Carl were generally absent from the premises, and Ethel and Jessie played increasingly important roles.

Who Will Succeed L.L.?

Working for L.L. and Carl again, making $80 a week while several of my friends were in law school or business school or other exciting careers, I should have felt frustrated. Much as I might have envied them, however, I had been eager to return. Graduate school did not have the real-life, compelling appeal of the here-and-now L.L.Bean.

I liked the idea of L.L.Bean and the way of life its products represented. L.L.'s Golden Rule of treating customers like human beings made a lot of sense. I liked the customers I had met in the store and those who corresponded with us by mail. Identifying with them and their outdoor interests appealed to me personally. L.L.'s notions of "good merchandise," although lacking in execution at the time, influenced me a lot.

I also liked the people who worked at L.L.Bean and their sincere and helpful attitudes. So a combination of duty to the people "to keep it going," along with a great fascination with the L.L.Bean potential—and some inertia—kept me there. I had no grand plans for the company, but I saw many opportunities to do a better job for our customers and for Bean people.

> SHAILER HAYES: Leon didn't always agree with L.L. and he'd say so. L.L. didn't pay any attention to him at all. That was a lot of trouble then. Not trouble, actually, but disagreement. Leon didn't hesitate. If he didn't agree, he'd say so. He wouldn't vote for anything he didn't agree on.

I guessed Carl would retire when L.L. died. That was the grapevine theory, but I had no way of knowing that. I'd simply have to deal with Carl in the event. It was clear our current relationship was not sustainable. It wasn't clear what his intentions were.

When I returned from the Navy I returned to my desk in the clothing department and picked up where I'd left off in 1961. I continued to work on all of our product assortments with our buyers, making up the catalogs with Ethel and reading all the customer correspondence, trade publications, catalogs, and whatever I could find that related to L.L.Bean. I began to develop my own thoughts on what products and merchandising strategies we should pursue. My black book notes written at the time include:

In upgrading lines do not neglect mid-priced items and alienate average customer—offer something to wider range—avoid isolation into A&F elitist area.

From working in the store I was aware that our customer base was largely a middle-class group of people, with some upper-income folks and a lot of working people. L.L.'s pricing had always been frugal. I liked the idea that many working people patronized the L.L.Bean store. I wanted to always have products that were of good value to them, as well as to those who were more affluent. "You get what you pay for" was the response I wanted.

All special requests rate prompt and careful attention—if customer takes time to write, deserves our time [in response].

I was frustrated by our inability to make timely responses to customers who had questions or to make the extra effort to fill special requests. In some cases we were even ignoring them. We weren't providing the service we should have been.

Stock line of merchandise to extent that if a person walked in without a stitch on he could be completely outfitted for a trip anywhere.

I wanted to be a complete outfitter in relation to the various activities we served, like fishing, hiking, and backpacking. There were real gaps in the line, and that bothered me.

Composite of various recommended camping [equipment] lists— refine in detail and be represented in each item with best appropriate [item for purpose].

Bean's is specialty house—merchandise should be new, unique, traditional but hard to find.

In catalog merchandising we had to have definitive products with their own identity that we could create stories about in our catalog copy. They couldn't be just run-of-the-mill products; they had to be special sorts of things that were unique and appealing.

Go easy on haberdashery items.

Who Will Succeed L.L.?

I was concerned about the company's becoming more of a clothing company than an outdoors company.

Assumption: Profits in camping equipment not significant (money made in clothing and shoes)—trade up and offer best available where possible and good value maintained—but don't price us out of our bracket.

A lot of the hard goods we sold then, such as camping gear and sleeping bags, were just poor quality and poor functional value as a result. Upgrading our camping equipment products would mean they would cost more money, but I wasn't concerned about being overpriced because we didn't sell that much at the lower prices. I didn't want to price ourselves into the high-end Abercrombie & Fitch area, but we still needed the most functional products we would find.

No gimmicks, games, etc. in catalog.

This came from dealing with customers in the store. They looked to Bean for no-nonsense products. Anything at all gimmicky would get a lot of negative comment. It was something L.L. always preached about.

Catalog: Keep it simple.

"Keep it simple" was another L.L. admonition that I subscribed to.

Continue to look for unique staple merchandise [and] avoid fads even though they may sell.

Yet another advisory from L.L. that made sense to me. Looking back all these years later, I was struck by the fact that many of these early comments foresaw many of the big merchandising issues the company would face over time, issues that would come up again and again through the years.

I had read somewhere that "Retail is detail," and I continued to immerse myself in growing my product knowledge both by using our products and by studying whatever material I could get on them. I honestly doubt whether there was anyone else in the industry who had the depth of knowledge I was to acquire on such a broad array of apparel, footwear, and sporting goods. Good retailing requires good intuitive judgment, based on absorbing a great many factual details about products and how they work and look. You had to be able to respond to many new product initiatives instinctively, based on both broad and deep factual knowledge as well as well-developed intuition and a good eye.

On rejoining L.L.Bean in 1962, I again picked up my formal business education and began evening courses at the University of Maine in Portland (now the University of Southern Maine). I was taking two courses per semester, learning a lot and thoroughly enjoying it. Course selections, which included business management, production management, business law, marketing, and data processing—related to my perceived needs for managing L.L.Bean.

In the process I was also learning a lot about what was not working at L.L.Bean. We had no sales reporting or inventory management systems, no operating budgets, no standard costing system in our manufacturing operations. We had no idea what it cost to make the Maine Hunting Shoe, or a duffle bag, or how much it cost to pack and ship a product. We didn't know the status of work in process or how long it took us to fulfill orders. We had no way of keeping track of anything and consequently couldn't tell what was going on in any part of the business without being there.

Those courses were useful, but they didn't help me understand how a business worked as a whole. I was beginning to understand the various parts of a company, such as merchandising or manufacturing or order fulfillment, but not how all the parts related to each other. The business model and overall dynamics finally came together for me, however, when I started taking accounting courses. Maybe I missed my calling, but there was something satisfying as well as enlightening in learning double-entry bookkeeping and tying together the diverse functions of a business by way of the general ledger. You could read the story of the enterprise there. I took seven semesters of debiting and crediting a multitude of T-accounts and studying accounting theory. Each course seemed to provide new revelations about the business model, until finally the lights went on and I felt I knew how all the parts worked together. Now I could relate, for example, the amount we paid our leather cutters to our overall costs of goods and ultimately to overall profitability. If profitability was up or down, I understood how you could trace it to its basic components and understand the causes.

I capped my night school education with a Dale Carnegie course. Public speaking intimidated me and I needed to overcome this. We'd periodically get requests from the Lions Club, the Chamber of Commerce, or some other local group to have somebody talk about the company. There was no one else in L.L.Bean to do it, and I saw that I'd be getting into more of that. The course was a great help to me, and I won a lot of automatic pencils for best speech of the week. But I never learned to enjoy public speaking.

> BANK LOAN OFFICER: L.L. Bean is still very active and will be leaving for Florida next week. Carl has not spent very much time in the office so far this summer . . . More and more active management is resting in the hands of Leon, the grandson. Leon and his brother Tom are both on the Board of Directors which continues to be strictly a company affair with Shailer Hayes, Carl Bean, L.L. Bean, and two men from the company. L.L.Bean, Inc. will rest rather soon on the shoulders of Leon Gorman. According to Shailer, Leon has good ideas and initiative. He expressed the wish that Leon understand the philosophy behind some of the procedures and methods of the company.

In our merchandising cycle, one opportunity was especially obvious. We had a gap in our catalog mailings between Fall and Spring and it was called Christmas. By enlisting Ethel's support I convinced L.L. we needed a thirty-two-page circular to fill the void for Christmas 1963. Our first mailing was a financial success, but, more importantly, it contained a lot of new products that were well accepted by our customers.

Through either lack of energy or interest, L.L. considered this circular and subsequent versions lesser publications. Products introduced in circulars didn't have to go through his approval process, and he didn't pay much attention to them or their contents. So circulars gave me the opportunity to test new products that I thought were appropriate for L.L.Bean. I encouraged the other buyers to use circulars as a vehicle for upgrading their product lines. (We also added a Summer circular in

1964.) If successful, the new products could be added to the regular catalog lines.

The reason circulars were a fairly painless way to add new products
to the line was the way L.L. reviewed new catalogs. As we were planning a new catalog, we would do a mock-up of each page by pasting in
clippings of product presentations—pictures and text—from prior catalogs. New products, of course, had no such clippings and so required
actual photographs and typed copy. As a result, when L.L. scanned the
mocked-up pages, he immediately saw what was new and what was not,
and he was likely to yank immediately any new item not already approved by him. If products had been introduced in a circular, however,
they were likely to escape L.L.'s notice because they already had a
printed clipping from the circular and no longer looked like new products on the mocked-up catalog pages. He was as likely to approve those
pages as he was pages filled only with products from previous catalogs,
because they all looked like carryover products. I remember he used to
give his approval by stamping every single page with a huge, double-
action mechanical stamp that put down "L.L. Bean" in red letters. He
would bang that stamp down with real authority.

I obviously had no authority to do what I was doing with the circulars, nor were the buyers under any obligation to cooperate with me,
but they knew that the company's future survival, and theirs as well, required this kind of initiative. I suppose it was subterfuge, but all the
products added to the catalog in this way had been proven via circular
sales and in fact were not "new." We never told L.L. the products had
been in previous catalogs. They just looked that way.

In any case, for reasons of timing or relevance, some new products
could be introduced only in the regular catalogs. So L.L. stayed involved, and even in 1965 I wrote to him in Florida, seeking his approval.

March 24, 1965
Dear Grandpa:

*I think you should definitely consider adding the following item
to our Fall 1965 Catalog.*
  THE OUTDOORSMAN STOCKING

This is an extra thick cotton thermal stocking. Fully lined with a terry pile of Hercules "Olefin" fiber. This is a unique construction as it wicks away moisture from the feet, keeping them dry as well as warm.

It actually works as several of us have used samples around here.

The company plans some national advertising of this stocking and would limit distribution to us and one other company. This would mean some valuable publicity at no cost.

I believe the stocking is warmer and more durable than any we have. It is of excellent quality and should prove profitable.

As to inventory, it comes in six sizes and retails for about $2.50. It's not cheap but it is more profitable for us to handle a stocking in this range.

By discontinuing our last year's Cotton Thermal Stocking (none in stock) and White Camp Stocking (Gray would be discontinued) we would not be adding to our stock.

Would be very pleased to get your reaction to the above.

Sincerely,
[Signed] Leon

The problem we faced in working on the product line was that there was no longer an L.L.Bean point of view, articulated or even just understood, as to what was special about our products or our positioning. Arthur Bartlett had expressed it as a reflection of L.L.'s lifestyle in his *Saturday Evening Post* article nearly twenty years earlier.[1] But L.L.'s lifestyle was no longer a guiding factor in the 1960s because of his age and infirmity.

Hence there were no guidelines as to the mix among our various product lines (apparel, footwear, fishing and hunting, and miscellaneous tools, bags, and home products) or the right balance between active and casual products. ("Active" products were for use in an outdoor activity, and "casual" products were for use in a relaxed, leisurely setting.) Everything had been L.L.'s personal choice. It was an important issue. The overall assortment of products is the key factor in creating a brand

and establishing what it means. As readers thumb through the catalog, the product displays create the impression in their minds of who you are, what you do, and who your customer is. If the assortment is irrelevant or inconsistent, readers don't know who you are, or care very much either. We were inventing a new L.L.Bean merchandising rationale and positioning strategy, very cognizant of our understanding of L.L.'s basic values but bringing them up-to-date.

Deleting irrelevant and inappropriate products (like the nurse's shoe, the CLB Oxford) was not a problem. People were simply not buying them. Dropping them presented no risk to our identity or our financial performance. Replacing them with relevant and attractive products across the board required trial and error. There were no quality standards as to materials, construction, and design, and little anecdotal information on L.L.'s expectations. In the years I worked for him, the closest he came was saying that things had to be "practical." But we, the buyers, shared a bias toward quality fabrications and design and commonsense functionality. Ern Griffin, Wid's brother and an experienced outdoorsman and trapper, was our buyer of outdoor tools. He was especially eager to upgrade the quality of our folding knives.

One area we did not change was L.L.'s pricing policy, which remained a tight 37½ percent markup on everything, rounded off to the nearest nickel, plus free shipping. I don't know where L.L. came up with his 37½ percent, but it represented exceptional value and challenging margins. It was not sustainable long term as we invested in updating our operations. Even with our tight pricing, Carl used to boast about buying his Chinos and sport shirts at a Portland bargain basement and not paying the prices I charged for ours.

Initially we added products to our men's and women's sportswear lines. Tartans, primary colors, natural fibers, and classic styling were some of our product characteristics.

We upgraded our utility and field wear, such as Heavy Duty Bush Pants, Tackle Pack Vests, down outerwear, and hiking boots, and we offered an insulated version of the Maine Hunting Shoe.

In 1965, we introduced one of the fishing industry's first ferrule-less fly rods, a rod made by Fenwick. Prior to this, fly rod sections were connected by a metal ferrule, or joint, which created an annoying flat spot as the rod flexed when casting. The new construction was a tapered "glass to glass" innovation that smoothed out the action and was a major advance in fly rod technology. The addition had to go through the regular approval process because it needed to be introduced in the Spring catalog in time for the fishing season. It required all of Wid's expertise and diplomacy to explain the technology to L.L.

We also introduced down-filled sleeping bags to the Bean line, as well as the newest synthetic fiberfills; external-frame family and expedition tents; external-frame backpacks; blaze orange hunting apparel in conjunction with the Maine Governor's Committee on Hunting Safety; propane gas camp stoves; and Old Town fiberglass canoes. Family camping, in tents and RVs (recreational vehicles), was booming, as was backpacking and wilderness camping. Lots of people were getting into the outdoors.

We also began establishing a position in the home and camp furnishings area with "Snowshoe Furniture," wool "Trapper Blankets," "Franklin Woodstoves," "Boat and Tote Bags," "Kitchen Cutlery," and extensions of our Hudson's Bay Blankets and some of L.L's domestic favorites.

Through all these changes, the Maine Hunting Shoe continued to be our benchmark for functional value and practical design. By 1967 we had comparable products and competitive positions in fly-fishing, upland and waterfowl hunting, hiking, backpacking, family camping, canoeing, and winter activities, including snowshoeing. We also had a base in men's and women's casual apparel and home and camp furnishings.

Our women's catalog products were distinctly unfashionable and utilitarian, which seemed to appeal to our no-nonsense customers. Carl's wife, Hazel, managed our Ladies' Department in the retail store. It had been opened in 1954 at the suggestion of Claire Bean to give the women something to do while their husbands browsed. Hazel refused to display most of our catalog offerings with her trendier sportswear assortment. Generally, I got along with Hazel quite well, but our points of view about appropriate sportswear for the L.L.Bean woman were far apart. Hazel was an attractive, stylish lady and liked attractive, stylish clothes. That's what we got, and that was the beginning of the ongoing debate about who the "Bean woman" was, a debate that persisted long after Hazel and me.

The catalog was printed in black-and-white letterpress, with the cover and inside cover pages in four-color. We resized all our product photographs to make them uniform, and we allocated catalog space in proportion to demand. For instance, L.L. had given a full page to his Sheepskin Innersoles, an accessory item for the Maine Hunting Shoe. They were certainly an important product, adding warmth, comfort, and support underfoot, but they were not a high-dollar item. We reduced the display to a quarter page and did the same amount of business.

Ethel and I set up a catalog makeup room in the old directors' room. We built racks and paperboard page holders on which we laid out all 100-plus pages of whatever catalog we were working on. It was a great help in organizing and sequencing the pages, and we brought more coherence and understanding to our overall product lines. (At least, Ethel and I could understand them better. Our customers still wanted an index.)

Overall we made the catalog easier to use and, I believe, more informative. I rewrote most of the product copy, keeping L.L.'s prose where it added color and made sense. I had no training in writing copy, but I had taken an excellent course in expository writing in college with a professor who appreciated the precise meaning of words as well as tight, to-the-point writing.

I tried to write from the customer's perspective and answer the questions I would have if I were considering a purchase. In addition I tried to create an identity for the product. We were not selling a flannel shirt but the Scotch Plaid Flannel Shirt, Bean's definitive version.

If the product had a good story, the chances were that it would be more successful than if it didn't have a good story. "Story" meant there was something interesting about the product—such as hand sewing—some way to romance it based on its materials or fabrics, its construction, its design, its use by somebody in a certain situation, or the fact that it was manufactured in an exotic place like Iceland.

I could almost sense how successful a product would be by the degree of enthusiasm I felt while writing about it. The ferrule-less Fenwick Fly Rods were a good example. I bought one as soon as they came in.

In all this, we were not trying to contrive a "look" or self-conscious "feel" to our catalog. We were simply trying to display our products and explain them as best we could with the tools and know-how we had, which included no professional training in marketing or graphics arts. We improved the organization of the catalogs and made them easier to shop. Things were grouped more logically. The pages were laid out in a much more orderly and easier-to-read fashion. In the process, without being fully aware of it, I think we were evolving an updated L.L.Bean personality and point of view, with a look and cohesiveness that were meaningful to our customers. It was a personality based on what we used ourselves in Freeport, Maine, but more related to the customers we were dealing with—and more reflective of what they wanted to buy than just what we wanted to sell. It was customer based, as opposed to "L.L." based.

We were complimented by a marketing expert in 1966. Paul Bringe wrote this in his newsletter, *Direct Mail Briefs*, of our Fall catalog:

> This is not a pretentious catalog and it should not be. Too much color and slick paper printing would hurt the quality-and-tested-products feel that is apparently important to Bean's customers.[2]

Customers followed our activities with intense and even proprietary interest. I kept an extensive card file of their suggestions. They wanted Chamois Cloth Shirts in every color of the rainbow. A man wanted a device for relieving himself without having to get out of his sleeping bag. We responded to all these customers.

Not everyone agreed with our responses or welcomed change. Sometime in the 1960s we put green carpeting on the salesroom floor. The carpet replaced a hardwood floor that was sanded down every winter to clean off the dirt and grime from thousands of customers' feet. It got to the point that the floor was too thin to sand again, so we put the carpet down. To this day many people say nothing's been the same at Bean since.

Another example is a product we used to sell that was a combination compass, matchbox, and whistle for deer hunters. A nonhunter confronted me in the store once and criticized me severely and personally for cheapening L.L.'s line of practical products with this touristy gimmick. Actually, although it looked like a gadget, it really was a practical emergency item, and it was in the line before I showed up. But I was beginning to be seen as the embodiment of all that was wrong with L.L.Bean, while L.L.'s deification continued undiminished with our newfound growth.

In the middle of all this, Charlie Leighton and Frank Tucker of Harvard Business School wrote its first case on the company:

> In the summer of 1965 Leon Arthur Gorman, a grandson of L.L. Bean and a vice president of the company, wondered if his grandfather's philosophy and business methods could be incorporated into new management systems, or whether there would have to be important changes to enable the company to continue its profitable growth. Gorman had recently made several recommendations that he thought would improve efficiency, cut costs, and increase sales, but they had been turned down by the company's two top officers. His grandfather and his uncle felt that since business was increasing there was no reason to make changes, even though Gorman's recommendations might have merit.[3]

The case positioned the upstart Gorman, who wanted change, versus the venerable L.L., who wanted the status quo. The professor invited me to sit in the class (anonymously, until the end, when I answered questions) while he led the case discussion. The majority of the students, several with their Bean Boots on, sided with L.L. I was surprised that L.L.'s legendary story carried the day in that citadel of young, aggressive, and aspiring businesspeople. The legend was powerful stuff.

I was reassured by the fact that the majority of our new products were successful. By 1967, three-quarters of our product assortment was new and our sales had doubled since 1960. Our mailing list had grown from 350,000 names to 600,000. We were beginning to grow at 20 percent or more annual rates.

Unfortunately, as our sales grew, our operational capabilities lagged further behind, with many out-of-stock situations and fulfillment delays. Carl continued to feel we didn't need to change anything since the business was doing so well.

> BANK LOAN OFFICER: Spoke to Leon Gorman and later with Shailer Hayes today. L.L. Bean is now 94 and in Florida.

No changes in the business anticipated . . . The company continues its policy of carefully avoiding any change or new procedures as long as L.L. is alive and Carl is running the business.

Our growing success attracted more media interest. Usually Ethel or I would escort the writer around the premises and embellish the L.L. story in any way we could to keep the publicity going. It was obvious that people loved L.L.'s personality and his core product, the Maine Hunting Shoe. They provided a solid foundation and got continuous attention and nurturing. We continued to stress that L.L. was doing everything of significance in the company. Of course, he would not be there when these writers came in, and that allowed us to talk about him as if he were full of life and energy and on top of everything, as he had been thirty years earlier.

L.L.'s persona was both our heritage and our brand. I was happy to attribute all that was good about the company to L.L., and to accept personally all that was not so good, including that combination compass and matchbox. We were building the L.L.Bean brand in our image of L.L. and his legendary story. It was our legacy, and we were more than willing to take advantage of it. Unfortunately we did not know how dependent our brand was on the living L.L., who many customers felt still personally tested all of our products and then handled their orders. Would the mystique and appeal of his name continue beyond his lifetime? This was a regular topic of anxious conversation at the company.

L.L. died peacefully on February 5, 1967. It was a moving moment for all of us who had worked for him. His loss was felt, I believe, by everyone who had ever bought anything from his company or had any contact with him. I heard the news at a sporting goods show in Chicago and wept at his loss. Despite my frustrations in working for him I had felt his presence, and now his absence, as much as anyone. His genius was in projecting himself, and his impact had been profound. We would all remember him long after he was gone.

BANK LOAN OFFICER: I attended the funeral of L.L. Bean today.

Time magazine wrote, "The catalog was his pride and joy, and Bean recently read galley proofs of the 100-page Spring 1967 edition, which came out last week the day after its originator's simple funeral in his beloved snow-covered Maine woods."[4]

The top-rated *Huntley-Brinkley Report* did eight minutes on L.L.'s story. Other national media paid tribute to his passing. We received more than 50,000 letters of condolence.

The letters also included requests for our Spring catalog. The legend had been institutionalized.

Carl chose not to announce L.L.'s death in the catalog. The only company acknowledgement appeared in the catalog copy for "Bean's Chamois Cloth Shirt." In the Spring catalog, being printed just as L.L. died, it read, "This is the shirt Mr. Bean personally uses on all his hunting and fishing trips." In the Fall catalog we changed to the past tense.

Carl succeeded his father as president of L.L.Bean. Months later, that summer, Jessie told me she had just learned from his doctor's nurse that Carl was suffering from a terminal illness. He had been ill for several years, probably much of the time I was at odds with him. He died in October 1967, eight months after his father, and I succeeded Carl as president of L.L.'s company. I was fully committed to L.L.Bean and ready to go.

PART TWO

1968–1975

Chamois Cloth Shirt

4

A Committee of One

THE BOARD OF DIRECTORS voted me president on October 18, 1967, four days after Carl's death. It received two column inches in *The Portland Press Herald,* about the same amount of space the paper would give to a baked bean supper announcement at our local Congregational Church. I felt a great sense of relief in having the freedom to run the company without worrying about L.L. and Carl. I knew how the business worked. I was now a committee of one, and I was excited about my new autonomy and responsibilities.

> JESSIE BEAL: So of course Leon had a meeting . . . within the next few days [after Carl's death] of the seven [department heads in the company]. Leon wanted us to continue as we were. He said, "Look, my grandfather had to be right, and we're not going to make a lot of changes fast. Everything's going to be thought through very carefully, because he couldn't have been the success he was unless he was right." So Leon wasn't anxious to change things, as some people might have been. If he'd been a person like that, I might have been skeptical, but I wasn't.

> That first meeting included Wid, Jessie, Shailer Hayes, and several others who made up the company's leadership group. To my knowledge

this was the first meeting of managers in the company's fifty-five-year history. But I wanted to formalize the group's status as leaders and heads of their various departments. I also needed a chain of management for communicating with the organization. Up to this point, there was no formal way to communicate, not even a bulletin board.

I also wanted to assure the group I had no intentions of replacing them. We would all be involved in managing L.L.Bean. There would be no significant changes in the way the business was currently being run. We would "stay the course." I gave each of the new leaders a significant pay increase.

The talk of not changing too fast was to keep people calm. Jessie and Wid knew as well as I did that we had an urgent need to change because we were beginning to grow. In 1967 we were growing by 25 percent over the prior year. Our sales were $4.75 million. Even before 1967 our sales growth had outstripped our fulfillment and inventory management capabilities. But we couldn't touch these areas because they were Carl's. Now we were officially free to update our operations.

To stay the course meant sustaining this 25 percent rate of growth. A compounding rate of growth of 25 percent means doubling in size about every three years. I've since been told that doubling the size of a business amounts to reinventing it. We doubled in size three times in the next eight years. Lots of change going on. To the credit of Wid, Jessie, and Ethel, they did not resist it but welcomed the opportunity to do a better job for our customers.

ART PERRY: We still had no computer systems. The warehouse was archaic. We didn't have any place to put things. We were warehousing in every building in town, it seemed like. Boxes in one building down the street and the Taylor Shoe Company down the other street where the manufacturing was going on. The Dingley Press was down in the cellar. Man oh man, it was something. I remember the inventories of Chamois Shirts. We kept them on pieces of yellow paper and by hand. And you'd run out and you'd count the red Chamois Shirts. Pretty soon, going from 12 to 25 million bucks, you couldn't do that anymore. It wasn't just red Chamois Shirts; it was hunting shoes and we were starting to boom at this time. Inventory management was brutal. I think it was a question of whether or not to try to hold it to the way L.L. saw it, you know, the small company where customers come well before the bottom line and this kind of thing. Or to do what fate was doing to the company and that was just exploding. Very early in my term it was obvious what was happening. L.L.Bean was going big time.

We weren't looking for ways to grow the company. Our formula was working very well. But we needed ways to manage the growth without much infrastructure. At least for the time being, we were able to retain some of the benefits of being small and uncomplicated.

K. C. PUTNAM: It was a big family . . . in the seventies. Everybody knew what the other people were doing. It wasn't "them and us." It was an "us and us" type of thing. The offices were just in back of the store. The warehouse was downstairs. You knew what came in [to Receiving] because sometimes you got called down to help them. You all had breaks at the same time. I was an avid ping-pong player, and so I played ping-pong with the custodial folks and I played ping-pong with the receiving agent. So you knew if somebody was busy. You knew if somebody was slow. You knew how the phones were doing, the whole thing.

In December 1967 we paid a 30 percent (of base pay) cash bonus to everyone for an exceptional performance that year, as well as a 15 percent profit-sharing contribution. (The practice of paying a cash bonus to all employees at the same percentage of base compensation went back to the 1940s. It was a credit to L.L. and Carl that they shared the profits with everyone in the company and, to my knowledge, quite unique.) I wrote my first annual letter "to our employees" and thanked them for their 100 percent effort and uncomplaining cooperation. The company's reputation and success were the responsibilities of all of us. We celebrated by holding the company's first Christmas party in many years. The man in charge of making our Maine Hunting Shoe played Santa.

I also stayed involved in everything that was going on and continued to work evenings and weekends. During the peak I wrote orders with everyone else in the front office and picked orders with our shipping room staff. My Navy experience made me sensitive to morale issues and the importance of being highly visible, especially during busy times. It was important for our employees to trust me and to identify with the business's success.

We had our first shareholders' meeting in August 1968, and L.L.'s widow, Claire Bean, was elected to the board. As administrator of L.L.'s estate, Claire voted the majority of the company's stock. I didn't need an MBA to recognize the importance of having Claire's support. Claire could be sharp-tongued and she upset a lot of people on occasion. Ethel and I put a lot of effort into keeping Claire happy and meeting her day-to-day living needs. Our maintenance crew was at her house daily, doing chores and running errands.

Claire was quite perceptive and had a good sense of what was going on. She felt a real responsibility to L.L.'s legacy, and I think she knew I was equally committed. She trusted Ethel completely and eventually trusted me, and I gained her full confidence in my judgment. I kept her fully informed amid all of the growth and change following L.L.'s death. Claire once wrote to me, "I know that you are very capable of handling the business and I am confident that anything you decide is what should be done, therefore, I am in agreement with whatever you wish to do concerning the financing of the new building." She lived until 1974, and we didn't have any disagreement during her years of majority control.

At the 1974 shareholders' meeting following Claire Bean's death, we elected all of the principal family shareholders of the company to be members of the board of directors. There were seven of us in all, five family. My aunt Hazel, my cousin Linda, my two brothers Tom and Jim, and me. This board membership policy, representing all segments of the family owners, was followed throughout the years.

We convened the board quarterly and discussed everything going on, sometimes in excessive detail. We never hid anything or held back any bad news. I think this openness was critical to the family's ongoing confidence in my leadership. It did not hurt that we were successfully growing the company, profitable, and paying regular dividends in increasing amounts.

A Committee of One

TOM GORMAN: Growth was what Leon wanted and, since he was the president, I figured I should support him and not undermine his efforts. I certainly wasn't enthusiastic as he was about it, but I still wanted to see the company prosper. I certainly never had the managerial talent that he has. Very few people do, to take the company almost from the brink of bankruptcy. That's how serious it was.

We set a policy on employment of family members (all were entitled to a job commensurate with their qualifications but subject to the company's employment practices). And we had a policy on which family members would be on the succession committee in the event of my death or disability.

These seemed to be sufficient to keep the family ownership arrangement an orderly one over the years. The family was not a cohesive one and never had been, going back to L.L.'s days. Relationships were generally cordial but not close. This may be one reason we were successful in maintaining family ownership over four generations to date. Our common interest was the well-being of the company, and personal relationships didn't get in the way.

Over the years we received a great many inquiries about selling the company or going public. I didn't follow up on any of them because no family member had ever expressed any interest to me in selling the company (and making a lot of money). And I was more than happy with our situation, not wanting to work for another company or to be subject to public market constraints.

At the initial 1968 shareholders' meeting I got approval to "investigate" a variety of initiatives. These included computerizing the order processing, inventory control, and mailing-list systems; acquiring land for new construction; erecting a new building for manufacturing; installing conveyor systems for warehousing and shipping; buying catalog labeling and mailing machinery; adding an escalator in the salesroom (which we never did); and even looking into acquiring other companies.

This was quite a laundry list, but I wanted almost open-ended approval to do whatever it took to bring our facilities and operations up to competitive standards and to continue our growth. I had little knowledge of corporate finance and no idea how we would pay for these projects. I felt the need for an experienced financial person on our staff. I knew we had to move ahead on all fronts and assumed the money would be there when we needed it.

Change came apace. In 1969 we converted our mailing list to a computerized operation, with a Maine bank providing the computer service. Our mailing list had reached 700,000 names, and there weren't enough typists in the Freeport area to continue our old practice of hand-typing it twice a year. We went straight to a keypunch paper-tape application for order entry and mailing-list maintenance. As a result we avoided the burdensome conversions to the older technologies of address plates and punched cards. This was one advantage of Carl Bean's do-nothing strategy, which had rejected these initiatives when they would have been relevant. To improve our service levels and manage our inventory, we later added a perpetual inventory control application to this computer system.

We leased 20,000 square feet in the old Davis shoe factory down the street for much needed warehouse space, and 13,000 square feet in the E.E. Taylor (another shoe company) building for manufacturing space. Moving our production department from its location of fifty-eight years in our old Main Street building was traumatic. But our people were soon producing Bean products in record numbers. Some even whispered that the new place looked like a factory. They took pride in the clean, well-lit space and in being productive as well as high-quality craftspeople. As late as 1975, one-fourth of our employees worked in manufacturing. They made unique, practical, and good-quality Bean Boots, hand-sewn moccasins, soft luggage and tote bags, and a variety of specialty items—in total, about 20 percent of our product line. They gave the L.L.Bean name a lot of authenticity. Many would have shut down our production facility as being "inefficient," but I saw a lot of nonfinancial value in doing our own manufacturing. For instance, writers and photographers from the outside were more taken by our manufacturing operations than by any other area except the store.

L.L. had always had a high regard for our manufacturing operation. He respected people who could do things with their hands, mainly because he wasn't very handy himself. I shared his admiration for craftspeople and seemed to have inherited his lack of handiness as well. Manufacturing was a genuine source of company pride for both of us.

We bought Claire Bean's eighty-acre blueberry farm outside town for future expansion. We enlarged and reengineered the picking and packing rooms in the old Main Street building for greater capacity, and we bought a labeling/bundling machine for our catalog mailings, releasing a dozen people for more productive work. Because we were growing so fast there was never any problem in reassigning people displaced by newer technology, and we were continually bringing in new and younger people and reenergizing the corporate culture and attitude.

Continued growth in the early 1970s caused us to think ahead to a new facility on the Claire Bean property. In 1970 we hired Dan Lord, an experienced local businessman, to be our controller. He was to help in planning our growth and in bringing a practical business perspective to our activities. One of his first acts was to hire an assistant to come in as chief accountant, a young man named Lee Surace, who was to become the personification of L.L.Bean values over the next thirty years. Dan and Lee put together some of our sales figures, projected our growth conservatively for the next five years, and told me we had to build a new distribution center. We hired an industrial engineering firm and an architectural firm to help us with the planning, design, and construction.

Prior to breaking ground on the Claire Bean property, where we were having some siting problems, we received an offer to buy the E.E. Taylor building and property (twenty-five acres), which was closer to town on Route 1. This we did and added 15,000 square feet for warehousing to the existing building we'd been renting. We also shifted plans to build our new distribution center to the Taylor site. Construction started in 1973.

LEE SURACE: I think [the new distribution center] was a huge turning point, when the company said, "We're going to take on this building and we're in growth mode now." It felt like if we wanted to continue to grow, we were going to have more of these things facing us in the future. We were going to have more growth and more buildings and this is what we wanted to do.

67

Until this point, we had used rental space to support our growth. This building would be our first major capital commitment. I was nervous about the new construction and the new debt. It would be difficult to pull back if our growth rate was not maintained, but I felt there was no alternative and we moved ahead. It was a point of no return.

IRVING ISAACSON: That probably marks the first major transformation of the company into a modern operation. It was the watershed between what they had been as a small, Maine company and what they were going to be as a national company.

The building was designed to handle $45 million in volume. At the time (1972) we were doing about $15 million, and I guessed the new building might last us ten years. (It lasted about five before a similar-sized addition was needed.) We started building facilities well beyond what we could use, with the idea of growing into them over time, which we did, and we continued that cycle over and over again. Growth and risk became automatic expectations. We had great confidence in the on-going appeal of L.L.Bean, but our projections were always conservative.

LEE SURACE: For us [the big issue] was suddenly the growing inventory. So now you had a company that never borrowed a nickel that had to start borrowing money. It was a big change. I know L.L. used to say things like, "Never borrow money." So, it began to be, "Wait a minute. We're borrowing money. We're actually borrowing and we have to pay it back. Is this a good thing?" We had to change that [attitude] because we wanted to grow. We were going to need some outside funds.

In 1972 we acquired our first computer, an IBM System 3. To many, the computer was going to be the downfall of L.L.Bean. It was the work of the devil. We would surely lose L.L.'s personal touch, and our unique products and individual customers would be reduced to anonymous numerical codes. How would L.L. feel if he could see what I was doing to his company? Two years later we moved up to an IBM 370 mainframe and converted all of our order entry and fulfillment, inventory control, and mailing-list systems to the new computer.

LEE SURACE: It used to be you called up and said, "I want that shirt on page 16," and you'd read off the name. I remember at one time, seventy-one or seventy-two, we even said, "We're going to have product codes . . . We'll use them ourselves internally, but we won't put them in the catalog" . . . because we thought maybe the customers would be upset if we had all these numbers and product codes. We were not that kind of a company. That was Sears or Penney's.

In 1972, we put stock numbers in our catalogs for the first time and disclosed to the world that L.L.Bean had finally succumbed to computerization. It proved not to be fatal and created less of a commotion than we'd thought it would. Besides being indispensable to our operations the computer served as the uncomplaining goat for any problems that arose in our mail-order transactions. Customers and employees alike were inclined to blame the computer for whatever ills arose in their relationships. And everyone felt better as a result.

The new distribution center started up in August 1974. It was 110,000 square feet, with thirty feet of clear vertical space. Its "horseshoe" layout followed the logical flow of receiving goods (at the incoming/outgoing loading docks), warehousing them, moving to ready stock, pick and pack, and then back out the door they'd come in. We used a combination of order picking machines, conveyors, and people to make it work. The spaces were clean and brightly colored, the work of an interior designer. And the new setup worked well. I had participated in all of the planning and was very familiar with the center's operation. In fact it was our last distribution center configuration where I was qualified to conduct a credible tour. The technology soon went well beyond me.

In 1974 we also redesigned and enlarged our retail store to 8,700 square feet (a 47 percent increase). We refurbished the interior with walls of spruce strip paneling and orange shellac finish, green carpeting, and wooden fixtures of our own making. Our staff was fully informed about our products, knew the outdoors from personal experience, and had a lot of laid-back Maine personality. The product line looked good—lots of plaid flannel shirts, down-filled parkas, and Chinos; Vibram-soled hiking boots, and hand-sewn moccasins; backpacking gear, fly rods, and all the right stuff. This iteration of the retail store had the atmosphere that still means L.L.Bean to a lot of people from my generation.

> K. C. PUTNAM: Bean, at the time, was selling spruce gum. Spruce gum was an acquired taste that many never lived long enough to acquire. There were a lot of times that people would actually chew it and end up being so sickened by it [Laughter] that they'd spit it out on the floor in the store . . . There was an accumulation, I wouldn't say a lot, but there was some around to be found.

A lot of the new, young outdoors people came to work in our store. Both the store manager and the assistant had the traditional hunting and fishing background and the traditional work ethic, and they weren't used to having their instructions questioned. We experienced a lively tension between them and the new outdoors generation. They just didn't understand each other. But the youngsters were better educated and usually won the work-scheduling debates. They also had a lot of good ideas on products, and if they didn't like what we had they wouldn't sell it. We tried a compact "Instant Gourmet Kit" of spices for trail cooks that was roundly rejected. They were in the outdoors every chance they got, and they helped us a lot in developing and upgrading our lightweight camping, canoeing, and winter sports gear. We had sold snowshoes for many years and introduced cross-country skiing in 1970.

> JOE MURRAY: Well, I always made fun of [their long hair] until my kid started growing his hair and then I said, "Now I can't say anything about it." They were honest, good people. But I couldn't see this long hair because I don't have any hair myself. I called them transients, because they'd work four or five years and get some money and then go to California or you don't know where they were going to go from here. They'd been to college and they'd come to work for us. More college people than we ever

had in our life were up there at the store. They knew the outdoors pretty well. If you taught them anything, they could catch right on. They'd either done it or you explained it to them.

In the summer of 1974, an outdoors writer from Memphis took his family on a tour of the Gaspe Peninsula in Quebec, Canada. He had been an L.L.Bean catalog fan since childhood and decided to visit our store on the way home. He was quite enthusiastic about the store's appearance and the gear available to sportsmen. In a later article, he went on to say, "The business is now being carried on by Bean's grandson, Leon Gorman, and everything is almost exactly like L.L. left it."

I was pleased with his reaction. Even though he'd never been to the store before, there was no doubt it was L.L.'s place. The mystique was very much alive. Gorman hadn't spoiled it.

In 1975, we established a new "customer service" department to promptly, accurately, and courteously respond to the hundreds of inquiries, suggestions, and complaints we received each week. Until this time, the handling had been spread throughout the company in a haphazard, unpredictable, and unsatisfactory way. The new system was designed by a consultant, Stanley Fenvessy, who was helped by a young colleague, Bill Henry.[1] I had heard Stan speak at an industry seminar the previous year. He took both a detailed and a comprehensive view of the order fulfillment and customer service functions, the "back end" of the business. Most consultants focused on the more glamorous marketing and advertising functions, but Stan specialized in the details of expeditiously researching and answering all of the individual customers' questions and complaints and keeping them happy in the process. He brought discipline to our caring attitude, and that resulted in a day-in, day-out commitment to superior customer satisfaction that was unique in the industry and, I think, a significant innovation in catalog marketing.

BILL HENRY: One of the most amazing things is that L.L.Bean at that time had a reputation for outstanding service . . . The way people at Bean reacted to customers was totally oriented towards making the customer happy, to the nth degree. But here's what was missing: the actual service level measured by standards, such as speed of response, was terrible . . . So many of the things they were doing were almost like cultural extensions of life on coastal Maine in the early twenties. It was really kind of wonderful, but not highly organized or efficient.

Because they did their best, people thought they were doing a good job. Unfortunately, their best wasn't good enough. If a problem happened, people would stand on their heads to fix it. But it would take them a long time to look up the original order and shipping documents in our cumbersome metal filing cabinets, then talk to whoever made the order filling error or could answer a product question, and finally get the information back to a typist. Nor was there any prioritization based on the magnitude of the problem or the urgency of response.

Stan's criteria for satisfactory order fulfillment (or inquiry response) time in 1975 was the calendar week following the week in which a customer placed the mail or phone order or query. With a lot of good effort we achieved this standard over the next year or so.

Our in-stock levels (the percentage of items in stock and available when the customer wants them) continued to be unsatisfactory (in the 70 to 80 percent range) as our high growth rates exceeded our abilities to forecast sales and manage inventory. L.L. used to say you can't do business with an empty wagon, and ours was empty too often. Inventory management became a priority and proved to be one of the most challenging disciplines for us in the catalog business.

The famous L.L.Bean guarantee of satisfaction was the final service element we dealt with in this period. The many magazine and newspaper stories about L.L. in the past had talked about his personal guarantee on everything he sold, but the guarantee hadn't been in print since his 1919 catalog. Nor was it practiced when I joined the company. I felt guilty that we were given credit for a satisfaction guaranteed policy we didn't practice.

Customer returns by mail or in the store were subject to an awkward, time-consuming, and generally unpleasant negotiating contest between the customer and one of our staff in the store or by mail. Neither party was ever satisfied with the outcome. The procedure didn't make any customer relations sense to me, nor was it economic. It cost us more in haggling time than a full refund or credit at the outset.

I started studying other catalog guarantees. There were a few in print, but they were mostly restricted to new or unused products or to unrealistically short time limits. Only Sears had an unqualified guarantee that made sense. I used it as a basis for writing our L.L.Bean product satisfaction guarantee. This was in 1967, and I had trouble convincing our staff of its feasibility. They were convinced we'd be overwhelmed with frivolous and fraudulent returns.

In the Spring 1968 catalog we included our first guarantee statement. It specified that any returns had to be new or unused but was purposely vague about what we would do if the product had been used. (Our practice was unconditional.) Disaster did not strike. The vast majority of customers could be trusted to be fair in returning unsatisfactory products, and this was a crucial lesson for L.L.Bean. If we expected customers to trust us in buying products through the mail, we had to trust them in deciding whether or not the products were satisfactory throughout their expected lifetime. The "expected lifetime" was to be determined by the customer, and sometimes it could extend to thirty years or more.

The next year we broadened our guarantee to make it unqualified, the broadest in the industry, and in 1970 we even printed it in boldface.

"Guarantee" Our products are guaranteed to be 100 percent satisfactory. Return anything purchased from us that proves otherwise. We will replace it or refund your money, as you wish, and return your postage costs. Please attach letter of instructions and our packing slip, if available, with returned merchandise.

Our customers continued to be trustworthy, and we validated a big part of the L.L. story.

I insisted that we comply with the satisfaction guaranteed policy, no matter what. It was necessary to follow the policy closely in its early years. I was on the sales floor one day when a customer came up, wearing one of our most expensive parkas. He'd had the parka some time but didn't like the pockets. Even though there was nothing wrong with them, he just didn't like them. I gave him a full refund with no further questions. One of our vendors happened to be on the floor and witnessed it.

He'd never seen such a thing and shook my hand. Our staff got the message I was serious.

> ART PERRY: This happened a couple times. Somebody would come through with their family and they'd buy a tent. They'd go to Baxter State Park for a couple of weeks and they'd come back and say, "The tent leaked." The poor sales guy would come in off the sales floor and say, "This guy's stealing us blind." I'd say, "I know it. Give him his money back." And they would, but I'd have to sit guys down because they'd get so hot at the customers for being takers. You'd have to explain that we'd get it back in the long run. It's a tough concept to get, but it did pay off, you know, and everyone realized it paid off. But, oh, it just killed the guys to be taken and smile at some son of a bitch who had his hand in your pocket. You know? It was awful. It didn't happen often, but often enough, in different contexts.

By 1975 our return rate had doubled. I thought this was a good thing. We got a lot of products out of our customers' hands that they were not happy with. And they became extremely loyal customers in the future. They also told many of their friends about L.L.Bean and helped to further build our reputation for trust. Our guarantee of 100 percent satisfaction became an L.L.Bean hallmark.

One thing we did not do in this period was to put in a budget system or any form of planning process or attempt to account for manufacturing as a profit center. I'd been grousing about these issues during my years with L.L. and Carl, but I still didn't do anything about them when I had the chance. We were too busy growing the business to allow time for planning and accounting. My general theory was that if you did everything you could for the customer with good-quality products and the best service you could provide, the bottom line would take care of itself. Our auditors annually disagreed with me and continued to recommend better systems of financial control.

The most important thing we did in the late 1960s and early 1970s was to upgrade our compensation and benefits programs and to improve working conditions and morale to attract good people. Jessie and I studied various material on job evaluation and job rating systems to come up with a basic structure to apply at L.L.Bean. It was quickly named the job "devaluation" system by our local wags, but it was essential to establishing internal equity among our various jobs. We used the jobs we could compare in our local employment area to increase our pay structure, first to competitive and then to more than competitive levels. It was our thinking that superior-paying jobs would attract superior-performing and younger people. It worked. By 1975 the average age of our employees was in the forties (it had been in the sixties in 1960). The dynamics of higher pay and high growth attracting high-performing people, and high-performing people contributing to high growth and higher pay (including bonuses), worked the way they were supposed to.

We increased our vacation days, installed a savings plan (with a 25 percent company match), and increased the employee discount to one-third off to get more Bean people using our products. We installed a pension plan. Our first retirees' party was in 1973. It was a happy event for many reasons. I had never let go any of our longtimers even though the pace of the business had gone well beyond some of their capabilities. So the pension plan, which was a good one, gave us all the chance to part company with good feelings, fully recognizing past contributions and a lot of pride in working for L.L.Bean.

We expanded our health-care plan, added group life insurance, continued our profit-sharing plan, and continued our annual cash bonus to all employees, now commensurate with truly superior corporate performance. We were committed to having the best wage and benefit package in the area, and I encouraged our people to compare it with their friends' and neighbors'.

There was a lot of energy and vitality in the younger employee group. Volunteers built an L.L.Bean float for Freeport's Fourth of July parade and held a fishing derby for area children that continues today. They formed softball and volleyball teams and held annual fishing and deer hunting contests as well as bridal showers and baby showers in our "rec room." In 1972, our people formed an "official" recreation committee, self-managed by volunteer leaders and self-funded. Soon we had a company picnic, a tournament for horseshoes (L.L.'s favorite pastime), ping-pong and cribbage contests, an outing club, an annual crafts fair, and "slimnastics" courses, as well as guitar, knitting, and ceramics classes. Something for everyone.

One year I was invited to the annual bowling league banquet to help award the trophies. There were fifty or sixty Bean people there and about twice as many trophies. I'd never seen so many in one place. Everybody got at least one trophy for some unique bowling accomplishment or personality attribute. And each was as thrilled as if they were the only winner in the group. I learned something about recognition that night: you can't do enough of it.

In 1970 we began an annual company publication, "*The Bean Scene*." I had a regular column, and the first year I talked about the implications of growth: "I think this opportunity for individual development and job satisfaction from jobs well done is the most important thing a company can offer. It's an opportunity not only to achieve your own goals, but to achieve them in working with others and enjoying the many satisfying personal relationships."

I think this idea was generally accepted in theory but not fully appreciated in practice. Many people simply didn't like the idea of their jobs regularly changing, nor did they have personal aspirations for growth. They wanted job security and predictability.

Mel Collins retired in 1974 after thirty years and noted in the local paper that older workers felt somewhat pressured by the efficiency techniques after Bean began to computerize the mailing lists and the inventory. Mel and a few others were never going to change to the new way. Mel didn't resist change, he just didn't.

LEE SURACE: Starting in the fall we worked Saturdays. We worked two nights a week during the holiday season. Some of us were probably working longer hours even in the off season. There was a sense of, "Wait a minute. There isn't a slow time anymore." So I think there was some stress there. I think a lot of people were being stressed just in their comprehension of what the business was now like. They had old skills and there really was a commitment to new skills and doing things in new ways, and I think some people just couldn't do it. They didn't want to do it, put it that way. "I just don't want to do that."

A Committee of One

I shared some of our people's skepticism of new technology and for several years even resisted buying a copying machine. But, in general, we prepared people as best we could and moved ahead. A few preferred the old ways with L.L. and Carl (although not the marginal wages) and wondered what the growth was all about. At times I wondered myself but I never seriously doubted our obligation to grow sales and then to keep up with it.

It was in this period that we began our outdoors trips. In June 1968, six of us—Wid, me, and four others from our staff—spent a week canoeing the Allagash River in northern Maine. Our stated purpose was to test equipment, but mostly we wanted to demonstrate that L.L.Bean was still an outdoors company and that Bean people were expected to enjoy the outdoors like our customers. Which we did—white water, black flies, and all.

It was a great experience for all of us and the first of many such "product testing" trips that were to take place in the years to come. This renewed emphasis on outdoors participation by Bean people was not confined to department heads.

JOE MURRAY: Seven days of rain, I mean rain. Everything was soaked, but when we got there, when we got to the Allagash, the sun shined . . . I said, "Someone up there doesn't like us." We turned one of the canoes over and ripped the bottom out. We had to repair that on the St. John. Some places we had to drag [the canoes] that year. That's a son of a gun. You drag three feet, rest, drag three feet, rest. The river had gotten bony on us.

We encouraged outdoor activities across the company and allocated a certain number of "outdoors days" for each department. A lot of lore quickly developed around the trips.

LEE SURACE: Leon didn't have to be the boss on those trips. He was very comfortable seeing what people did. Leon sometimes would say to me, "Oh, it's really funny. You always had people who want to just take the lead and do things." He said, "It's almost like they fight for it. 'I'll wash the dishes; I'll pack this up.'"

He would sit back and see who was doing those sorts of things. He seemed to enjoy them.

I didn't think it was appropriate to carry over business relationships into the outdoors. I thought we were out to enjoy the outdoors as a group and not be boss and subordinate but more or less peers sharing the experience. So I did not attempt to be the leader of the trips. I just wanted to see how the dynamics worked. If someone was the best ca-noeist, he led that part. The best camp cook was in charge of the meals.

There's no denying, however, that I was the boss back at Freeport and that we all had our places in the company's pecking order. But this wasn't, to me, an obvious issue on the trips.

ART PERRY: I think the trips probably worked out about the way they were intended. They were 80 percent socializing proba-bly, 20 percent business maybe. Maybe a little bit more socializing intended but, you know, the president's there and the core of the thing was the L.L.Bean Company. Now Leon's very much all the time the leader. The boss was there. Summer of seventy-three I [went on a trip] and back in the office the following Monday, Leon said, "You did a good job." It was as if he'd been watching me all week to see if I helped with the dishes, if I got up, if I did my part in the camp, how I paddled the canoe or tossed a fly, that kind of a thing.

Once in a while I'd get some feedback in relation to something I said on the trips that wasn't quite right. It made me increasingly aware I couldn't escape being the boss. I was constantly being watched, and every move and word analyzed.

5

Living the L.L. Story

I STILL PAID a lot of attention to the competition, particularly Abercrombie and Fitch. By the time I took over L.L.Bean, they had expanded their product lines to include a dominant assortment of men's and women's sportswear and home furnishings, all in typically good Abercrombie & Fitch taste and quality. Their extensive product assortments had grown from hunting, fishing, and camping to tennis, yachting, golf, and almost anything that was used outdoors, which included the backyard, the beach, or Central Park.

The evolution of Abercrombie & Fitch was upsetting to outdoors purists, but their assortments and merchandising approach in their stores and catalogs, which I still looked forward to receiving each season, all fit together very nicely to meet the full array of recreational needs appropriate to their traditional clientele. Unfortunately, their traditional clientele was aging, moving to the suburbs and the malls or being targeted by more focused catalog and specialty shop competitors. They were committed to their downtown stores in New York, Chicago, and San Francisco as well as in several fancy resort areas. Their pricing was not close to being competitive and their margins not sustainable.

Specialist outdoors companies like Orvis, REI, Cabela's, Eddie Bauer, and L.L.Bean were more relevant and provided better service and value.

By the mid-1970s, Abercrombie & Fitch was in serious financial trouble. We had actually overtaken them in revenue (something that at one time had been an idle dream on my part). They went into bankruptcy and one of America's great retail institutions was gone.

Nat Ross, the highly esteemed historian of direct marketing of L.L.Bean at the time, wrote "The company [L.L.Bean] was quick to recognize that profound social changes were taking place in the 1960's which would transform the outdoor sports and recreation field from a 'class' to a 'mass' market. As the recreation boom was on its way, L.L.Bean innovated with additional men's and women's quality products, displayed in 4-color catalogs, to satisfy the emerging interests of the mass of new customers."[1]

I never disputed this observation on our strategic astuteness, but more realistically we happened to be in the right place because we were what we were—real people who enjoyed the outdoors. Our innovation was to do what came naturally in expanding our product lines for people like us. Nat Ross was probably correct in observing that we were the first to bring high-quality, practical outdoors apparel and equipment, reasonably priced, to the emerging mass, or middle-class, market. We were just trying to do better at being L.L.Bean.

Other competitors in the outdoors business in the 1960s and 1970s included Corcoran, Inc., of Stoughton, Massachusetts. It put out a creditable and competitive catalog of outdoor gear in an L.L.Bean lookalike format. In fact Corcoran's core product was a "Paratrooper Boot" that they originally had made for the military. They didn't really lend themselves to civilian outdoor activities, and the company eventually discontinued their catalog. The Alaska Sleeping Bag Company of Beaverton, Oregon, published a catalog of good-quality down outerwear, down sleeping bags, utility apparel, and miscellaneous outdoors equipment. They were well positioned for the emerging outdoors business in the late 1960s, and a serious competitor. They ran into major inventory problems, however; out-of-stock in their best selling items and holding excessive inventories in the balance. In addition to causing the Federal Trade Commission to issue new regulations on mail-order selling, the Oregon company ran out of cash.

George Herter was still publishing his perfect-bound, phone-book-sized catalog from Herter's of Waseca, Minnesota. It contained everything imaginable in fishing and hunting paraphernalia, camping equipment, and a wide variety of unrelated products, all endorsed by his mythical Hudson Bay Guide Association. Herter described his products in the most grandiose (and often humorous) copy I have ever read. I wish I had saved my copies.

Eddie Bauer was the single strongest competitor we had in the outdoors catalog business. They were a first-class operation in every respect, with high-quality products, competitive pricing, excellent customer service, and superior catalog merchandising and marketing. I studied their catalogs in great detail. In many ways L.L.Bean and Eddie Bauer were mirror-image concepts. Both had legendary outdoors founders, one from the Northeast and the other from the Northwest. Eddie Bauer started his business in 1920, only eight years after L.L. had started his, and he retired the year after L.L. died. The two companies' value systems and reputations were quite similar. Both companies believed in superior product quality and customer service. *National Lampoon* magazine once did a parody on "Eddie Bean," treating the two companies as complementary.

Eddie Bauer made their own down jackets, parkas, and sleeping bags. Their down products were more than half their business and were without question the best available. Eddie Bauer outfitted several major expeditions. We were probably more competitive in other apparel categories, footwear, and equipment, but all in all, the two companies were quite comparable and very competitive, and both tried hard to be the number one outdoors catalog company. Our sales volumes were about the same.

In 1971, General Mills acquired Eddie Bauer. Management determined that a strategy of national retail expansion was the best way to go for Eddie Bauer. They subsequently reduced their emphasis on the catalog business and shifted their retail store product emphasis to men's and women's casual apparel. I had enjoyed competing with Eddie Bauer during those years, and I missed their strong presence in our part of the catalog business.

There were a variety of other catalog companies of the day, including the Charles F. Orvis Co., famous for fly-fishing and upland hunting equipment as well as "country" clothing; Eastern Mountain Sports, now a retail chain of backpacking, climbing, camping, and winter sports gear; and REI (Recreational Equipment, Inc.), a major Seattle-based retailer and cataloger of backpacking, camping, expedition, and winter sports apparel and equipment. Cabela's was just getting started as a complete outfitter for hunters and general fishing. The Lands' End catalog in those days specialized in sailing hardware for yachtsmen. Quite a few others were also entering the growing catalog marketplace.

We benefited from what was happening in the broader society and economy. The late 1960s and early 1970s were banner years for people in the recreation business. The disposable income of American consumers was increasing significantly, and most people were enjoying shorter work weeks and correspondingly more leisure time. There was a lot of interest in personal health and fitness as well as in the outdoors.

Family camping, backpacking, canoe tripping, and skiing (downhill and cross-country) were among the fast-growing activities among our customer base. Hunting and fishing were growing but at lesser rates. The outdoors market was beginning to divide into distinct groupings of activities, each with its own demographic and lifestyle characteristics. The basic split was between the hunting/fishing group and the so-called nonconsumptive sports such as hiking, family camping, canoeing, and cross-country skiing. L.L.Bean was beginning to stretch to accommodate the new diversity among our customers. We were also attracting less active customers but, we hoped, people who still had some kind of outdoors orientation.

Product technology was changing at a pace at least as fast as the markets were growing. Dick Kelty invented the first external-frame backpack; Sierra Designs developed the "60/40" parka; Jansport built dome tents; and Bob Gore invented Gore-Tex. This period also saw the introduction of fiberglass canoes and skis, graphite fly rods, sea kayaks, "Therma-Rest" sleeping pads, polypropylene underwear, and technical running shoes. All these were beneficial advances in functionality. But a lot of technological junk came along as well, and there was a need for knowledgeable and trustworthy retailers.

Living the L.L. Story

In the early 1970s, the catalog business was also taking off. Catalog titles published in 1974 doubled the number of a decade earlier. High gasoline prices due to the oil embargo restricted store shopping, and specialty catalogs were reaching narrow segments of consumers having unique product interests. Mainframe computers made it feasible to finely divide mailing lists to reach these segments. They also facilitated the availability of many mailing lists on the rental market.

Boston Magazine wrote of L.L.Bean in the seventies, "So how did Bean's run past every competitor? The answer is beautifully simple. It mailed more catalogs."[2] And so we did. In 1967, we mailed about 1.8 million catalogs, and in 1975, about 5.9 million. Our sales grew from $4.7 million to $29.5 million, and our profitability increased six and one-half times. We were mailing catalogs four times a year—the traditional Spring and Fall catalogs and the more recently developed Summer and Christmas circulars—to our customers and prospects. Between 1967 and 1975, the catalogs grew from 100 to 128 pages, and the circulars from 32 to 64 pages. We were offering about 600 products in 1967, and 1,500 in 1975.

So we mailed more catalogs, as would any cataloger that was growing rapidly. But if you don't know what you're doing, simply mailing more catalogs can be a fast road to nowhere. The secret requires finding and developing enough names of new and repeat customers who will respond in sufficient numbers to make mailing more catalogs economical. We were able to "run past every competitor" because our products and mystique had greater market appeal and so we found and added new customers more easily. We had a compelling story and product assortment.

We were more-or-less independent of the general economy. During the recession of 1974–1975, our annual rate of increase was still 20 percent. The energy crisis boosted the sale of our woodstoves and wood-burning tools and especially warm clothing and flannel pajamas. Double-digit inflation gave us pricing and inventory challenges, but we dealt with them. We tended to operate with heavy inventories to support high service levels, and the higher replacement cost that went into our pricing actually helped our margins on the carryover merchandise.

The increased consumer interest and spending on outdoor recreation, the updated L.L.Bean product lines, and our improved service performance reinvigorated the L.L.Bean mystique and gave us a power-ful model for growth. The mystique based on the L.L. story gave us an enormous competitive advantage. We quadrupled our advertising spend-ing to $250,000 and placed dozens of small coupon ads in our traditional outdoors group, men's magazines, shelter magazines, and special inter-est publications as well as our more upscale media such as the *Atlantic Monthly,* the *New York Times,* the *Wall Street Journal,* and the *New Yorker* magazine. Our greatly enhanced presence substantially multi-plied our catalog requests. We were spending to the point of diminish-ing return, and we weren't finding that point. Catalog inquiries were costing us about $0.30 each, and 25 percent of them were converting to customers. These were unheard-of numbers in the catalog business.

As we increased and broadened the number of magazines we used, we couldn't tell whether our best long-term customers were coming from our traditional outdoors magazines or from the upscale media. But we seemed to be attracting a diversity of customers, from *Fur, Fish and Game* readers to those from *Better Homes and Gardens* to the younger outdoors people, whatever they were reading. We never rented other companies' mailing lists, the conventional way to grow catalog circulation. Only in the mid-1970s did we start to need more than the print media to generate new catalog buyers. It was also well into the 1970s before we could tell where our best customers were coming from. We didn't have the data processing capability to do conversion rates or long-term value calculations by source of the inquiry.

I had concerns about developing too much of an upper-demographics mailing list. We had always seen ourselves as a middle-class company catering to the kinds of people we were and those we hunted and fished and enjoyed the outdoors with. We knew what gear worked for us and for them and what didn't. I wanted to stay in this market, continue to offer high-value, practical products, and not get too far into the high end of things. I was always pleased to see a new jacket or boot of ours being worn on the streets of Freeport. Our local customers set the func-tional value standard.

Our traditional sport of hunting was most problematic because we didn't sell firearms. For federal paperwork reasons as well as shipping restrictions, selling guns by catalog did not make sense. As a result, staying in hunting without selling shotguns or rifles was like running a restaurant without selling the main courses. But we tried to maintain a viable position based on footwear—with L.L.'s Maine Hunting Shoe at the center—along with apparel and specialty equipment like our famous Coastal Decoys. These were still being made by George Soule of South Freeport, longtime friend of L.L. and renowned duck caller and grouse hunter.

By 1975 we continued to support our traditional outdoors market of hunters and fishermen and had become a leading provider of functional apparel and lightweight equipment for the new outdoors people, men and women alike. These new buyers of outdoors products were young people and young, active families engaged in the "newer" outdoors activities, and some in alternative lifestyles, living off the land. L.L.'s customers were the traditional outdoors people. I'm not sure how he'd have reacted to the new crowd. But they liked L.L.Bean and, although young, shared the old-fashioned values we stood for. Perhaps this was a reaction to the Vietnam War or more likely to the environmental movement. Their focus was on the "nonconsumptive" sports (no fish or game involved) such as backpacking, canoe tripping, bike touring, and cross-country skiing and winter camping.

Our catalog page content and creative evolved more deliberately than our circulation grew. New people were coming to L.L.Bean from our advertising and from word of mouth. As a result we did not have to rely on a lot of product turnover and "newness" for the sake of newness in our catalogs. We could focus more on perfecting, or continually improving, the assortment with better quality, more fully tested, and more relevant products, at the same time trying to improve the catalogs' readability—the layouts, page sequencing, photography, and copy. I say "trying to improve" because we never got high marks from the pros in the graphics area, but our customers liked our format.

I had written or heavily edited most of the product descriptions, including rewriting a lot of L.L.'s copy, to create a more consistent and straightforward voice. L.L. had written, "Our Maine Hunting Shoe is made on a swing last that fits the foot like a dress shoe fits over a silk stocking." This was the kind of quirky language we revised throughout the catalog. L.L. could get away with it because he was L.L. and it sounded like him and his customers liked it. But it would have been foolish as well as impossible to try to imitate his unique genius in expressing himself.

> TOBY SOULE: Leon's copy was long, not super-long, but a little bit longer than L.L.'s, because L.L.'s had gotten so short. [L.L.] had really taken a lot of the meat out of the copy . . . and cut some of the best stuff out. But Leon didn't want to do L.L.'s voice. He wanted to change and yet he wanted the company to still be L.L. So they kept what he calls "the myth of L.L." He wanted to keep that alive for as long as possible.

I put more facts and a little touch of Bean-ness in the copy. Part of that was to make sure the customers had all they needed to know about a product before they bought it. My test was to ask myself what information I would expect to have if I were buying the product. Additionally, a lot of Federal Trade Commission requirements came out in those days—what was "virgin wool," what was "used" wool, fiber content, washing instructions, and all that sort of thing. We had to become more disciplined in the copy as well. The challenge on the Bean-ness side was to keep L.L. alive—the practicality and the authenticity, without any attempt to copy his voice.

I pictured our customers as I wrote copy, and, depending on the product, it could be a longtime AMC (Appalachian Mountain Club) member hiking in the White Mountains, or one of my hunting and fishing friends in the fields and streams of Maine, or an old acquaintance who had a lot of canoe tripping experience in the United States and Canada, or the summer people who'd traded with L.L. for years. I saw them all as being critical and demanding and wanting practical, long-lasting products described without exaggeration or a trace of fluff.

We had a distinct point of view in our copy, and a distinct L.L.Bean look in our catalog. We started commissioning original cover art featuring seasonal outdoors illustrations—for example, of two canoeists surprising a moose for the Spring catalog, or a group of hikers coming across a black bear for the Fall catalog. Our scenes were always Maine based, with Maine fish and game, and our logo (and registered trademark) was our name in upper- and lowercase Cheltenham type.

We never did put an index in the catalogs, but our consistency in paginating or sequencing product groups in each book from year to year helped make it easier to shop. Reading the catalog wasn't complicated, and we wanted people to go through the whole thing (which was L.L.'s old theory). We had our "Page 3" opening page densely packed with ordering information and terms, including our guarantee. Our page layouts had four or five products per page using every square inch of paper. The position of the photographs alternated from left to right sides of the page. We'd never gotten into eye flow studies; our format just seemed a sensible way to put the pages together, and we'd done it for years. We rarely used headlines. A few line art elements illustrated unique features, and almost no models appeared in our pages. In 1972 a *Sports Illustrated* writer noted, "When [the reader] does run across a model in Bean's catalog, it is easy to dismiss him. The model looks like the madman who installed the plumbing at your cottage, or the guy who sold you the camper. It is a sort of democratic catalog élan."[3]

Our photographs were straight out of Mel Collins's darkroom. We never used fancy setups or airbrushed anything, so there was lots of credibility. Usually there wasn't time to reshoot a product, and once in a while we had to go to print with some really unattractive photography. Our printing, which had once been referred to as "country style," had improved significantly, thanks to Ethel's and Dingley's good efforts. Dingley brought in new offset printing presses and expanded their capability of four-color printing from front and back covers only (in 1967) to 40 four-color pages per 128-page catalog and 24 four-color pages per 64-page circular in 1975.

The catalog preparation and printing cycle became the critical path in our business cycle. Our advertising, product development and selection, forecasting and planning, inventory logistics, fulfillment operations, employment, and cash flow all depended on our mailing schedules. Dingley could economically add pages only eight at a time, and that helped to discipline the growth of our product lines. We needed a solid group of high-potential new products to justify the big increase in pages.

Our products were functional ("Bean's Warden Jacket," "Bean's Pine Tree Lodge" tents, and "Bean's Boat and Tote Bags") with our version of styling, which was neat, clean, and modestly attractive and mostly unique to L.L.Bean. We had a good assortment of outdoors gear (although still too much general fishing equipment), strong positions in outerwear and footwear, an emerging line of casual sportswear for men and women, and a small collection of outdoorsy furnishings and specialties for home or camp.

In 1967, we offered eighteen pages of women's apparel; in 1975, thirty-four pages. My Aunt Hazel continued to run the Ladies' Department in the retail store and continued her preference for much dressier sportswear than I was putting in the catalogs. It was almost 100 percent inconsistent with our outdoors and utilitarian product assortments in the rest of the store. I used to cringe when I walked through Hazel's department. She still resisted displaying our Alpaca Lined Walking Coat, Corduroy Wrap Skirts, Field Trial Boots, and other more functional catalog products. Hazel was very supportive of my leadership of L.L.Bean, and we maintained our very friendly relationship. I just kept my mouth shut as far as her merchandising preferences were concerned.

Actually, Hazel's little department in our store did quite well, adding to my frustration. She began selling Fair Isle Shetland sweaters in the early 1970s, and they soon became our most successful women's product, retail or catalog—and a harbinger of things to come.

At the same time, our product lines were evolving to meet the needs of the emerging outdoor lifestyles I was seeing. We clearly had the traditional Bean sportsmen who hunted and fished, and we were attracting the young "back to nature" people, who were backpacking, canoe tripping, and cross-country skiing. We also had a lot of family campers and RV travelers, "summer people" who did a lot of sailing in the summer and downhill skiing in the winter, less active types who did some light hiking or walking for exercise, and others who simply found us by accident.

They all seemed to wear our sportswear for their weekend pursuits. We were starting to build a significant apparel business for both men and women with Boat Mocs and Penny Loafers, our Chino pants and Scotch Plaid cotton flannel shirts, our Norwegian sweaters, and our old favorite Field Coats. These came to be known as "preppy" and were starting to equal our outdoors gear in volume.

We described our men's wear in our catalogs as "sturdy," "durable," "handsome in appearance," and "light in weight." Our women's wear, on the other hand, was "practical and stylish," "practical and attractive," and "durable but soft." Or, as noted by one newspaper reporter at the time, "downright dowdy."

Our sportswear was generally made of natural fibers, such as wool and cotton. But we used synthetics or blends whenever they added strength or reduced weight or provided superior warmth—mostly in our active outdoors apparel, where we used the rapidly developing textile technologies whenever appropriate. We added our first serious hiking boot, a Raichle model for men and women, in 1969. By the mid-1970s we had an assortment of functional, high-quality, well-priced active gear in all of our outdoors categories. I used camping equipment checklists recommended by various outdoor experts to ensure the completeness of our assortments. We were more than competitive with any other cataloger.

Our sources for new products and new product ideas included our regular vendor base who kept us current on their understanding of the marketplace and their own products. Some of our best vendors were Woolrich Woolen Mills, Willis and Geiger, Duofold, Eureka Tent and Awning Company, and Bass Shoe. They would all "special make" products for us under our label. It was important to get our name on our products and not have Bean confused with any other brand names. I went to every apparel, footwear, and sporting goods show in the country; I also read every magazine related to what we were doing, to check the advertising and editorials on new products. I looked at all the customer suggestions as well as reports from our own trips on the Allagash and elsewhere. I studied all the other catalogs. Depending on the space they devoted to an item you could tell how important it was.

We always had a surplus of new-product possibilities, and so, given our catalog space limitations, we were pretty selective in what we chose. The choice wasn't based strictly on potential sales. I wanted to keep a balance of active wear, sportswear and sports equipment, and L.L.Bean "miscellaneous" (cribbage boards, sandwich spreaders, maple syrup, weather forecasters, and more). I had different sales expectations for each category depending on how much the product supported our positioning as well as its volume. We had no way of calculating the profitability by item, and so I simply went by the sales number. Quite often I'd keep an item like trout flies in the catalog because it belonged there even if the sales were below average for the space. Even at that time hard goods sales (camping equipment, canoes, and so on) were not keeping up with the soft goods. It was tempting to follow the demand trends, but I was trying to support all the hard goods categories to keep our position in the outdoors marketplace.

K. C. PUTNAM: I brought Mad River Canoe into the catalog, and a company called Snow Lion and one called Wilderness Experience. Snow Lion was a pack manufacturer. Wilderness Experience was a backpack line . . . I presented all these products to Leon and he agreed to put them in. But I will never forget, he said to me, "OK, KC, we'll do this but I need to put things in perspective for you. I could take a flannel shirt, a single flannel shirt, I could put it in the bottom corner of any page in the catalog, and that one flannel shirt will do more business than this whole four- or five- or six-page spread." Well, I mean to tell you, those are words that I have listened to in my mind for a long, long time because what bothered me is that they were absolutely true. And this is part of the continuing evolution of Bean, that it was becoming increasingly a clothing-driven company. He was right. The one flannel shirt in the bottom corner of any page in the catalog would do more than my sleeping bag, backpack, and canoe line would ever do . . . The flannel shirt was more important in terms of sales than all this other stuff. Yet he approved the lines, because they were, at that time, the right sleeping bags, backpacks, and canoes to be putting in the Bean program, and they were successful, all of them . . . But it was a drop in the bucket in comparison to *the clothing*.

Product selection wasn't a scientific process by any means. I'd become so immersed in every detail of our products—their features, construction, cost, positioning, relative value versus competing products, sales of comparable items, and so on—that my intuition was pretty well informed. I could make decisions quickly, something I had to do because there were so many and not a lot of time to spend thinking about them.

ART PERRY: Go back to L.L.'s company. You put a knife in the catalog if you like it, not whether or not it's saleable. Dammit, everybody ought to have it because I like it, you know, that's L.L.'s company and the bottom line will take care of itself. That's before my time but I worked for a company like that and that would be my image of it. Then, Leon's company. There's a way to do it. Just like his grandfather, it's my way. [The same way as his grandfather?] I think so.

When L.L. liked a product, he carried it. And so did I. We both had a point of view on what was right for Bean and what wasn't, although I had a much broader concept of L.L.Bean and its marketplace than he did. Ours was an idiosyncratic approach to merchandising, versus a market-driven approach. Success depends on which approach best reflects your customers' preferences. Idiosyncratic is more unique and compelling when done right. The market approach is safer but more generic and tends to be more like what everybody else does.

A lot of my weekends were spent in the outdoors, hiking, camping, fishing, skiing, and so on. I could think like a customer in using samples of our products. For me this went beyond the rational pros and cons to an emotional involvement. I loved the activities and the products and couldn't imagine working for a company where I couldn't use the products and develop a passion for them.

Above all, it seemed to me that our product line was the mainstay of our success. You are what you sell. I wanted to have the better mousetrap. Our assortment had to be superior in quality and uniqueness and appeal. Service was important, and so were advertising and attractive catalogs. But they could never make up for faulty products and second-rate assortments, at least not for long. If you have faulty products, the customers will catch up with you.

Each item had to have its own story as well as a specific role to play in our overall assortment. We wanted minimal redundancy, and so the line was highly edited for what we considered the best value for the use intended. Our chamois cloth was woven for us to the right density, weight, and nap. It was comfortable, wore well, and was washable. There was no need for any other flannel shirt in that weight class.

We would also try to special-order almost anything our customers requested that we didn't carry. We'd even send them to competitors if we couldn't furnish the product. Our manufacturers considered this special order policy a major nuisance but usually cooperated with these single-item orders. We ordered a fellow from Massachusetts a set of size 60 down-filled underwear. We didn't dare charge him anything near what it cost for us to have it made.

We also began our practice of repairing anything we sold if our customers wanted it done. Sometimes they'd get attached to a pair of boots or a field coat and wanted to keep them going. If we didn't have the skills in house to repair a binocular, for instance, we'd ship it to the vendor. I thought this repair service was good for our customers and a way to recycle our products consistent with good environmental practices. We charged nominal amounts for repairs and special orders and hoped we'd break even on them. We were doing it more for goodwill.

Our product line was growing at about 20 percent a year, but we kept to the same photographic style and we rarely reshot continuing products. This practice created a sameness and familiarity to our catalog assortments that suggested to people we never changed. I think it helped reinforce our reputation for dependability and credibility. Our advertising constantly added new customers to our mailing list, and to these people our products were all new.

I thought our concept of Bean in the 1970s—our "brand," in today's language—was well communicated in our products, our outdoors heritage, and our commitment to quality and value, all backed by our 100 percent guarantee. The cohesiveness of our product assortments in their functionality and their aesthetics also defined L.L.Bean. We'd gotten all the extraneous stuff out of the product line and had an assortment we could all be proud of—a sense of Bean-ness you could see and feel in the store and the catalog.

The word *mystique* continued to come up in the press. We had a kind of magic, some kind of special status in the public eye that we hadn't tried to achieve but that had emerged. It was not contrived, although we were certainly conscious of it and protective of our public image. L.L.'s story continued to have a magnetic appeal. And everything we were doing in our products and in improving our mail-order service and in talking with our customers in the store reinforced and enlarged his legend. As late as 1975, Ethel told a reporter, "There is a saying around here that 'Mr. Bean casts a long shadow.' I always have the idea he's right there looking over my shoulder."

> ART PERRY: [The Bean mystique was about] quality and reliability. And a little bit of country cousin. Things that are good, red-white-and-blue. It was in touch with the past, I think. It was almost sort of resistance to the loss of innocence. Bean's was basic. Bean's didn't tell lies. Bean's gave you back something that broke. Bean's pants lasted. What a wonderful name. The value of the label was just fantastic.

Our catalog was the Bible and our store was Mecca, adding a sectarian metaphor to our mystique. Customers made "pilgrimages" to Freeport. And if they couldn't do that, they browsed Bean's "homey cluttered catalog." Berkeley Rice wrote, "Bean's products mark their users as members of a special fraternity. 'Bean people' tend to be proud of their purchases, and like to point out their virtues to the uninitiated. Every spring, thousands of fishermen somehow manage to find uses for all seven pockets on Bean's 'Warden's Jacket.' Every fall, thousands of duck hunters wait more comfortably out in the marshes because of the rubberized game pocket on Bean's 'Field Coat.'"[4]

He went on to say, however, that most of Bean's products could be worn "with pleasure by those whose outdoors activities are limited to the wilds of suburbia," adding that the secret of L.L.Bean's mystique was making urban or suburban people feel like real woodsmen and part of the "great urban escape."

The *Wall Street Journal* called us "homey hustlers" in a wonderful 1973 front-page update of the L.L. story. The author concluded, "In a retailing world of plastic, neon and the get-with-it sell, Bean's rambling wooden store remains a reassuring haven of durable wood, hand-stitched leather and no-nonsense styling."[5]

Another writer called us "the people's Abercrombie and Fitch" and a company "you feel you can talk to." The *Village Voice* asked, "What idea animates the L.L.Bean Hunting Boot or the L.L.Bean Chamois Cloth Shirt?" and went on to tell the L.L. story, including his discovery of the Maine Hunting Shoe and his catalog business.[6] "Even those of us who will never tread the backwoods in any serious capacity must admire the kind of mind which can envision such [outdoor] situations and imagine a solution to them. We must respect and even trust such a man. And that, of course, is the secret of L.L.Bean's success." The article went on to extol the L.L.Bean values of functional integrity and the romantic ideal of the dependable and enduring woodsman, albeit containing a subtle reference to L.L. as being a "modest hustler." I liked this article because it got into a lot of what we aspired to in our culture and values. At the same time, whenever the writer started getting carried away with his grandiose imagery (the "Gothic prose" of our catalog, for instance), he'd catch himself with a bit of humor and bring us back to reality.

> LEE SURACE: I identified with the stuff we sold . . . I would say that was the thread that sort of bound us all together. If you weren't into something outdoors, camping, hunting or fishing, you wouldn't have anybody to talk to. You would have nothing in common with them . . . I think we felt pretty special, working inside a pretty unique company that had a lot written about us. We were always in the news. We had all the college students that were coming by and stopping at midnight. This ideal company. We had this [sense] that we were just different in our business. It was the sense that we were focused, we knew what we were doing, our products were environmentally friendly. There was sort of a first environmental wave that came and here was this company up in Maine and all that. People were moving to Vermont and coming to Maine, going back to the land and here was L.L.Bean, this family company, great products, sleep outdoors, tents. It was a wonderful feeling. You were so proud to be L.L.Bean. We were winning catalog awards. We'd go to a seminar in New York City . . . "Where are you from?" . . . L.L.Bean! . . . "Well, L.L.Bean, what a wonderful

company!" It's like everybody thought instantly you had credibility because you came from L.L.Bean.

I remember in those years our people from all areas—the retail store, marketing, operations—would go to conventions and seminars. They were treated like celebrities. They were heroes. Then they started to be put on panels and make speeches. I remember data processing people going to seminars and coming back and telling us, "I said I was from L.L.Bean, and, oh my God, you know. You wouldn't believe it." They all felt like stars. That was a common feeling in those days. People even asked for our autographs.

There were other articles similar to those quoted. They seemed to feed off each other. Collectively they were making L.L.Bean into a national presence with an engaging personality and a resonant set of values. They were also identifying L.L.Bean with a distinctive and romanticized way of life and a Maine lifestyle that was to define our personality in customers' minds for years to come.

A recurring theme of the mystique articles was that L.L.Bean was a self-perpetuating phenomenon still driven by momentum L.L. had initiated and requiring little effort on our part. Despite the high growth rate and constant change, everything appeared to the writers to be tried and true. We didn't challenge this belief. We wanted to make it look easy, or at least not make it look like we were trying too hard. We were working hard, however, to manage L.L.Bean's growth and to live up to our mystique and its increasing popularity.

There certainly was a momentum factor. With all of the publicity focused on the L.L. story, all of us at L.L.Bean began to take the values and the heritage even more seriously and to act accordingly. These values of trust and reliability and service to others were internalized by all of us at Bean and became a living, growing part of our company's character and culture. I think we achieved the L.L.Bean persona that most longtime customers think of as the original, the real L.L.Bean.

6

"To Run a Perfect Company"

A S THE COMPANY DOUBLED IN SIZE every three years, it grew more complex and difficult to manage. The leadership skills required of the company president were becoming such that I began to wonder about my ability or desire to acquire them. Nor was I certain I wanted to lead an organization that had grown beyond a certain size. A case writer captured my thoughts in 1974 in the second case the Harvard Business School did on L.L.Bean:

> Although he was pleased with L.L.Bean's record ... Mr. Gorman questioned whether or not his own management style was appropriate for the size of company L.L.Bean had become. While the company was now over six times its size just eight years ago, his day had hardly changed at all.[1]

The business had reached the point where I couldn't keep up with all of the merchandising and general management jobs I was trying to do. We also lacked certain technical skills, such as data processing and direct marketing, that we didn't have within the company. I needed help.

In the early 1970s I had interviewed several potential new managers from the outside. These people were all intelligent, of good character, and sufficiently competent based on their experience. I liked them and hired them. Unfortunately they couldn't manage effectively in our (or my) way of doing things and left the company after only two or three years. I felt very much at fault. In one case, with a first-class guy—an outdoorsman and all that—things were just not getting done. I sat down one day and used up one and one-half pages of a legal pad listing items I'd asked him to look into and had never heard about since. We had a problem and it wasn't fun.

If this was what growth was all about in addition to distancing me further from the things I liked to do, I began to wonder if I was in the right job. I started looking for advice. It turned out our bank was using an industrial psychologist from Portland named Jim Mahoney to help train its managers in people skills. Bank officials recommended Jim to me.

We were to use Jim's advice for many years in successfully bringing outsiders into L.L.Bean, as well as in other personnel assessment and management development initiatives and in advising me personally. L.L.Bean still had a paternalistic culture, and I had a strong belief in what we were doing—which products were appropriate for L.L.Bean and how we should treat our employees. There was not a lot of leeway. Plus, I had my own idiosyncrasies that had to be dealt with. Jim's genius, and his great value, was in assessing the cultural or psychological fit of candidates with L.L.Bean and with me and vice versa.

JIM MAHONEY: I got a call one evening from my secretary and she said that Leon was on the tube. He hadn't told me a thing about it. It was on a game show in the seventies called "What's My Line?" This show had a panel of various well-known show business personalities and their task, blindfolded, was to determine who the mystery guest was. Leon was [the guest]. The panel was supposed to identify the hard-driving president of the dynamic L.L.Bean Company among three men sitting before them, Leon and two imposters. Well, Leon is about as far removed from the stereotypical, charismatic, hard-driving CEO as you can imagine, and so the panel had some trouble. The two fakes, whenever they were asked a question, would talk in an animated voice about how decisive they were going to be and how they were going to wave swords and get up on top of tables and inspire the troops and whatever. And then they came around to Leon and they asked him some question and he looked off into the distance and he said, "Well, I'm not sure how I would handle that. I have to think about it." Eventually, they did get him because I think one of the panelists had been a customer for some time. But it certainly took them a while because of the fact that Leon was so far removed from the stereotype, at least on the surface.

To understand L.L.Bean better, Jim interviewed most of our management group, as well as me. His conclusion after talking with me for several hours was that I "exhibited fewer characteristics commonly found in successful chief executives" than anyone he'd ever interviewed. (I did well on the Rorschach test.) I felt good about Jim's observation because I didn't want to be a conventional manager. On the other hand, I had deficiencies that I should probably have taken more seriously.

My only real exposure to formal leadership models prior to joining L.L.Bean had been with the Boy Scouts and the U.S. Navy. Both organizations stressed the importance of leadership and prided themselves on developing effective leadership skills. But neither attempted to define what leadership was and the specific skills involved. My old *Boy Scout Manual* was virtually silent on the subject. ("If you prove yourself the right kind of Scout, the fellows may someday elect you for a patrol leader," the manual said, without beginning to explain "the right kind.")[2] But the Scouts were very strong on values ("the Scout Law") and doing one's best. My *Division Officer's Guide* and *Watch Officer's Guide* from my Navy days expanded on the notion of leadership. They stressed the critical importance of motivating "the men," preparedness (like the Boy Scouts), and leadership by example. Otherwise, the "art of leadership," according to these guides, was not learned from books but was developed only with experience.

The Navy also believed in developing leadership experience fast, with total immersion in "on-the-job training." At age twenty-two, three or four weeks after reporting to my ship, I was put in charge of an operations division—the Combat Information Center (CIC)—with responsibility for the division's operating performance and the thirty-five men assigned to it. More responsibility than many get in a lifetime. I got little advice from my predecessor or my department head on what to do and was pretty much on my own. The crew members, fortunately, were used to periodic turnovers in their division officers and gave me fair latitude to learn how things were done. We also had some good officers on board who served as helpful role models and advisers.

I was smart enough to establish a good relationship with my division's chief petty officer and had enough common sense to treat my men with respect and fairness. But I was never able to get into the habit of being highly directive and "chewing out" my men regularly—both actions considered good leadership attributes, at least by my captain. My style was more participative and team oriented, with lots of positive reinforcement. I also focused on learning all of the jobs that were done by my division members as well as how they all worked together in making the CIC team perform its mission. I had a desire to develop the perfect Combat Information Center and a need to know everything that was going on.

We won our share of competitive fleet awards and came close to the highest score in our biennial evaluation at Guantanamo Bay refresher training. Successful outcomes reinforce the behaviors that went into them, so whatever strengths and weaknesses I had in my managerial skills or leadership characteristics were formed largely by my Naval experience.

I came across the famous Lao Tse quote on leadership during my early years at Bean. "A leader is best when people barely know he exists ... When his work is done, his aim is fulfilled. They will all say, 'We did this ourselves.'" This concept seemed to fit my thinking on the ideal leadership outcome—the importance of humility and competence and of attributing success to those most responsible.

TOM GORMAN: I didn't have the drive or the ambition that Leon has. He was always ambitious, even as a kid. He was always near the top of his class. Leon and L.L. were both ambitious, driving, managerial types of people. Oh, yes, they were similar in many ways.

The similarities between L.L. and me were not obvious to everyone, and writers often noted the contrast between us. "In personality [Gorman] reminds no one of Mr. Bean, and doesn't try to," said one writer.

"Where L.L. was bluff, hearty and outgoing, Leon is careful, quiet and reserved." "Low-key," "soft sell," and "easy-going manner" were terms applied to me that no one would ever have used to describe L.L.

> When asked to explain in an interview recently his enviable busi-
> ness record, Gorman said, "Well, we did our best." When pressed,
> he volunteered this much: "Oh, we don't have a grandiose market-
> ing plan. We sell products that work, that we like. We brought our
> product line up to date. We used better advertising methods. It
> was in the 60's, the economy was on our side. There was interest in
> the environment, in the outdoors. We just had the right product
> line at the right time. There were no real miracles."[3]

In 1970 I attended a seminar in Boston on entrepreneurialism. The attributes of entrepreneurs and their pros and cons were discussed and seemed to match my style. Among these were taking personal responsi-bility for seeing jobs well done (a healthy fear of failure helps); the need for concrete feedback on how well one is doing (strong sales results for the catalog products I selected were most gratifying); taking some risks but only those calculated to be successful (that was me); and a lack of consistency in approaches to achieving goals and solving problems. I also think most successful entrepreneurs have a strong idea of what they are out to accomplish. It all sounded as if the company was in an entre-preneurial mode during the 1970s, as it had been during L.L.'s tenure.

Years later I took some tests (answering for myself and for L.L. as I thought he would) that attempted to compare L.L.'s leadership style with mine. The results indicated that L.L. and I shared strong, personal visions for the company, but he tended to be a real salesman and shoot from the hip at times. I was more deliberate and more often looked for cooperation by others than being directive. Neither of us was much good at giving feedback on performance, although we both took deci-sive action as required.

L.L. was not very strategic, and this was one of my strong points. I constantly, perhaps excessively, tried to relate to the big picture. L.L. was a much better communicator, and there was rarely any doubt where he stood. We both had a results orientation and high expectations. I was a lot more innovative and open to change than L.L. was, at least in his later years, but he'd taken his share of risks and made his share of innovations as a young man.

L.L. was a lot more expressive and could show a lot of concern for people, whereas I was more reserved and yet equally empathic in my way. Neither of us would have fit into a large organization. Our entrepreneurial styles wouldn't work there. Conventional wisdom said that entrepreneurs could not grow their companies beyond what they could personally control. Delegation of responsibility was not one of L.L.'s strengths. My Navy experience made me more comfortable with delegation although less so in the product area.

One thing entrepreneurs could do well, I believed, was to effectively lead their companies, despite their managerial idiosyncrasies, through their vision, commitment, and sheer energy. There was no question that L.L. had a strong notion of the kind of company he was building, as did I. Although neither of us was able to articulate it in purple prose, people seemed to know that we had high aspirations for the company. We both were honest in our business dealings and competent in the business we were in. We were also energetic in supporting the concepts we believed in, and, to a great extent, we both led by example. By the end of his career, however, L.L. had lost any desire to grow his company. But growth was extremely important to me.

BILL HENRY: There was such a gap between the management group that was there and Leon's ambition . . . His ambition was not stated in the sense of ambition but you could just tell in dealing with him, he wanted things to be at a totally different level . . . I remember Leon communicating at the time that . . . he did not like the quality of the communications that were going out to customers in the written form and that in general he felt that the service was not where it should be. At that time, back in the mid-seventies, great service and customer satisfaction were not something that drove management thinking . . . I could tell he was really on top of it. He just expressed that he was not happy with service and he had also thought pretty deeply about it, which was really part of the culture of L.L Bean, the man as well as the company . . . I said [to myself], this company is going to go somewhere. [Leon] obviously wanted to go somewhere; I could figure that out about him. And he, for all his strengths, which are extreme, he is not a great communicator. But I could tell, based on just the questions he asked, that this was a mind that was pretty deep into what he wanted to do.

I was obsessed with making Bean a bigger and better company. I've forgotten how much time I put in, but I was really living the company twenty-four hours a day, seven days a week. I didn't take a vacation until 1975 or so. It wasn't fair to my family, and I started trying to do more with them. I had three young children at the time, and my work/home balance was slightly out of whack.

BUCKY BUCKLIN: Somebody would give me a call; the furnace was out or something happened. Well, I'd come in at night and he would be in his office or here weekends. If there was a storm or something, I'd come in and check, you know. He was here, and he was everywhere.

People ask why I was so committed. The answer may be genetic, but it was also related to striving for something more than business goals.

LEE SURACE: I really do think L.L.Bean, the company, gives something of value to society. I really do think that we have something that enriches people's lives and for me, that's what it is. I think that has to be from Leon because I think that's where I got it . . . It's not just trying to make a buck. It's when you wear our raincoat out in the outdoors, you're going to be dry and you're going to have a better experience. When you take our sleeping bag and you sleep out at Mt. Katahdin, you're going to be warm.

A lot of people at L.L.Bean, then and today, think that they're doing something more than taking phone calls or picking orders, that they're really adding value to people's lives. We weren't doing what we were doing just to line our pockets with bonus money. I think most people want to think their lives are more than putting food on the table. I think the people at Bean believed that. But at that time we, or I, talked about it only indirectly. The L.L. story was our way of expressing all that.

LEE SURACE: Leon talked about L.L. quite a bit in my recollection. The outdoors, how L.L. felt, you can't do business with an empty wagon, you never want to argue with a customer, those things. We all knew that stuff and it just came through. Things L.L. had said. Sort of a different way of doing business and treating the customer as a human being . . . I'd say a strong sense of commitment that you could trust L.L.Bean. I take that back to, "If I say this knife will work, it's because I tried it." I certainly got that feeling from the people in the company, not just Leon. We all felt that, hey, this is an honest company. If we say something, it's true because we've tried it, we know it will work.

At the core of the L.L. story was a belief in the importance of outdoor experiences to the overall quality of life. The whole point of providing quality products was to enhance our customers' outdoors experiences. It's as basic as having a good sleeping bag to get a good night's rest or good hiking shoes to comfortably support and protect the feet or a fly reel that doesn't fail under pressure. All contribute to the outdoors experience. This is the kind of added value you'd expect from a competent Maine Guide. This is what we were, without being self-conscious about it, and it was a big part of our mystique at the time. This is why the magazines and newspapers were saying that Bean was unique. I believe our character, our values, were what separated L.L.Bean from all the others, what created the mystique that had grown up around the company.

Still, as much as we tried to build on L.L.'s philosophy and values and spirit, it was a different way of running the company that I had in mind—a broader concept. I used to say that the L.L. story was something that evolved over time with new and richer meanings.

IRVING ISAACSON: Leon had a vision, apparently, which we didn't discuss in terms of vision but in terms of what he wanted to do. It was a transition from a corporation which was essentially the alter ego of L.L., to a corporation which truly operated as a corporation and had as its primary interest what Leon always called the stakeholders—the employees, the family, and the public.

I think I wanted Bean to be all things to all people and do everything right. Profit maximization was not my goal. And this didn't always sit well with some in management or the family. But most over time came to believe in L.L.Bean's values and to take great pride in the ongoing L.L. story.

JIM MAHONEY: To do a job, to do a perfect job. Leon once told me that he wanted to run a perfect company.

Part of what was driving me was this notion of the good company or the perfect company—the perfect catalog and the perfect retail store and successful outcomes for all of the stakeholders. I had somehow taken to heart this notion of building the "perfect" company.

ART PERRY: Oh, I think [it meant] every letter would be answered the right way. That everybody's boots would fit perfectly. That the pants wouldn't tear. That you wouldn't need the cut-rate outlets. Out of that old yellow framed building you can design the company from the foundation up the way it ought to be . . . Behind it was this notion that there's a right way to do everything. And a great part of that was just plain good ethics too. I think that's where a lot of the strength came from. I just think Leon's as ethical as they come. He has a very strong sense of right and wrong, doesn't have to fret about things.

The "perfect" company was the ethically correct company. And it was all about doing the right thing. This was part of the culture and was shared among all Bean people: the right quality level in manufacturing; the right kind of service in our retail store; the right way of treating an employee with a problem; the right commitment to a community project. We had an official company color, Bean Green, and the notion of "bleeding green" was used to describe the true believers.

JIM MAHONEY: L.L.Bean has always been a fiercely ideological company. It was much more than just, treat the customer right and they'll come back and that sort of stuff. It was an environmental company long before that became a fashionable term. It had very much an identification with the outdoors, with the state of Maine, with Yankee values. The company really tried to encourage, at least in the early days, the image that the customer might have of old L.L. Bean himself . . . They never really wanted to advertise that they were a significant corporate entity. They have never advertised the corporate offices. I'm sure they say that this is because they don't want to confuse people and have them all drive in there. I'm sure that's true. I think it's also true that they did not want to encourage people to think of them as this big, huge expanse of offices and warehouses.

It wasn't until 1974, when the distribution center was built, that we became concerned that our size might make people think of us as just another big commercial enterprise. We had never had a sign at the entrance to the distribution center because we thought we'd have too many customers driving in thinking the store was there. Perhaps concern about creating the image of a big corporation was a part of it. It was not wanting to put product numbers in our catalog for several years after we'd installed a computer. We'd have looked too businesslike. We eventually got over this. What we stood for didn't depend on having or not having a big warehouse or a big computer.

JIM MAHONEY: Part of it was a mystical relationship with the outdoors—the idea of the outdoors being the vehicle for getting in touch with the spiritual side of yourself and other people. I think that has always been there. Leon would go off with a few buddies fishing or hiking all day and they'd hardly say a word to each other but have a marvelous time, just feeling the relationship with nature. I don't know if Leon has ever been explicit about that. I would suspect he hasn't been, but I think it's always been fairly clear that there have been ethical dimensions perhaps flow out of the spirituality. The idea of having a kind of understanding with nature, a partnership with nature, a partnership with your own people, your customers, I think, has always been there.

In the late 1970s, as we got more into formal planning, I tried to express some of these aspirations in writing. But until then, we had never tried to express formally how we felt about what we were doing. I, for one, wasn't comfortable in talking about such soft subjects. It wasn't part of my generation.

Besides, there wasn't a lot of time then for discussion and consensus. We made decisions on the fly, and I kept a pretty tight rein on things. As a manager in those days, I had a hands-on style that fell somewhere between directive and participative. The reason was in part my Navy experience, and in part my obsession with doing things my way, which I was convinced was the right way but which I wanted others to share.

> BUCKY BUCKLIN: I used to work for Carl, and you'd go in and have a discussion with him and he may say, "I want that thermostat fixed right now." So, you'd go fix the thermostat, and you'd go in to see Carl the next day and it was just like you never even talked about it. I'd say, "I fixed the thermostat, Carl," and he'd say, "Oh, that's all right." So, when I first went to work for Leon, I remember we had a big discussion of things going on, what he wanted done. I guess I was meeting with him once a week. I went up the next time and he went right down, you know, "Have you done this and this?" Wow. [Laughing] I left there saying, "This guy's got a terrific memory." You know what he was doing? He wrote everything on a 3x5 card and I think he had a drawer or a box or something that said "Bucklin." He wrote down everything. That was new to me. [Laughing] I never operated that way. I made sure that I did what was discussed, what he wanted. And, you know, he did that to all the employees.

There had been no system of accountability before me. Carl and L.L. had simply never checked up on anything. So something as simple as making notes of what was going on would have been a radical change at Bean.

> K. C. PUTNAM: I was the buyer for hard goods, but Leon somehow seemed to know more of the product specifics many times than the buyer would. And I guess that was part of the tension

because you knew he was active, interested, and he would tell you that that particular feature doesn't work . . . I mean, he had analyzed it already and knew if that made sense or this didn't or whatever. He knew more about fabrics. He knew more about construction. He knew more about whatever. Yeah, he was phenomenal . . . He never tried to be the authority. [But] you couldn't slip one past Leon . . . Leon never came across as the expert until you said something that wasn't absolutely right. And then he would call you [on] it.

I was definitely a nitpicker. In part, my defense is that retailing is not about periodic strokes of genius and major deal making, but day-in, day-out execution at a very detailed level. To operate in a superior manner everything has to be right—not only product quality and completeness of assortments and proper displays but also having the right buttons and pocket details on a shirt or including the height of a stocking in our catalog copy.

I remember that the buyers I worked for at Filene's never walked across the selling floor without straightening out the display of sweaters and folding shirts and giving information to the salespeople. It's what you instinctively do. I think one of my skills was that I could operate at a fairly detailed level. Then I could move to a fairly high conceptual level, as well, and see how all the details fit together. My operating at these two very different levels probably confused some people.

In any case, a kind of folklore started emerging from my management style. Stories began to accumulate. I'd become the walking compendium of management practices at L.L.Bean. The folklore was good in a way, because I could influence things without being there. It also helped reinforce and bring focus to our culture.

JIM MAHONEY: The values have always been there . . . It's been a strength for the organization. I think it has led to a lot of ownership on the part of the employees in the organization . . . He was as dominant a CEO in his organization as any I've ever seen. It's not because he's a domineering personality but everybody in the organization felt they worked for Leon, and if the janitor was feeling good in the morning, he'd give an extra sweep and "This is for

Leon." If he was ticked off at the company, he'd say, "Okay, take that, Leon."

However, there were definitely shortcomings in my communication skills, and those most likely contributed to the folklore. I just have never talked a lot. I listened a lot. People had trouble knowing what was on my mind, so they improvised on what they thought I was thinking.

K. C. PUTNAM: I've never known Leon to be wishy-washy about anything, but I do remember him as very contemplative . . . I remember going into Leon's office, and I would . . . make a point and talk about it, and Leon would ask questions about it . . . Then there would be silence. For a long time silence bothered me. So I'd go on and I'd try and explain something else or I'd go on to the next item, and it didn't really work. So one time, I remember I just sat there. I said [to myself], I'm just going to sit here and see what happens . . . He wasn't just silent. He looked distant . . . You would think that he was thinking about something entirely different, but then he would ask you a question, and you'd answer that question. I finally learned to shut up. Then he would ask another question or he'd say, "OK," or he would say, "No, I don't want to do that." I don't remember long involved whys, but he would make his decision and then that was it. But the decision was made after a period of reflection. He wasn't hurrying into a decision, and I think when he made his decision, he was comfortable with it. And that was it.

Most people figured all this out and knew where I stood on most issues. But it was a problem for some. I'm not sure how aware I was of my effect on others. Conversations that I considered relaxed were probably not relaxed at all for others. My lack of communication tended to fuel the folklore with some misinformation.

NANCY MARSTON: The quietness was more intimidating . . . You have to wait for him to finish. And you have to get to know him. Once you get to know him, it takes a while to understand all the little things. You can tell when he's sitting in a meeting, and he'd either be scowling or he'd be doing something and those wheels would be turning. What is he thinking? What's he going to come up with? What's going on in there? [Laughter]

I always thought he was fairly easy to talk to, most of the time, because I probably did most of the talking. We'd get word that he was coming . . . Somebody would say, "Leon's in the building." Or, "Leon's coming up the stairs at the retail store." . . . He may have intimidated more people than he realized.

My management style was nonconfrontational. My preference was to work collaboratively with others and support their work. Formal performance management was a cumbersome process but a good opportunity to discuss job and personnel issues at length with my direct reports.

JIM MAHONEY: Leon has many strengths but confronting unpleasant personnel decisions is not one of them.

I avoided negative criticism. Nonetheless I was close enough to the people working directly for me that there was no secret about my expectations or how well they were meeting them. In the few cases where there was an individual performance problem I was probably late in dealing with them. But in these situations I'd rather be late and fair than quick and wrong.

Mostly, Bean people and L.L.Bean were growing in leaps and bounds. In my regular letter to employees in "*The Bean Scene*," I wrote about growth and change in generating and increasing the flow of profits. Profits ("the "*P*" word" to some of our idealists) enabled us to provide better products and services for our customers, cash bonuses and job security for our employees, increased dividends for our owners, and greater participation in our local and state communities. It was my version of the "virtuous cycle," rewarding all of our stakeholders.

By the mid-1970s, the opportunities for L.L.Bean seemed enormous, but we were growing so fast I didn't have time to look into all of them. Our advertising program and every segment of our mailing list were working. We were experiencing a kind of special appeal to our public, our "mystique," that we didn't entirely understand. Nor did we know how sustainable it was. Yet we were making significant long-term investments in facilities, systems, and people based on continuing high growth rates.

In addition to our mystique, or our unique positioning, several external factors were working in our favor. The mail-order industry was entering a period of dramatic growth. More women were entering the workforce and had less time for traditional shopping, and there was more discretionary household income. Wide area telephone service (in 1975 our telephone orders were insignificant; in 1980 they were 15 percent of our orders, or 270,000 and growing) and credit card services (we began honoring credit cards in 1976) greatly accelerated telephone ordering. And, most important, our product line was increasingly relevant, with its outdoors orientation and emphasis on functional value—two important consumer values, especially among the coming-of-age baby boomers.

> NANCY MARSTON: [Some of the longtime employees] just didn't comprehend what the outlook was for the company. Some people just really had a difficult time. They would say, "We're doing fine right now. We're making money. Why do we need to be huge?" Consultants would come in with a whole brand new way of doing something. And [the reaction] was, "This is not going to work." That would be the mind-set. "Why do we need to do that?"

Many people in the company wanted to know, Why so much growth and change? Where were we headed? Was it really worth it? Would growth spoil L.L.Bean? It was becoming important to me, too, to have answers to those questions. Growth for its own sake was a form of managerial adventurism and didn't interest me. On the other hand, I believed strongly that if we could keep adding value to people's lives, we had an obligation to grow. I told this to a business reporter once, and an incredulous look came over his face. A rationale for growth, other than making more money, may have been news, but I thought it essential for making meaningful sense out of any business strategy.

So I believed in growth—but with two conditions. First, we should grow as long as it didn't work against any of our stakeholders. For example, there was no reason for the owners or employees of the company to take unnecessary financial risks with L.L.Bean or to grow faster than we could keep up and provide quality products and superior service to our customers. We were committed to adding optimum value for all our constituents.

Second, and equally important, growth shouldn't ruin our unique positioning, or "image" as it was called in those days. "Image" has a kind of superficial meaning that I never liked. I actually preferred the notion of corporate "character." I thought L.L.Bean should grow as long as it didn't change our character—who we were and what we believed in—which was based on the L.L. story.

But I was having problems keeping up and, at the same time, anticipating future growth. I was running into the limits of how much I could do on my own. I needed help to deal with our marketing issues and especially our opportunities in direct marketing. I needed help in operations management. I needed help with financial strategies. L.L.Bean needed to make a transition from entrepreneurial management to professional management, beginning with marketing.

The Harvard Business School had done two case studies on L.L.Bean and I'd been impressed by the people I'd met. So I prepared a letter to the school's placement office: "We are presently looking for a qualified person to serve as our Marketing Manager," it began. It went on to describe the laundry list of exceptional business qualifications I was looking for.

Further, it said, "the candidate must have a strong, personal and proven interest in some of our outdoors sports such as fly-fishing, upland game or duck hunting, family camping, backpacking, canoe camping, or cross-country skiing. Plus an interest in country living." I was looking for the perfect L.L.Bean fit.

Specifically, the successful candidate would be someone who could get us into the more technical and best-practice areas of direct marketing: mailing-list rentals and circulation building; advertising; catalog merchandising; and growth strategies. The economy was in a slump in the mid-1970s, but I continued to be optimistic and felt we had a great adventure ahead of us. I looked forward to sharing it and to the search.

A second purpose was to find a "professional" manager to be my second-in-command. I don't think I was overly concerned with this issue, but the company did about $30 million in sales that year (1975).

We were at or approaching a size where my type of entrepreneurial style might not be appropriate. The company could probably benefit from a more disciplined management approach.

I still had not instituted any budgeting or profit planning systems, and we'd been working on a personnel policy manual for three years with no end in sight. I was a little skeptical of "modernization," but mainly administrative functions were not my favorite things. I much preferred developing and selecting the product lines, catalog merchandising, and advertising. Operationally, I was on the floor a lot and knew most of our employees, and I was more hands-on with problem solving and daily updates with our department heads. I let them handle their own administrative responsibilities. Maybe I could learn from a "professional" manager and move beyond the entrepreneurial stage.

In summing up this period, the March 8, 1976, issue of Fairchild Publications' authoritative apparel retailing publication, *Daily News Record*, in a story about ten great stores, articulated the L.L.Bean paradigm:

> Long before survival became chic, there was L.L.Bean, an institution that has taken on the human qualities of an old friend in the minds of its many faithful followers. A true down-Easterner, Bean has let others' flirtations with fashion bring them around to this year's fascination with the practical, the comfortable and the durable. When the others have gone on to the next big thing, dependable Bean will be steady as a rock with its offerings of good, common sense merchandise. Of course, the faithful all over the world have known this for years, and the twice-yearly arrival of the Bean catalog is for them like receiving a little security in the mailbox. For while the Whole Earth Catalog and its mystique may bear much of the responsibility for the armies of down-vested, Frye-booted pavement pounders on the loose in our cities, the Bean Catalog came first. And when fashion has fled the woods, Bean will still be there—with style.[4]

Whether L.L.Bean would "still be there"—another form of the question being asked within the company, "Will growth spoil L.L.Bean?"—would depend on my ability to blend professional managers and business practices with the Bean mystique and everything behind it. Until the mid-1970s I had been able to avoid hiring the kind of professional manager I just described. In part it was because I was a penny-pincher. I didn't want to pay the salaries that professional managers got. Second, I didn't know whether I had enough work to fully occupy them. But I think I probably didn't really want conflicting points of view in the place, because I had this vision and it was my company, and, I guess, I just didn't want people challenging it. I was also concerned about what might happen if I hired really good people. Could I manage them? Could I stay ahead of them? Or would they run away with the business?

The more obvious concern was whether they would really buy in to the L.L.Bean concept, or whether they would be pure bottom-line people who forgot the heritage and all the rest of it. But I had reached the point that I simply could not do it all, and I had to have help if we were to keep growing. So I sent the letter to Harvard. The business school there responded by giving me the name of a search firm, which I subsequently engaged.

PART THREE

1976–1990

Blucher + Boat #Tote

7

Taking L.L.Bean Professional

IN JULY 1975, we hired Bill End as our marketing director and my second-in-command. This was about eleven months after we had commenced the search. I'd gone through dozens of résumés and personally interviewed fifteen candidates in Freeport. I used eight criteria, including an active interest in outdoor sports, which significantly reduced the field.

Bill was the winner by a wide margin. He was twenty-six years old and had an MBA from Harvard. Extremely bright and highly energetic, Bill had accumulated a wealth of marketing experience and confidence with the Gillette Company in Boston. Following my first interview with him, he sent me a nine-page typewritten marketing plan for L.L.Bean. Jim Mahoney called him a "super marketer," "a helluva manager," and a "meteor" in the business world. I felt very good the day Bill accepted our offer and looked forward to exciting times ahead for L.L.Bean.

BILL END: I had a particular interest in working for Bean, as I've always been a very avid outdoorsman. When I got out of graduate business school I wanted to go into either the outdoors industry or brand management. One of the companies that I interviewed with was the Browning Arms Company in Morgan, Utah, and I applied for a job at the Orvis Company. I came up to Maine a great deal. I rented a home up at Sugarloaf for a couple of years and did a lot of skiing up there, did some hunting and fishing. So I was very familiar with Bean at the time. The move to Bean was very positive, moving from a large company to a small company into a fairly senior position. But it was not necessarily a great career move for me at the time because the opportunity at Gillette was a terrific one. I think the only thing that caused me to move was real interest in the brand and the outdoor industry in general.

Just prior to Bill End's joining the company, Bill Henry had also come to work for L.L.Bean as budget manager. This meant designing and implementing our long-awaited budgetary planning and control system, with all the practices and disciplines that go with it. Bill was in his early thirties and had a variety of business and direct marketing experience. Prior to coming to work for L.L.Bean he had been the consultant on-site for Stanley Fenvessy in upgrading our customer service operations. Bill and his wife, Dagny, loved Maine and the outdoors, and he simply insisted on coming to work for us. After getting the budget system installed, he joined Bill End in the direct marketing department. He was smart, meticulous, innovative, and hardworking. Together, the two Bills proved to be a powerful team. Bill Henry went on to become our vice president for direct marketing and one of the leading experts in the direct marketing industry.

John Findlay joined L.L.Bean in the fall of 1976. John was thirty-four and had been a good friend of Bill Henry's at William & Mary College. John had served as an officer in the Marine Corps and, after that, had substantial experience in data processing and general management. John became our director of data processing and, soon after, our vice president for operations. John also had an active outdoors family and readily adjusted to living in Maine. Jim Mahoney said that if you were ever marooned in the Alaskan wilderness, John Findlay was the guy you wanted to lead you out. He proved to be a great leader in our operations area and saw L.L.Bean achieve the highest industry standards in customer service.

I hadn't been significantly involved in direct marketing. Improving product assortments and managing advertising had been enough to increase the business tenfold since I had become president. I knew there was a whole world of list rentals and list management out there. I had studied direct marketing; in fact I wrote a paper about it for one of my night courses. But I just hadn't had time or the need to implement a direct marketing strategy at L.L.Bean. So it was Bill End's first assignment to get us more deeply involved in direct marketing.

As a customer of Bean's and an outdoors enthusiast, Bill was personally committed to the catalog business and our focus on the outdoor life. He and I talked briefly about growth options, such as opening retail stores and more manufacturing, but it didn't take a lot of thought to recognize that we still had great potential in direct marketing. The catalog channel was growing all across the country; it tended to have greater profit margins than retail; it was relatively less crowded at the time; and L.L.Bean knew the catalog business.

> BILL END: One of the things Leon asked me during the interview was to write up a memo on what I would change if I came to Bean, and I think my answer was I wouldn't change much of anything having to do with the brand. I thought it was a great brand, well positioned to grow, and had a huge opportunity going forward. My intent would be to do more of what they had been doing, just to get the brand a much broader circulation. That was the primary growth direction.

Completing our senior management team during this period was Norm Poole, who joined us in 1980 as our senior finance person. He was very smart, with significant retail and catalog experience and an outgoing personality. Norm provided the company with exceptional leadership overall and in our financial area. He was highly regarded by all, and he understood L.L.Bean. When Norm showed up for his first interview he had a full beard and was driving a big Cadillac. For the second interview he was clean-shaven and driving a Ford Bronco.

Now we would see whether professional management could keep our momentum going. It was a direct marketing truism that specialty catalog businesses tended to plateau in the $30 million to $50 million range. Could L.L.Bean break through the $50 million ceiling, or should we look harder for alternative growth opportunities? We decided to ignore this bit of catalog folklore and stay the course.

In 1976, Bill End got a group of us together—including a direct marketing consultant, our ad agency representative, and a well-known mailing-list broker—at a brainstorming meeting in Portland to begin developing a direct marketing strategy. We felt that with increased knowledge of the list rental business and mailing-list management, we could not only continue our high rates of growth but also control the rates.

> BILL END: It was a very exciting time to be with the company . . . Probably the biggest early breakthrough was figuring out how to circulate catalogs to outside mailing lists. The company primarily grew early on through an advertising program where they would basically advertise their catalog in magazine advertising . . . When I got there we . . . learned something about renting other people's mailing lists. In the first year that we rented mailing lists virtually all of the lists worked for us, so we had very clearly a great deal of opportunity to extend the number of lists that we were using, go much deeper into the lists that we were using.

At Bill's strategy meeting we planned our first effort to calculate the values of various kinds of L.L.Bean buyers. This would tell us how often we could afford to mail catalogs to them. We discussed various techniques for segmenting our mailing list to determine the relative likelihood of buying among our customers. This was what direct marketers called RFM analysis (recency of purchase, frequency, and monetary value). Almost invariably it revealed that your best prospects for future sales were recent customers who'd bought a lot in total and had bought from you a number of times. That wasn't a big surprise on the face of it, but the analysis lent itself to supporting much more efficient and extensive catalog mailing plans.

We also talked about a wide range of other direct marketing techniques and opportunities: testing techniques for prospecting for new customers by renting other catalogers' mailing lists; market research for people's likes and dislikes about L.L.Bean; package inserts; sale mailings;

timing and frequency of mailings; mini-catalogs for prospecting with inquiries and rental lists; geographic penetration outside our Northeastern regional customer base; shipping and handling charges (L.L.Bean was one of the last to continue free shipping, but we were reluctant to publicize it because we didn't know how much longer we could afford it); early order discounts to move up Christmas shopping; more precision in cost/benefit analysis of various inquiry advertising sources; store sales as a function of catalog circulation; the success we were having with women's and gift lists; and a wide range of direct marketing strategies and tactics including a mathematical technique called regression analysis, which can sort people out by their likelihood to buy based on various buying behaviors. This made it possible to forecast sales from a specific catalog mailing.

So there was no lack of opportunity in Bean's catalog business. In 1975, when our sales had been $30 million, I'd hoped to reach $50 million in the next five years. But a year later, after our 1976 planning meeting, we projected 1980 sales at $109.5 million. It represented a continuation, even a speed-up, in our growth since the late 1960s. We had been growing at an average annual rate of 25 percent since that time.

Moving to professional management meant more than hiring experienced managers. I myself had a lot to learn about managing a large and complex organization. We needed systems and processes, ways of thinking and planning and doing work, that were effective and let the company grow profitably while maintaining its character. We needed to learn to work together.

I'd never had any training in modern management practices, and so in 1977 I went to a week-long American Management Association (AMA) seminar in Florida for company presidents. It was a revelation. I got caught up in strategic planning as well as the process of management, with its clearly defined goals, action plans, and performance standards, executive committees and good communications, decentralization and consensus decision making, position descriptions and performance management, climate studies, good listening skills, and all the other trappings of professional management.

Not all those concepts and practices were new to me. I'd certainly read a lot and heard a lot about strategic planning, management techniques, human resource practices, and so on. But this course put it all together. It turned the lights on for me on what management was all about—how people should be managed and the way companies' strategies should be developed.

The notion of responsible autonomy, for instance, showed me, in a simple way, the need to give managers the freedom to do their jobs and the need for overall company guidelines. This idea is best understood by envisioning a four-sided box. Two sides of the box represent mandates: company beliefs and policies, and legal and ethical standards within which the manager is expected to act. The other two sides represent negotiated limits: budgets and operating plans. These the managers work out with their supervisors. Once everyone agrees on the goals, the plans and budgets became guidelines within which the manager is expected to operate. The space within the box represents the area where the manager can operate with responsible autonomy.

The notion of stakeholders also became central to my view of how a business should operate.

> WES DEVRIES: Leon is one of the few people I've met who really believes in . . . the balancing of stakeholders' interests. I work with many different companies of many different sizes. He is the only CEO I know who truly was committed to trying to balance all stakeholders' interests. Many articulate that. I mean, it's a typical thing in the schools. "Yes, we've got this constituency and that and the other one and we're going to balance all the interests." He really did his best to try to do that and it's a very difficult thing to do.

"Stakeholders" meant the constituents who had a vested interest in our business. I believed we had responsibilities to all of them. We owed our customers superior-quality products and personal service, our employees fair wages and benefits and superior working conditions, our owners a fair and secure return on their investment, and our communities good citizenship and active participation.

Several years ago I was on the board of our local utility company, Central Maine Power. I remember one of the other directors saying that the board's only role is to advance the interests of the stockholders. That bothered me. I had a big argument with him. I said, "What about the customers? What about the people who work here? What about our communities? Don't they count? Just the stockholders? Advancing stockholders' wealth—is that all we're about?"

At L.L.Bean I believed in paying our family owners a fair and significant dividend and in securing their investment in the company as best I could. But making the most money wasn't why I was working here. I saw myself as working for all of the stakeholders: customers, employees, and communities, even our natural environment, as well as our owners. That's what made the whole thing worthwhile.

I continued to believe that people want to feel they're serving a higher purpose. Not to sound pretentious, but I think people in business can do noble things, just like doctors and educators and people in public service. Sure, we sell Bean Boots and backpacks and fleece jackets, but they enable people to enjoy the outdoors and that adds value to their lives. What do they get from the outdoors? All kinds of physical and spiritual rewards. That's what it's all about and what we're all about; what we're promoting and supporting and enabling people to do. I think most people at L.L.Bean, including our new senior management group, shared in this belief.

We recognized that in the short term our various stakeholder interests could be competitive, but in the long term—and we are a long-term company—their interests are interdependent and mutually beneficial. No one could benefit in the long term at the expense of another. But the customers were foremost in importance to us. If we did well by them, we'd do well by the others. We never forgot that all these lofty aspirations were carried out through a business enterprise. To serve all our stakeholders well, we needed to do well in business terms.

I'd studied enough accounting to understand income statements and balance sheets, but I knew very little about formulating a longer-term financial strategy that would incorporate a high rate of growth, decent profitability, and a strong balance sheet. We had ambitious marketing plans, and I needed financial goals and guidelines.

I had the good fortune to attend one of John Childs's seminars in December 1978. John was a financial guru, an adviser, lecturer, and writer on corporate finance, and a man of great integrity. When I met him, he was working for a large investment banking firm. One of his jobs was to conduct seminars and week-long courses on financial strategy for client and prospective client companies.

John emphasized two broad goals: always producing a satisfactory return on capital, and ensuring that outside capital would always be available at a reasonable cost when it was needed for expansion. To achieve these goals, three financial ratios provided the basis for financial strategy:

1. Long-term debt to total long-term capital (the debt-to-equity ratio)

2. Return on equity (ROE), the ratio of earnings to equity or book value

3. The ratio of dividends to book value (the amount of earnings that should be paid out in dividends)

Setting targets for these ratios and achieving them over time, John said, would ensure high-quality financial performance for the enterprise, the owners, and all the stakeholders.

The three key ratios interact dynamically on the financial statements. Given an ROE goal and a return on sales assumption, we could project pro forma financial statements into the future, which then provided a context for marketing and operating plans that we could implement without excessive borrowing.[1]

MARK FASOLD: I always start with return on equity because, although it's a standard financial measure, net income divided by stockholders' equity, it really for L.L.Bean is the foundation for serving all the stakeholders. If we have good ROEs we can pay employees well, we can pay bonuses, we can retain enough money in the company, we can pay a return to shareholders, and it means you have to be doing something good with your customers or else you couldn't be generating good returns.

I think you can relate more to an ROE ratio than you can to a concept like return on sales, which is only part of the story. ROE equates to what you might be earning on your own money if you had invested in the stock market and you were getting, say, a 10 percent return. Because it can be compared with almost any other kind of investment, return on equity is also a way of comparing your investment performance with that of other companies in varied industries. Maybe in the retail industry alone you could compare returns on sales, but it would be comparing apples to oranges if you tried to take it to different industries.

What especially appealed to me about John's approach and focus on the three ratios was that, as he said, "They will determine the future of your company, regardless of its type." In other words, if you get those three right, everything else has to be right. They are at the core of any strategic business plan you may have.

In 1982, John met with our family board of directors and we formally adopted the key ratios as our basic financial strategy. We set the dividend rate at 6 percent of book value. (Later in the decade we also began adding fourth-generation members of the L.L.Bean family to the board.)

John continued to be our chief financial adviser over the next twenty years or so and was a good and valued friend of the company. Most of our senior financial people attended his week-long course in New York City. During our high-growth years in the mid-1980s John said our financial performance compared with the 86th percentile of the *Fortune* 500.

I believed that the planning process based on the three ratios should provide the framework of management at L.L.Bean. The planning process brought everyone together, departments and work units, in periodic meetings to discuss the various elements of the plan and their roles in achieving the planned results, the financial ones based on the three ratios. It was the process that got us to agree on priorities for the coming year. And it was the process that got us to evaluate the results of initiatives and come up with newer and better ones for the next planning cycle. In speaking of our planning, people sometimes used the term *process bound* as a pejorative, but the process was the whole point. The *process* of planning *was* the plan. The plan was the never-ending series of steps and activities that led to our getting better. The process spun off periodic operating and capital budgets and strategic initiatives, all in a context of continuous improvement and within the L.L.Bean concept and strategies.

The planning process was intended to engage all parts of the organization. It required participation at all levels. It wouldn't work, for example, if our senior group went off by itself and came up with a grand plan. The goal was to involve as many people in the organization as we could, in order to create understanding and commitment.

The process of planning was my idea of a management model. That's how I intended to bring together and align all the parts of the organization, from direct marketing and customer service to human resources and facilities maintenance. It would continually bring people together in ongoing discussions and decision making and advancing L.L.Bean. That was the important thing.

Our senior managers didn't resist the process of planning as I saw it and its central role, but I don't think they shared my enthusiasm for it. They were already stretched thin keeping up with our growing business. We were fully occupied with getting the work out and didn't have much time for the niceties of professional management. I used to think of the late 1970s as the time we became a professionally managed company, but we were probably more hands-on and entrepreneurial in our leadership style as the company continued its rapid growth.

BILL END: I think what happened when the outside management team was hired, we started putting in place some things that hadn't been there before, for example a budget. I think for the first time we actually had a month by month budget and a full year budget and a plan that we were reporting against, and we started to do some of the things that are done in a professional management organization. I'm sure we began to do three year plans at that time. I think where there's perhaps some disagreement was about the level of detail behind the plans. I think we were planning in an operating mode, using the plans as an operating tool. And I think what Leon saw in this process, and I'm guessing, was planning at a whole different level of detail and things like that. I think we were not staffed terribly well early on. We were all pretty busy and there may have been some pushback there, but we generally, I think as a management team, were highly cooperative with Leon, worked well with Leon throughout the end of the seventies and the eighties. I think everyone had a high degree of respect for Leon, so if he asked us to do something we did it. I don't recall pushback or anything of that type early on.

The ongoing dilemma of maintaining our old-fashioned values in a rapid growth environment needed a rationale that we all could understand. Strategic planning—with its mission statements, overarching strategies, and situation assessments—promised to provide this. There was a lot being written on the subject. It was trendy, and most organizations I was familiar with were giving strategic planning a try. And so did we.

A young man showed up for an interview while this notion of planning was taking shape. He was bright and energetic, and he wanted to come to work for Bean in the worst way and for all the right reasons. Although he'd never done any formal business planning (his background was in logistics at Sears), he was eager to give it a try. We hired him as our director of strategic planning.

We both started reading whatever material we could get on planning, including American Management Association publications and books by George Steiner and especially Peter Drucker.[2] In reading Professor Drucker's books we found two versions of his eight key results areas. Our new director immediately jumped on the telephone and called the professor in his California office to clarify our interpretation.

Professor Drucker turned out to be a longtime customer of ours and was a bit taken aback that the venerable L.L.Bean, of all companies, would be engaged in strategic planning. He gave us some excellent advice: that our prime objective should be in maintaining our character, both inside and outside the company. He confirmed our basic approach and told us, "Don't change until there is no other alternative."

Taking Professor Drucker's advice, we drafted the first part of our strategy statement in 1978 to elaborate on the character of our business. This statement would provide the strategic context within which our planning process would work. The character statement read as follows (somewhat shortened):

Leon L. Bean founded our company in 1912 and incorporated it under the laws of the State of Maine in 1934. This statement of our purpose serves to clarify our current corporate situation . . . The critical factor in our success has been the unique character of our company and its way of doing business. This character is a product of Leon L. Bean's unique personal qualities and the fundamental human qualities we all share as part of our common Maine heritage. The most tangible results are the superior value of our line of specialty products and the superior services we give to our customers. Our future success is dependent not only upon how well we continue to fulfill our corporate purpose, but also upon how well we understand our unique character and maintain it in our corporate activities.

The first element of our purpose (and our character) is based on our specialty products. Our products are recreational apparel and footwear, sporting equipment and other merchandise associated with outdoor recreation. They are designed or selected by us to meet the practical needs of people like us who enjoy the outdoors, whether it be for hunting, fishing, camping, backpacking, canoeing, winter sports or related activities . . .

The second element of our purpose (and our character) is based on the service we give to our customers. Our marketing and advertising techniques are intended to efficiently and accurately communicate our line of specialty products to outdoors oriented American people. Our primary means of communication are our mail order catalogs and our Freeport, Maine, retail store . . . Being users of our own products, as well as distributors, we are aware that their value depends on their quality and performance at a reasonable price.

The third element of our purpose (and our character) is our unique way of doing business. We are aware that our customers are human beings like ourselves. We not only guarantee our products to be 100% satisfactory as to quality, performance and price. We also guarantee in all of our transactions with our customers, whether for purchase or for information, that we will treat them with respect and personal consideration as we ourselves would like to be treated.

We were proud of our character and our reputation. People liked and trusted L.L.Bean. We were all part of the L.L. story and its appealing human values and felt responsible for perpetuating it. Our character was our most important asset and the key to our competitive advantage.

After beginning with our corporate character, we spent considerable time writing purpose statements and assumptions and basic values built around the L.L. story and getting consensus on the words. Our first purpose statement read as follows:

> To market high quality recreational products of the best functional value to outdoor oriented American consumers with the kind of personal service we would like to receive.

This statement was factually correct but painfully lacking in inspiration. People instinctively gravitated toward L.L.'s Golden Rule: "Sell good merchandise for a reasonable profit; treat your customers like human beings and they'll always come back for more." L.L.'s words prevailed. We continued to use his pithy statement as the cornerstone of L.L.Bean.

> BOB PEIXOTTO: The corporate purpose statement is actually about a 38-page document that pretty clearly outlines what [Leon] wants for this company. It appeared in the early eighties ... It's a planning document, but it doesn't lend itself to any particular year. It's more, "This is how I think about the business." And in it Leon addresses things like how fast we should be growing, what our responsibilities are for each of the various stakeholders in the business. What people should be getting out of the business. The way we think about our environment. It's really very uplifting, forward looking, it's the description of a model company in my estimation.

As the company grew in size and complexity I was spending more time on people management issues. These could get complicated, subjective, judgmental, and ambiguous. In human resource management, you have variables—such as performance management, hiring and training, motivation and leadership, and legal requirements—that I needed to put together in an understandable context. I wanted to see the whole picture, all the HR elements, in an overall, coherent way. So we developed what we called a "model of organizational behavior." It outlined a straightforward and systematic way to manage and motivate a large group of people effectively, fairly, and, I thought, respectfully. The heart of the model was this belief:

> People with ability, given the opportunity to perform in a motivating environment, will achieve the best performance and in the most productive manner.

The "people with ability" part meant recruiting, training, developing, and placing or promoting good Bean people. "Opportunity to perform" meant effective use of our performance management program of planning, coaching, and evaluating individual performance—that is, executing the responsible autonomy concept.

Every company does these basic elements of the HR model, although companies obviously differ in how well they do them. We had no problem in recruiting people, because of our appealing mystique and the opportunities to perform that growth provided. Our contribution to the equation, I think, was in consciously and systematically trying to identify the elements of a motivating environment. We worked out a motivational model with Jim Mahoney based on his experience as an industrial psychologist and our own experience at Bean.

In the model, we identified the eight dimensions of a motivating environment: (1) clarity of objectives, (2) integration of efforts across units, (3) teamwork within units, (4) commitment or willingness to serve, (5) adequacy of recognition systems, (6) degree of experienced autonomy, (7) openness of communication, and (8) company reputation and identification with it. We felt these dimensions were critically related to our ability to achieve our goals. We believed that if we surveyed Bean employees on a regular (biennial) basis, we would know what it was like to work at L.L.Bean and would learn how to deal with any deficiencies. Continuous improvement.

We conducted our first such "climate study" in 1980. It attempted to measure those dimensions of our work environment that determined people's motivation. It was accompanied by a fair amount of apprehension and skepticism on the part of all of us in senior management. We didn't know what was going to come out of it.

In fact, it gave us valuable insights into the current environment at L.L.Bean, highlighted priority issues, and set a baseline for future studies. We learned so much that it convinced me you had to do formal surveys regularly if you wanted to really know what people were thinking and feeling in a way you could do something about. Our climate studies were more than surveys. They were followed up with discussion groups and individual interviews. Outside professionals sat with a dozen or twenty people in various areas and got a lot of narrative, anecdotal feedback to expand on the survey results.

That first study revealed a great deal of pride in the company and its reputation, and a strong sense of integrity and commitment. There was concern about what our longer-range goals were and how to prioritize work. Most employees wanted more participation in decision making for the longer term (a key reason we opened up our planning process). Communications in general, vertically and laterally, could be better. But interpersonal relationships were perceived to be first rate, and there was a great deal of comradeship across departments.

Unfortunately, the HR model could seem mechanistic when it was outlined and explained with formal definitions for each of its parts. This upset some people, who felt employee relationships were dehumanized by such a structured approach. But it sure helped me understand the HR issues and theories and grasp the dynamics of how people worked together in a common enterprise. I didn't push the model itself very hard publicly, but our personnel director and I used it for prioritizing our human resource strategies.

JOHN FINDLAY: Bean was never a hard-nosed, ruthless, internally and externally competitive company. It treated its employees really well, paid them well, didn't put too many hardships on them and, I think, kept people around too long before they got rid of them. I was to blame for that too. I think the idea fit with my personality too well, which was to support people and make them better.

As our new and highly competent senior managers put their ideas and energy in place, I felt we had the foundation for continued dramatic growth. I said earlier we'd projected that our sales in 1980 would be $109.5 million. In fact, sales in 1980 reached $121.5 million, a quadrupling of our sales ($30 million) in 1975. We also maintained our profit margins and earned more than 30 percent on our equity.

Moving to professional management, and managers, had taken L.L.Bean way beyond that mythical ceiling for specialty catalogers, and far beyond my original goal of $50 million by 1980. We had moved to a different world.

Catalog circulation and list management became major strengths of the company in the 1970s and 1980s because of Bill End and Bill Henry. Both had exceptional math minds as well as innovative ways of looking at direct marketing problems, and they weren't afraid to hire bright and computer-literate people to help them. It was under Bill End's guidance that L.L.Bean earned a reputation as one of the best, if not the best, direct marketers in the country.

BOB PEIXOTTO: I think at the beginning [the senior managers] were a really good, tight group. They socialized together. At least outwardly they showed a lot of mutual admiration for one another. I think it was a pretty strong leadership group for the company at that time.

Bill [End] was highly respected for his business expertise. Leon represented the heart and soul of merchandising of the company, and Bill represented the science of the company, the numbers. Bill probably was more restless than Leon was. Bill was the kind of guy, if you went in and gave him a presentation, you would start on page one, Bill automatically flipped to the back to see what the conclusion was. He didn't have a lot of patience for going through the whole presentation; he just wanted to get right to the facts. Leon would be much more methodical going through things, because the logic of it all and how you arrived at a conclusion was very important to him. They actually were a great duo, working together.

[Bill] . . . was a straight arrow, told it like it was, was young and hungry, but also really respected what Leon and Bean stood for. He did the outdoors in a different way, a big game hunter. He always took the time to write a personal note to anybody who had a birthday, and if you got promoted he would write you a nice note. He was writing notes all the time. Just highly respected, because everybody thought he was a business genius, because we felt like he modernized the direct mail part of this business. There's lore that comes along with being the first MBA in the company.

John Findlay. He was an interesting sort. He was honest, upstanding, probably not as young and hungry as, say, Bill End. He was just far more laid back. Very practical, pragmatic, and down to earth. He'd always say, "It's just a simple business. Customers place orders and we send them out."

Norm Poole was a little flashier, and a little eccentric in many ways. He was kind of flamboyant. He loved people. He loved being in front of people. He loved to go through manufacturing and shake hands with people and talk and laugh. He was a huge jokester. He cared a lot about what Leon wanted to do here and was highly willing to support it. It wasn't as much who he was as how much he admired Leon and wanted to help Leon accomplish what Leon wanted out of the company. Norm was a deep sea fisherman. He had these huge yachts. Times were good! He had these huge yachts and he would take people out fishing in the afternoon, numerous times, go fishing and call it business, talk about a little business and we'd be reeling in bluefish.

I think all of us in senior management worked together very well. We were all committed to L.L.Bean, and we worked hard. Each of us had our individual area of responsibility. I was functioning as chief merchant as well as president. Bill was marketing; John, operations; and Norm, finance. John once said we each had our own fiefdom, which implied a certain independence, but the group was respectful of one another's prerogatives, and we had easy and frequent communications, daily and even hourly as necessary. We usually had lunch together in the Beanery, our company cafeteria. The chemistry was good. We were well aligned as to what L.L.Bean was all about.

JOHN FINDLAY: Never once did he stand in my way. I think he knew that the customer was important to me and he never once wavered in terms of providing the resources I asked for to serve the customers as well as I could do it. You could plan a distribution center of 100,000 square feet, if you needed it, and have the money, and not rob Peter to pay Paul. That's huge. I mean, none of this taking three years, going through five levels of finance. We had to come up with some numbers, but basically once you put the numbers together, if that's what you need, that's what you got. He'd have to understand it and buy in to it, but that was a good part of working there, that I was able to feel that Leon and I had an understanding about the customer. He had won me over early. [Customer service] was one of Bean's hallmarks and damned if I was going to let it go when I was there, and he certainly wasn't going to let it go, or let me let it go—the fact that the customer was extremely important. I think he looked to me, as to himself, as being the two people who would be a barrier against the barbarians. I mean, Bill End and I are good friends, I see him all the time, [but] in terms of marketing, in terms of catalog, in terms of inventory management, all those things have an effect on the customer, and it was fair game for me to bitch and complain on behalf of the customer. I think it was understood. It was. It was important to Leon that that be taken care of. So I think we demanded and got responses from other people, whereas some companies . . . you're so far down the pecking order from the marketing and creative types, that you just do the best you can and keep your head down, keep your mouth shut, that kind of thing. Bean was not that way and that was very refreshing, to be on the operations side of a company like that. It was very positive.

We continued our tradition of annual or semiannual directors' trips to various parts of Maine's great outdoors. We hiked or biked or canoed or kayaked or skied or whatever was in season. Participation in the trips came to mean that the participant had "arrived" at L.L.Bean. The outings were looked upon as a good time, but newcomers found them a lot more strenuous than they'd anticipated. We spent six days canoeing the St. John River one year, with its several sections of classified white water and its occasional rainy days, every day. Another time we backpacked the Carter-Mahoosuc range of mountains connecting New Hampshire and Maine. It's considered the most challenging stretch of the entire Appalachian Trail, and the temperatures were in the 90s. It lived on in corporate lore as the Death March.

In 1980 I was inducted into the Woolrich Outdoors Hall of Fame. Bean was one of its largest customers if not the largest. Representing the real outdoors heroes were Lowell Thomas, the great radio newscaster and world explorer, and Jim Whittaker, the premier mountain climber and in 1963 the first American on Mt. Everest. We were being interviewed by a local Wilkes-Barre, Pennsylvania, television station and I was in the third position, following these two legends of the outdoors. What exploits could I possibly discuss in the company of these two adventurers and great storytellers? As the camera turned my way, it occurred to me, because of my involvement in all the activities that Bean catered to, that I was probably mediocre in more outdoor activities than anyone else, possibly, in the world. This observation got laughs from Lowell and Jim, and the interviewer and I had a nice discussion of my "average guy" adventures hunting, fishing, hiking, biking, skiing, and so on.

In 1980, Bill End and I presented L.L.Bean as a case study at the Colby College Institute for Management in Waterville, Maine. We prepared our parts separately as to L.L.Bean's market position, strategic issues, growth within the catalog channel, and the importance of maintaining L.L.Bean's image or character throughout. We presented our parts at the institute, and they perfectly complemented each other. We had worked together closely for five years and were in complete agreement regarding the present and future of L.L.Bean.

BILL END: I would say any company that's growing the way Bean was growing was just a terribly exciting place to work. It was just fun, a really, really exciting place to watch stuff happen, watch the business grow. You have to build a new distribution center and you have to build a new footwear facility and you've got to crank up the phone center, and now you've got to start another new distribution center. It was exciting and fun and challenging during that period of time, for sure. That would be the overriding thing. I think it probably was a little constrained as a company just because of Leon's management style. It wasn't a free flowing everybody-does-their-own-thing-and-coordinate-after-the-fact. But again, with all due respect, Leon did a hell of a job of running the business and the controls that he ultimately put on the business I think were generally positive. And he preserved and protected the brand very effectively as a result.

8

Fashion Boom and Bust

I N 1978, we changed our logo to read "Outdoor Sporting Specialties," replacing L.L.'s "Hunting Fishing and Camping," to reflect the
broadening scope of L.L.Bean.

Outdoor activities we now supported, along with L.L.'s hunting
and fishing interests, included hiking, backpacking, and family camping, canoeing and kayaking, recreational bicycling, and winter sports,
including cross-country skiing and snowshoeing. Criteria for an L.L.
Bean activity were that it be, for the most part, people-powered and
noncompetitive and that it generally take place in a natural environment. I put together these three criteria in an effort to encompass everything we were in that seemed appropriate, and to clarify what we weren't
in, such as tennis and golf and team sports.

The notion of noncompetitiveness went back to L.L. We go outdoors "to forget the mean and petty things of life," he said. It's not
about winning and losing. Trying to catch the most fish misses the
whole point of the outdoors experience. A friend of mine considers any
fish caught a bonus. It's being there that counts.

The three criteria weren't perfect but provided direction for our
product and creative people. They also gave cohesiveness and meaning

to our outdoors positioning. Bill, John, and I did not golf, and those golfers on our staff took a fair amount of friendly criticism for being off strategy. Being people-powered, however, meant that an activity supported a healthy, physically fit lifestyle and taking place in a natural environment attended to the spiritual side of our outdoors heritage.

Our overall strength was functional value—products that did what they were supposed to do, did it every time, and did it for a long time, all for a reasonable price. This was what L.L.Bean was known for. In November 1981, *Gentlemen's Quarterly* wrote, "Uniting the diverse garments and outdoor accoutrements under the Bean banner is the emphasis on simplicity, practicality and durability. Unlike 'high fashion' where 'look' is foremost and function secondary, the appearance of Bean apparel is guided by what the clothes are intended to do."[1]

Most of our active assortment was aimed at the intermediate performance level ("people like us"), with enough entry-level products to get people started in the activity and enough at the expert level to keep advanced users interested in L.L.Bean. But beginners tended to buy at discount stores, and experts at highly specialized outdoors shops. Some 70 to 75 percent of our products, all categories, were made to our specifications by contractors or in our own factory, another 20 percent private label, and the balance national brands. We used branded products where the product was preeminent in its class—for instance, Coleman stoves—or in categories such as optics (Nikon binoculars) where we did not have credibility.

We wanted each product to have its own unique story and role to play. We were "item merchants," and the aggregate of our items was our assortment. We did not, for example, merchandise an assortment of sport shirts by price points of good, better, and best. Each of our shirts was intended to be an optimum of quality fabrication, design, and price. Each season we reviewed the assortments, deleted products that customers were telling us they didn't want, and added new ones to fill voids with new and fully tested concepts. We had relatively stable product lines that lent themselves to our continuous improvement strategy. Much like the popular Volkswagen Beetle of that day, we were continually improving products or improving the line with new products while always maintaining an L.L.Bean familiarity and look.

This strategy enabled us to put a lot of value in our pricing because we had minimal obsolescence and liquidation costs. We also had a narrow line of products in relation to our volume and passed on the manufacturing economies of scale to our customers. We intended to be lower in price than anyone with comparable products, and we didn't add extra margin for "on-sale" promotions. People could count on the consistency and fairness of our pricing.

One of the reasons I continued to be committed to our own manufacturing capability, which in the mid-1980s accounted for 15 percent or so of our retail revenues, was that it gave us a lot of authenticity. The products we made were indeed unique, our benchmarks in functional value and not available to others, although our Boat and Tote bags, Bean Boots, and Blucher Mocs inspired a fair number of creative imitations that showed up in competitors' lines.

In 1982 I spoke to a group of consumer affairs professionals visiting L.L.Bean. One of the ways we served our customers, I noted, was by selecting products on the basis of their functionality, durability, and safety. We tested them accordingly, and then through customer surveys and other feedback we confirmed our assessments. It was an application of our Golden Rule to provide customers only with products we used ourselves and found to be 100 percent satisfactory. One of the listeners said she was not surprised at the Golden Rule metaphor, but, after observing our customer service reps and noting the bond of trust they had with our customers, she said it was "exciting" to see the Golden Rule actually working.

Back in 1976, shortly after Bill End arrived, we had asked the people at our new ad agency to critique our catalogs. In a written report, they commented on the mediocre quality of our paper stock, the inconsistent density of our black-and-white printing, and the poor registration and color fidelity of our four-color printing. About one-third of our pages were in color and two-thirds in black-and-white. Their critique went on, "The layout is a perfect example of the 'cut 'n paste' school of design. There is simply no consistency, either item by item or page by page. Many products are jammed into areas that are too small to adequately display the item or describe it in readable type . . . Typographically, everything has been done to make it more difficult for the reader."

Other comments related to our flat and unimaginative photography, our Cheltenham typeface ("Don't even consider making a change"), and our copy ("This is the best copy in any catalog in America").

We began a process of continuous improvement within the constraints of our five major graphic elements: our catalog size (a once common but now distinctive 7¼-inch x 8½-inch format); silhouetted (no background) product photographs (although we were adding more "square-ups" with outdoors backgrounds in photos); large copy blocks in proximity to the appropriate product photograph; Cheltenham typeface; and employee models.

We continued to use our employees and their families, friends, and dogs as models. We didn't want to come across as slick or sophisticated (and we didn't want to pay expensive fees for professional models). Our home-grown models acquired some renown. A writer in the 1980s noted, "Nobody is ugly, mind you, just plain and self conscious, the way most of us would be if we posed for a catalog picture. You know, nerdy." I think the use of real people added a lot of credibility and was consistent with Bean's personal and friendly feeling. Also, if one of our people were holding a fly rod as a prop in an outdoors background shot, they didn't hold it like a broomstick. John Findlay once modeled one of our parkas in a Fall catalog. The next year his head was cropped off to save a little space on the page. One of John's old school friends wrote to ask if everything was OK.

We hired a professional art director who was an ardent fly fisherman and had a good feel for L.L.Bean. He responded to the agency's creative suggestions. In 1979 we converted all of our catalog printing to full color. In 1983 we hired our first professional copywriter. Until that time I had either written the copy or edited copy written by our product managers.

Perhaps the biggest change was that of printers in 1981. We had grown beyond the capacity of our local printer, Dingley Press, and changed to one of the world's largest printers, RR Donnelly of Chicago, and its Gravure printing presses. We had planned this move with Dingley to make sure they had sufficient time to replace our volume with smaller catalog print runs.

The most immediate effect for our catalogs was a marked increase in the color clarity, registration, and consistency, thanks to the huge Gravure cylinders and rollers. This improvement was a significant factor in our 42 percent sales increase that year.

We still didn't put an index in our catalog. It would have taken up too much space to put together a useful one, and our catalogs weren't so large that a person couldn't skim through them easily. But we continued to paginate product groupings in the same sequence from year to year. We started with a joint apparel section (for example, men's and women's Down Jac-Shirts), followed by men's-only apparel, then women's-only, then joint footwear (to position our signature product, Bean Boots, in the centerfold), then outdoors equipment appropriate to the season (fly-fishing, hiking, canoeing and kayaking, bicycling, hunting, cross-country skiing, and winter sports), then camp (or home) furnishings and miscellaneous, and ending with another section of joint apparel. Hopefully this consistent sequencing helped our customers find the products of interest, although nobody ever said it did. At least it gave us an internal rationale for putting the books together.

We also never put a lot of editorial content or outdoors imagery in our catalogs. We relied on our products and their descriptions to tell who we were. The Maine Hunting Shoe copy, for instance, always contained a short version of the L.L. founding story.

Upon receiving our catalog in the 1980s, a writer for the *Christian Science Monitor* wrote, "In a world surging with change we have just received for our annual summer reading that reassuring symbol of security and continuity, the L.L.Bean Fall Catalog."[2] Despite all the changes we thought we were making, we were still very much the same old L.L.Bean to this observer.

BILL HENRY: During the seventies, I did L.L.Bean's first focus group. I was out somewhere north of Chicago in a very affluent area, and we were bringing in groups of customers and groups of prospects. I was dumbfounded by some of the things I learned. I had the moderator go around and ask the people in the room what the L.L.Bean store was like. I asked, if anybody had ever been there, don't mention it. And I let these people free-associate around this. The customers came out saying things like, "It's a little, old, country store in a small town up in Maine, you know, wooden floors, dogs lined up against the side, scratching, maybe a pot-bellied stove, merchandise piled up and down, guys in red suspenders and plaid jackets." It was this Midwestern group of people, who were L.L.Bean customers, describing something that did not exist. It was the power of all those catalogs, the millions of catalogs Bean put out, slightly funky compared to the standard of its day, and yet very powerful. The customers that had never been to the L.L.Bean store had a real image of what Bean was that was profound and wonderful.

We worked hard to sustain and communicate our outdoors heritage in many ways. In 1980 we significantly increased our Freeport store's outdoors education program by adding seminars and training sessions for cross-country skiing, fly-tying, game cooking, hunting safety, canoeing, backpacking, and a variety of other activities. Dave Whitlock— one of the world's great fly fishermen, brilliant at tying flies, skilled artist, and the best teacher of any subject that I've experienced—took over our fly-fishing school. We also put on an annual three-day kayaking symposium at Castine, a lovely Maine coastal community.

In 1981 we published with Random House a 384-page book, *The L.L.Bean Guide to the Outdoors*.[3] It was written by Bill Riviere, a well-known outdoors expert who lived in Maine, and members of our staff. It provided a complete source of information on apparel, footwear, and equipment for outdoor comfort, performance, and safety. The information was in-depth and fully tested, practical, up-to-date, and sufficient for beginners to experienced outdoors people. I thought it was the most authoritative book on outdoors gear that had been written since Horace Kephart's *Camping and Woodcraft* in 1917.[4] Our book was featured on NBC's *Today Show* and sold more than 100,000 copies.

Two years later we published, again with Random House, *The L.L.Bean Game & Fish Cookbook*.[5] It was written by Angus Cameron, a longtime Random House editor and experienced hunter, fisherman, and chef-level cook. It contained 450 recipes—many from our staff, including a couple of L.L.'s—and sold well for many years.

But in spite of all our efforts to remain who we were, consistent from year to year, L.L.Bean became fashionable, at least for a time. In 1976, we were surprised to win the prestigious Coty fashion award, presented in New York City for inspiring the so-called gear look of function in fashion that was in vogue. The award resulted from an unusual convergence of fashion trends with our functional value merchandising strategy. The *Cleveland Press* said the award "would have been enough to knock old L.L.Bean out of a pair of his long red woolen underwear."

I made an eleven-minute appearance on NBC's *Today Show*. I remember the producer telling me in the waiting room that a live audience of more than eight million people was watching and that my interviewer Cassie Mackin was new at the job and nervous. If she started to get off track, he said, I was to take over the interview. I was not even sure whether my own voice would work, and I was being asked to manage the interview. The segment went well and the interviewer asked how it felt to be "radical chic." I told her L.L.Bean had never been called "radical" to my knowledge, and I didn't even know what "chic" meant. Tom Brokaw, the program's host, who knew Bean, had a good laugh in the background. Dan Rather from CBS was soon on his way to Freeport for a similar look at L.L.Bean's functional, and now fashionable, apparel.

This kind of notoriety stimulated business significantly and was compounded by the "preppy" boom. In 1980, Lisa Birnbach published her best-selling *The Official Preppy Handbook*.[6] It was a well-done caricature of the lifestyles, schools, clothing preferences, and mannerisms of teenagers, as well as their parents, from upper-income, well-educated households. To a great extent the demographics were similar to those on our customer list, and L.L.Bean products were prominently featured — for example, Chinos, Blucher Moccasins, Shetland sweaters, and down vests. The handbook said of us, "A Down-East extravaganza, the Bean catalog is the biggest seller of the rugged New England Prep look. Never mind that you don't really need a game pocket in your back-to-school field coat. Home of the ubiquitous rubber moccasin and the Norwegian sweater. Let that label show!"

BILL END: The preppy fashion boom helped us a great deal. If we ran an ad, we got more response. If we sent catalogs to a rental list, more people looked at them because they had heard of Bean, and that all was very positive for us. The outdoor look was at least as important. When people started knocking off Bean product and taking a shooting vest, for example, and modifying it for street wear, or taking a camera vest and modifying it, or Chamois Shirts, all those sorts of things—the Bean boot being worn in New York City as regular casual footwear. All of those things really helped us for a period of time. Bean wasn't in the fashion business, but fashion came to Bean in both of those scenarios and certainly helped the business and got some real recognition for the company. It helped a great deal to get Bean to become more of a national brand.

The publication of *Preppy Handbook* represented a fashion trend that had been growing for several years and reached its peak in the early 1980s. Many people, especially young women, began shopping our catalog because many of our products and our persona were in style. Reliability and durability were not the appeal. We had a "look" and we had a lot of copycats.

This led to another Coty citation in 1981 for our contributions to preppy fashions. Two years later L.L.Bean was included with other designers, such as Oscar de la Renta and Diane von Furstenberg, in providing outfits for Snoopy and Belle, the popular cartoon pups, for a fashion tour of Europe. Our Snoopy wore traditional Bird Shooting Pants, Bean Boots, and a Chamois Shirt, and he carried a rucksack. Belle was preppily dressed in Chinos, a button-down Oxford shirt, Blucher Mocs, and a Norwegian Sweater, and she carried a Tote Bag.

L.L.Bean as fashion was a mixed blessing for us, and we all knew it. Our sales increased markedly in the near term but were unlikely to be sustainable long term. In addition, being fashionable was a serious contradiction of our character and brand positioning. It confused our positioning internally as well as in the marketplace.

The year 1981 was a record year for us, with a sales increase of 42 percent, followed in 1982 by an increase of 30 percent. Our business nearly doubled in two years. Then, in 1983, the fashion wave crested, and, as one writer put it, we "ran out of preppies." Our sales increase for the year fell to 6 percent, little more than inflation. Suddenly, for the first time under my leadership, our growth had stalled.

MARK FASOLD: Well, you can imagine when things slowed down. It's life, it's not L.L.Bean. It's life. People second-guess. "We're not doing the right thing."

Besides our problems with fashion, we faced an overall economy that had slowed down in the early 1980s, and we were hearing more about junk mail and mailbox clutter from the general public. Our traditional competitors were mailing more (as were we), and new competitors were entering our marketplace and the direct marketing channel. Catalog saturation and customer tolerance for it were becoming issues.

BILL END: Any time the business slowed there was consternation and we all scrambled trying to figure out ways to turn it around and get it going again. Regardless of what the reason was, it wasn't acceptable to have that level of growth and we wanted to get it cranked up again.

On September 30, 1983, we issued a press release announcing postponement of the planned construction of a new distribution center on our Desert Road property just outside Freeport.

JOHN FINDLAY: I remember thinking that growth used to cover up many ills. Then, when the growth stopped, your warts became more apparent. So there was, on the one hand, longing for growth because it's fun. Everybody is working six, seven days a week, the way a business is supposed to be. You're profitable, you're growing. Then no growth, and maybe, out of laziness, some relief. It was nice not to go to work all day Saturday and half of Sunday every week. But that didn't last that long, in terms of how we felt. It was so unusual that I think we were, scared is not the right word, but after six or eight months of not working on Sunday, "Hey, where are the sales? This isn't the way a company is supposed to be. What's the issue? The preppy thing is dying a little bit, so what's next?"

Some people in the company said that I deliberately slowed sales. I was glad to see the slowdown in 1983, but we didn't pull sales back on purpose. The customers took care of that. However, it gave us the opportunity, I thought, to get back to what Bean was all about—basics and core values. Too many people were buying our products for the wrong reasons, which had little to do with functional value.

In September 1983 I wrote a letter to employees describing our sales slowdown as part of a general slowing down of the country's retail economy, especially mail-order buying, which it was. The weather, of course, was not helpful. (It's always too warm or too cold for retailers.) I noted that the growth rates of the prior years were not sustainable and a slowdown would give us time to rethink where we were going. We were clearly in a new and highly competitive business environment, given our larger size and visibility. And our customer demographics and lifestyles were changing significantly. Our sales in 1983 were $237 million compared with $30 million in 1975.

In 1984 we mailed only 7.5 percent more catalogs than the prior year (whose circulation increase had been 30 percent). We shifted our mailing emphasis more to current customers and less to acquiring new customers. Bill End drafted an eight-page memo to our marketing and merchandising people listing a variety of large and small improvements in our catalog graphics (correct use of models, more fresh photography, pagination and copy style), our product development (quarterly line reviews, more new products for more differentiated mailings, the testing of new concepts in specialty outdoors catalogs), and our circulation plans (changes in book sizes, timing of seasonal mailings, cover strategies, and thematic content).

We had been doing nicely without all the fashion recognition. It distorted our growth rate and took us to a volume our traditional outdoors positioning could not sustain. We had built the infrastructure to support the increased volume, and that in turn had increased our dependence on the casual or weekend apparel business, especially women's.

In spite of my relief, the slowdown created serious concern inside L.L.Bean, especially among the marketing and product people. It brought forward some fundamental issues related to growth that were already being debated around the company. Until now, those issues had lacked urgency, because our growth through catalogs had been so strong.

BOB PEIXOTTO: I think anybody looking at a brand as strong as L.L.Bean . . . looking at the penetration we had and the direct mail business, would say the first card that you play, almost the easiest card that you play, would be to take this retail. Because more than half of the U.S. population doesn't shop by mail.

Central to these questions was the fear that L.L.Bean had reached the limits of its current business model, that there was no more room to grow without changing who we were or the ways we did business. So the first issue raised by the slowdown was whether we should expand our business model by exploring retail stores.

JOHN FINDLAY: It made some sense to have flagship stores, five or six of them, around the country. Sort of tailor some of the products by region. I mean, don't go crazy because SKUs [stock-keeping units—the number of products carried] were always the big issue at Bean, too many SKUs, too much to keep track of. But the idea was both to drive awareness up in these areas where we didn't have much penetration, or as much penetration, and in some of the areas where we had it, like the middle Atlantic, trade on the fact that we were well known there. [It would] bring us new customers and probably wouldn't lose the old customers. Then, in the Northwest, to fight Eddie Bauer and REI and the fact that they own the Northwest. [If] we had a retail store there, it would bring Bean into people's faces and they would then, perhaps, order from the mail too from us. They would see that we were better than Bauer or REI or whatever.

I opposed retail expansion. I had never seen another retailer that was successful in both retail and catalog. The two channels required different sets of merchandising skills, logistics technology, corporate cultures, and customer services. None of the people advocating retail expansion at L.L.Bean had any experience in retailing, and, I thought, they didn't understand the fundamental differences between the two channels and the challenges of a retail expansion.

CHRIS MCCORMICK: Well, I remember the big retail discussion. And, in fact, that was coming from Bill End more than anybody else. I reported through Bill End. I was three layers or two layers below him . . . What he was promoting back then was retail expansion—that we could gain new customers through retail and penetrate markets through retail that we were not traditionally strong in.

My brief experience at Filene's was enough to tell me Bean wasn't ready for the retail environment. Nor did retail feel like L.L.Bean. It had a much faster pace, a "crisis management" style, was more intuitive than deliberative, and was much more promotional.

BILL END: I think [Leon] believed that [retail] was a completely different business and that it required a very different expertise that we didn't have. I think he believed that [L.L.Bean] is a Northeast business, rather than a national business. And I don't think he wanted to risk the family jewels and run the risk of a possible failure in that side of the business.

Catalogers such as Talbots and Eddie Bauer had gone into retail stores and soon moved away from their catalog strengths in favor of retail. Retailers (such as the old Abercrombie & Fitch and some major department stores) were also going into catalogs and never achieved significant success in the direct marketing channel. Why would L.L.Bean suddenly be able to do what all the others had not been able to do?

BOB PEIXOTTO: Leon was always very steadfast in saying, "The retail industry and the mail industry are very, very different, and we're going to stake our claim, as long as we can see the growth opportunities in mail order, on being the best mail-order company out there." We actually added in our purpose statement a section called "Concentration Decision." We said, if we see enough opportunities in the mail-order business, we're going to stick to our knitting, in our own product categories.

A second major idea for new growth that we'd talked about in the past was to acquire other mail-order companies. The sales slowdown, in the eyes of acquisition advocates, only made the idea even more attractive.

BILL END: We had a chance to bid on Abercrombie & Fitch. We had a chance to bid on Eddie Bauer. We had a chance to bid on Talbots. You can say, I'm going to build this business, L.L.Bean . . . or you can say, we've got a huge mailing list, we've got a huge fulfillment operation. Why don't we buy additional mail-order businesses, leverage the list, leverage the fulfillment, leverage all the merchandising, leverage all the buying, all of that . . . Those could have been additive businesses at Bean and could have taken pressure off how far you push the brand and cause you not to have to go into women's or have to go too far into commodities or whatever. There's a right size for every business. If you try to push beyond that it's going to cost you an arm and a leg to do it and cause you potentially to move outside your sweet spot and get yourself in trouble as a brand.

The advocates of retail expansion and acquisition of other direct marketers wanted to engage consultants to investigate the possibilities for L.L.Bean. This may have seemed like a fair and straightforward approach, but I had rarely seen an exploratory project by consultants not lead to a recommendation to proceed. Objectivity always got lost in enthusiasm for the project and in loading all the assumptions in favor of it. I had no interest in proceeding in either direction—retail or acquisitions—or in opposing, ignoring, or rejecting the inevitable positive recommendations. I felt we should stick to our knitting and that there continued to be growth opportunities in the catalog business. More than that, I liked the L.L.Bean model, our specialty product mix, and our ability to offer value-added service by mail. With better merchandising execution we could achieve "quality" growth, sufficient growth that would reward all of our stakeholders and avoid unwanted risk by any of them.

CHRIS MCCORMICK: There [was] a group of people who bought in to [retail expansion]. But I would say there was a bigger group who did not. Two reasons for that. One is, even when things slowed down in the eighties, we were still growing, whatever the number was . . . and our return on equity was 20 percent or better. So we were still performing. We're getting 15 percent bonuses paid out every year. Why do we need retail? The other thought back then was, we don't know anything about retail. We're a catalog company. We're organized, our infrastructure is for a catalog. We don't really understand retail.

We also had geographic expansion opportunities by mail; the potential of specialty catalogs (fishing, home furnishings, winter sports, etc.) to develop targeted markets; and emerging direct marketing technologies (for example, lifetime value analyses) to do what we were already doing but do it better and more productively. We had a lot of strengths under the Bean umbrella we weren't fully exploiting.

Needless to say, opposing retail and acquisitions at the time did nothing for my risk-taking reputation, especially since I opposed even looking into them. There were certainly potential limits to growth in our catalog business. Prospective buyer sources were not infinite, and saturation mailing was already a problem. Ever-increasing postal rates and the emerging privacy issue were significant concerns. But I preferred to deal with the problems we knew about than the myriad of unknowns we would face in the retail business.

Finally, of all the issues brought forward by the slowdown, the most basic was the question of L.L.Bean's merchandising direction and focus. Slowing sales seemed to generate a feeling of panic among our product people, who had never experienced the vagaries of the fashion market. There was a flurry of meetings and memos and recommendations saying that L.L.Bean should focus on sportswear or even dressy casual clothing. The advocates of this option wanted L.L.Bean to shift to casual clothing and get out of the active sports business. We should become a purveyor of trendy sportswear rather than our traditional mix of relaxed weekend wear and our core rugged utility apparel. The idea was to change the company into a Lands' End or the current version of Eddie Bauer. There was serious controversy within the company over this fundamental issue.

TOM SIDAR: The concern was that there's a tendency to go more toward casual than to outdoors to achieve sales potential. A lot of people saw casual as greater potential. It's harder to come up with a new functional outdoor product than it is to come up with a new assortment of casual shirts or pants or sweaters. What Leon said when we'd do blue books [a review of new product recommendations] and line reviews was, "I want as much attention spent on the active business as the casual business." So you couldn't just come in and say, "Boy, I had the greatest line review ever and it was all casual and everyone was happy." Because it was like, "OK, but what do we have for the active side?" That would cause the merchants to stay immersed in what's the best functional apparel for an active outdoor lifestyle.

The idea of focusing on sportswear and fashiony apparel seemed to me extremely misguided. It would compromise our character and our outdoors positioning and would move away from our fundamental product strengths. It would clearly be a move away from traditional L.L.Bean and toward a more contemporary and gentrified L.L.Bean.

RON CAMPO: I don't think L.L.Bean took Lands' End very seriously maybe the first couple of years they entered apparel. But soon thereafter it became obvious they were in for the long haul and their creative execution was always very excellent and after a few years we began to take them very seriously . . . They were interpreting—that's maybe a better word than "knocking off"—a lot of our product and using a lot of our same vendors to secure that product. I had direct feedback from vendors. But it was obvious, if you were a merchant, that we were a leader in that niche and they were trying to catch up and they caught up fairly quickly over a five- to ten-year period.

I didn't like the idea of L.L.Bean being defined by our competition. But the casualization of American dress was beginning. And everybody except us and the hard-core outdoors catalogers were heading in this direction. In 1980 there were some 3,300 consumer catalogs, and in 1985 there were more than 5,000. And a great many of the new entries, as well as department stores, were focused on casual apparel for business and for weekends.

The unhappy experience of my old ideal, Abercrombie & Fitch, came to mind. Their outdoors lifestyle concept and positioning were similar to my aspirations for L.L.Bean. Yet they had gone bankrupt in the late 1970s. *The Official Preppy Handbook* said Abercrombie & Fitch had "passed away with dignity, with customers still awaiting their leather-trimmed canvas shoulder bags." I think their original positioning had been generally correct, but weekend and dressy casual had begun to dominate their product mix. In addition, their pricing, operations, and store locations had become uncompetitive. I was sorry to see them go.

Lands' End had also emerged with the preppy boom in 1980 as a significant casual apparel competitor. We knew they were growing at least as fast as we were, and there was a lot of concern about keeping pace. Feelings about Lands' End in Freeport were ambivalent. Many felt it was piggybacking off L.L.Bean. They hired some of our people, used our suppliers, and copied many of our most popular products. Others felt we should follow their lead in casual apparel and their engaging catalog style.

We tracked Lands' End in our customer research almost from the beginning. The customer perceptions of the differences between Lands' End and L.L.Bean were strongly felt. L.L.Bean fans preferred our product quality, and Lands' End fans preferred its color assortment and fashionableness. Lands' End's appeal was slightly younger and more to women, and ours was just the opposite. We sold to active outdoors people, and Lands' End to people who had a more casual lifestyle. Their catalog graphics and copy were attractive, effective, and innovative, and they cultivated a friendly, lighthearted, and helpful attitude. Good communicators.

JOHN FINDLAY: I think the feeling was that Bean was an old-line, quality company with products and service that you could count on, and Lands' End was an upstart, veneered kind of copy-cat, taking the best parts of Bean and sort of putting a little splash of paint on it and putting a little bit of catalog out maybe, and snagging these customers who didn't know any better. [Laughter]

We used to call it Lands' Envy . . . because none of us would have predicted that Lands' End would turn out to be bigger than Bean.

It used to annoy me to no end that many of our merchants and creative people were obsessed with Lands' End and its more stylish sportswear positioning. I'd go to product meetings and hear, "Lands' End did this, that, and the other thing and we have to do this and that as well." L.L.Bean had its own position and we didn't need to copy anyone else. Nor did we intend to copy Abercrombie & Fitch's demise. We could succeed with our own active/casual lifestyle approach by better execution of our merchandising strategies.

It wasn't a matter of simply continuing to do what L.L.Bean had always done. We knew the world was changing. Customer research in the late 1970s revealed what we had intuitively known for years: that our newer outdoors customers preferred outdoor activities other than hunting and fishing. Good catalog buyers were, almost by definition, upper income and well educated. Our customer profile trended inevitably in that direction as we grew our catalog business by renting mailing lists and advertising in general-interest magazines. People with these demographics tended to participate more in hiking, skiing, water sports, and cycling, and not in hunting and fishing. Our challenge in our outdoors offerings was to be more inclusive of these new outdoors customers without losing our traditional hunting and fishing clientele.

At the same time, we needed to address the fact that increasing numbers of women were coming to L.L.Bean for casual apparel for themselves and their families. In 1975, one-quarter of our customers were women. By 1980, women accounted for half our customers.

BILL HENRY: L.L.Bean was growing primarily because the company was bringing a lot of women onto the file. The company really had an appeal to women. All the sources of names that were working for us were all mainly targeted towards women. For which I took a little bit of heat, I might add, particularly from Bill End, who thought that that was the wrong direction to go. Leon shared that [point of view]. We had this schizophrenia going on. On one hand, we wanted to be an outdoor company. On the other hand, I could see clearly where the growth in sales was coming from. If we really said that we didn't want to be in the women's business, we wanted to limit it, we were going to have some problems. Up until eighty-three within the company there was a general feeling that we could grow at 30 percent, or whatever, into the future, doing what we were basically doing. But I was looking at how we grew the customer file, how we invested in acquiring new customers, and what our opportunity was in eighty-two and eighty-three . . .

There was tension between holding on to the image and the outdoor element of the business and the fact that the opportunity, in terms of growing the business and selling and the customer, was somewhere else. People like myself would lose sleep thinking that I've been told, on one hand, "We've been growing 25 percent a year" and, on the other hand, "We don't want to grow the way you're trying to grow us." For me it was an unbelievable personal strain to be caught in that.

The market—*our* market, not the fashion market—was forcing change on us. Our product line was evolving to respond both to changes in the outdoors interests of our customers and to their gender and lifestyles. Women buyers from L.L.Bean were much more active in the outdoors than the general population. Although their product interests may have been in the more stylish casual side of the business, they were also buying for outdoors-oriented households. The gender shift, as well as the idea of mailing to households and not individuals, was changing the dynamic of the business. It was hard to figure out what it meant and how we should respond.

BOB PEIXOTTO: I think that was a concern, especially with Leon. He wrote down at one point a corporate personality statement, that we were "a little bit more male than female, but that's OK." That's actually what was written. Because that was sort of the shape of the brand, and the shape of the brand that he was trying to create, that we would not lose our appeal to men. And the rise of the female, as the chief shopper in the family, I think that was a little bit of a challenge.

Growth presented problems all by itself. As we tried to continue growing on an ever-larger base of sales from year to year, it was hard to maintain uniqueness in our products. We needed items with broader appeal and higher volume potential than in the past, and that took us closer to mainstream trends in the overall retail marketplace. At the same time we were being copied ("tasteful digressions," per one observer) by a great many designers and other retailers, as our outdoorsy look became "rugged casual" and a lasting apparel category. According to *Time* magazine, even Ralph Lauren was a reader of our catalogs.[7]

> BILL END: I don't think we ever let the business be described as fashion, and I don't think we ever aggressively went after that. A few exceptions, you know — we put Hawaiian shirts in and did some things like that once in a while. But I would say generally the company had a pretty solid understanding that we're not a fashion business, and in particular not a women's fashion business. And that's where you would have really shot yourself in the foot, if we had gone too far in those directions.

We needed to grow traditional L.L.Bean in order to catch up to a more organic fit with our current operating capacity. Otherwise we would simply drift toward the more generic middle market. I didn't oppose the growth strategies that had been proposed because I opposed growth. Rather, I resisted them because they were not likely to work in the first place and were likely to change our unique character.

Bill and I both believed in growth and yet keeping faith with traditional L.L.Bean at the same time. We both knew that women's fashion and the casual apparel market were not where we should be. But we needed growth for the reasons I've mentioned, and we had to deal with the aspirations of all those managers we'd hired, including fifteen MBAs by 1980, and to provide job enrichment and career opportunities for all our people. We needed a minimum rate of growth to maintain the basic vitality of the organization. I arbitrarily picked the 10 to 15 percent range. We needed a new growth strategy for the new marketplace and its changing demographics and lifestyles.

It was important to come to terms with the fundamental issue of our merchandising strategy. The company was starting to divide between those who saw Bean as a business and wanted to follow fashion, because that seemed to present the most opportunity for growth, and those who saw Bean as a value system or "religion" ("bleeding green") and who wanted to stick to the traditional outdoors L.L.Bean. We needed to put together an inclusive L.L.Bean concept.

We were being tugged in several directions. The right wing said we should be in hunting and fishing, period. "Bleeding green" referred more to the nonconsumptive sports crowd. They joined with the hunting-and-fishing people to keep Bean on the active side. The hunters, more than the fly fishers, were angry about Bean's selling out to the yuppies and abandoning our heritage. The irony was that through the 1980s our assortment of hunting gear was far broader than anything L.L. ever offered. For example, along with Bill End, one of the best hunters and outdoorsmen I ever met, I introduced firearms to L.L.Bean in our retail store. L.L. never sold firearms. Yet these traditionalist hunters would constantly accuse us of abandoning the hunter.

To those who feared we were going to abandon Bean's heritage, I pointed out that the company had always been in relaxed weekend apparel, such as polo shirts and Chinos. L.L. was never in "hunting and fishing, period." He was in casual apparel; it was L.L.'s lifestyle approach ("He sold what he liked and he liked what he sold"). In response to those at the other end of the spectrum, I refused to expand into what was called "dressy casual"—tailored clothing and sport coats and women's dressy apparel. That was not my idea of L.L.Bean. But I didn't have any problem with our being in relaxed weekend apparel—denim shirts and corduroy slacks and lambswool sweaters—which I think was very much a part of the company and its heritage and the lifestyle we supported.

We decided to follow both product tracks: the traditional outdoors track and the contemporary casual apparel track. We intended to continue to pursue the casual weekend sportswear business (*not* the fashion end of it) and at the same time keep an equivalent presence in the active side of L.L.Bean to maintain the integrity of our brand. The outdoors would continue to define who we were.

This was no offhand decision, but one we pursued with as much discipline and rigor as possible. We categorized all of our products as either "active" or "casual." If a product lent itself to any of the specific outdoors activities we supported, it was classified as active. If the end use was general recreation or streetwear, it was casual. Active products needed to be 90 percent functional. A parka, for instance, needed to be warm, waterproof, and durable, and to fit comfortably. Ten percent of its value was for styling or color. Casual products, such as a woman's skirt, needed to be 50 to 60 percent functional in fit and fabrication, with the balance in styling and aesthetics. Obviously we placed function ahead of fashion, with lots of emphasis on the physical quality of the product.

Our decision to pursue the two tracks represented formal adoption at L.L.Bean of an evolving lifestyle concept. It was based on the idea that our customers were outdoors-oriented people and we were catering to the leisure-time parts of their lives. This was the crucial distinction. Our goal was to serve a particular kind of people, those who valued the outdoors just as we did, and our goal was to sell them the products, active and casual, they needed to enjoy their outdoors-oriented lifestyles. These people—"people like us"—work; they have families, and they have recreational time. We would cater to their recreational time—both their active recreation and their casual recreation.

We also formalized the definitions of active recreation and casual recreation. "Active" meant those outdoor activities, like fly-fishing, hiking, and winter sports, that we were formally committed to supporting. "Casual" included outdoor photography, bird-watching, backyard and beach barbeques, and a host of other casual outdoor pursuits, including a relaxed social evening with friends. The categorization seemed to encompass things that L.L.Bean people did in their recreational time. There was a cohesiveness among the activities that felt like an L.L.Bean lifestyle, that possessed what we came to call Bean-ness, and that described our market position.

I thought L.L.Bean could embrace occasional practitioners, including weekend adventurers or armchair enthusiasts, as well as the more avid outdoors people and expert practitioners. The important distinction was having a love and respect for the outdoors and a lifestyle that required our kind of active and casual recreational products.

We continued to develop and introduce high-visibility products to help reinforce our commitment to the outdoors tradition, such as our own high-performance fly rods, touring canoes, recreational bicycles, and cross-country skis. We produced our own video library, with instructional tapes on fly-fishing, canoeing, bicycle touring, and outdoor photography.

> WES DEVRIES: I encourage clients to consider including products that say a lot about them, what I call editorial products, even if they lose money. Competitors won't offer them because they're not going to intentionally lose money. So you end up with a differentiated product mix.

This lifestyle strategy would allow us to stay in casual apparel without diluting our identity. It was also the only way we could grow and stay in the active sports business, which by itself did not offer us sufficient growth opportunities. And it was entirely consistent with L.L.'s approach and the company's historic product mix.

Putting the strategy into practice, however, would get a little tricky. It would lead us to a new, and much more complicated, catalog strategy, a reorganization of our product development department (and a tendency for product proliferation), and strict adherence to our active and casual product classification scheme. That scheme comprised four categories: active, soft active, relaxed weekend (casual), and updated traditional (casual). The core of L.L.Bean was soft active, which comprised Bean Boots, Chamois Shirts, and similar general-purpose outdoors products.

Despite our best efforts, though, the distinctions among these categories weren't always crystal clear. So, in a sense, adopting the lifestyle strategy institutionalized the ongoing debate between the two sides of the business, active and casual, and raised a never-ending debate about the right balance of products. We said our customers were people like us, but "us" included everybody from bird hunters to bird-watchers. So pursuing this approach would require an unusual combination of understanding and collaboration in our merchandising point of view.

The lifestyle strategy never fully satisfied purists in either camp within L.L.Bean. Active outdoors proponents continued to believe we were threatening our heritage. The businesspeople could never fully accept our commitment to less profitable active outdoors products, beyond window dressing. They saw more growth in contemporary and stylish sportswear. The tension, which was a healthy one, would continue long after the decision was made.

L.L. modeling his first Maine Hunting Coat, sometime before World War I.
He made frequent catalog appearances in these early product photographs.

MAINE
HUNTING SHOE

Outside of your gun, nothing is so important to your outfit as your foot-wear. You cannot expect success hunting deer or moose if your feet are not properly dressed.

The Maine Hunting Shoe is designed by a hunter who has tramped Maine woods for the past eighteen years. They are light as a pair of moccasins with the protection of a heavy hunting boot. The vamps are made of the very best gum rubber money will buy. The tops ($7\frac{1}{2}$ in. high) are soft tan willow calf that never grow hard by wetting and drying. Leather inner soles keep the feet off the rubber and prevent "drawing" that is so objectionable with most rubber shoes.

Skeleton cork-filled heels keep the shoes from slipping and make them much more comfortable to one accustomed to wearing shoes with heels.

For those hunters who go just before the first snow it is next to impossible to find footwear that is adapted to both bare ground and snow hunting. The Maine Hunting Shoe is perfect for both. For bare ground, its extreme light weight and leather inner soles keep it from drawing the feet while the rubber soles keep it from slipping. For snow, by using a heavier stocking, you have warm light, dry footwear that is ideal for still hunting.

L.L.'s first direct mail piece went out in 1912. It was a four-page circular with a silhouette illustration of the "boot." This earliest piece already included the direct, highly personalized prose that would make the expanded L.L.Bean catalog famous.

Above: L.L. talking to Don Williams, 1962. *Below:* The original Bean store in the 1960s. By this time, the Warren Block building (front right) had aged enough to need an exterior support truss. In 1977, it was demolished to make room for parking.

Above: Ensign Gorman, May 3, 1957. *Below:* Christmas party, 1967. From left to right: Wid Griffin, Ken Stilkey, Shailer Hayes, and Leon.

Above: Ethel Williams taking dictation from L.L. in 1962. *Below:* A product-testing group prepares to head out for the Allagash river and canoe trip in 1969. From left to right: Ed Whitmarsh, Maurice Hilton, Don Williams, Wid Griffin, Joe Murray, and Leon Gorman.

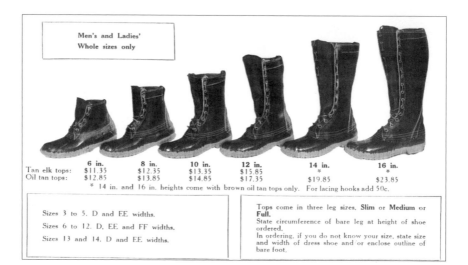

	6 in.	8 in.	10 in.	12 in.	14 in.	16 in.
Tan elk tops:	$11.35	$12.35	$13.35	$15.85	*	*
Oil tan tops:	$12.85	$13.85	$14.85	$17.35	$19.85	$23.85

Men's and Ladies'
Whole sizes only

* 14 in. and 16 in. heights come with brown oil tan tops only. For lacing hooks add 50c.

Sizes 3 to 5. D and EE widths.

Sizes 6 to 12. D, EE and FF widths.

Sizes 13 and 14. D and EE widths.

Tops come in three leg sizes, **Slim** or **Medium** or **Full.**
State circumference of bare leg at height of shoe ordered.
In ordering, if you do not know your size, state size and width of dress shoe and/or enclose outline of bare foot.

The Fall 1960 lineup of the Maine Hunting Shoe.

Donald E. Johnson

Above: Opening mail orders in the front office. In 1962, all work was still done by hand. Front to back: Eunice Pitts, Thelma Summers, Idalyn Cummings, Helen Stilkey, and Mary Dyer.
Left: Jessie Beal (left), a key administrator in Bean's early days, can be seen here working with Nancy Marston, another Bean employee.

Above: Leon Gorman at the office, May 6, 1977. *Below:* Board of directors' meeting in the mid-sixties. From left to right: Tom Gorman, L.L. Bean, Warren Bean, Carl Bean, and Leon Gorman.

Above: Howard Wilson waiting on a footwear customer in the retail showroom in 1968. *Below:* A *New Yorker* cartoon from 1972. (Drawing by Weber; ©1972, *The New Yorker* magazine.)

"While I'm at it, is there anything I can order you from L.L. Bean?"

"THE GOLDEN RULE OF L.L.BEAN"

"Sell good merchandise at a reasonable profit, treat your customers like human beings and they'll always come back for more." Leon Leonwood Bean started a company 73 years ago based on this simply stated business philosophy. We call it L.L.'s Golden Rule and today we still practice it.

Everything we sell is backed by a 100% unconditional guarantee. We do not want you to have anything from L. L. Bean that is not completely satisfactory. Return anything you buy from us at any time for any reason if it proves otherwise.

L. L. Bean pays all regular postage and handling charges. This means the price you see is the final cost. There are no additional charges.

All of our products are regularly tested by us in the field as well as in the lab. Each product continues to be made with the best materials, construction and design that we think is appropriate to the needs of our customers. They represent a solid value and deliver a fair return for the money.

The L. L. Bean Customer Service Department operates on L. L.'s belief that "A customer is the most important person ever in this office — in person or by mail." Telephone representatives are available 24 hours a day, 365 days a year for customer assistance and order taking. Your order is shipped promptly and accurately.

☐ **Send for our FREE 1985 Christmas Catalog!**

Name_____
Address_____
City_____
State_____Zip_____

L. L. Bean, Inc., 1055 Casco St., Freeport, ME 04033

L.L.Bean®

L.L.Bean's "Golden Rule" advertisement—one of the company's most successful.

Above, left: Lee Surace, Bean's chief financial officer for many years. *Above, right:* Bill End, marketing director at Bean and Leon's second in command, at his desk in 1976.

John Findlay, Bean's vice president for operations, in 1977.

Above: From the Snoopy in Fashion tour, 1983–1984. Snoopy and his sister, Belle (right), showcasing some classic Bean outfits. *Below:* The diversity of Bean's catalog offerings grew over the years to include both kids' and women's categories as well as outdoor catalogs.

Above, left: Leon with good friend and fellow traveler Lloyd Holmes at Mount Everest, 1990. *Above, right:* TQ on the "Roof of Africa," Mount Kilimanjaro, 1989. *Below:* Leon with his wife, Lisa, on the Milford Track in New Zealand, 1992.

Above, left: Biscuit is well known at Bean and often accompanies Leon to the office as well as to various bird covers. *Above, right:* Leon fishing at Grand Lake Stream, Maine. *Below:* Leon with his children (Ainslie, Jennifer, and Jeff), 1980.

Above: The new Bean team—Chris McCormick (in front), Fran Philip, Mark Fasold, and Bob Peixotto, 2006. *Right:* Chris McCormick and Leon at the order fulfillment center, 2003.

Above: Freeport Retail Store, 2006. *Left:* Leon's last day as president, 2001. L.L.'s Parker shotgun is on the wall.

9

Back on Track

G ROWTH WAS BACK. After two flat years, we grew 20 percent in 1985. There had been talk of people leaving in the post-preppy slowdown for lack of growth opportunities, but it never happened. With the return of growth, adding retail stores became a dead issue.

> JOHN FINDLAY: Twenty percent growth? Great! Let's just forget retail for a while. As an operations guy, I had my hands full. Why would we want to dissipate energy, money, and time doing something when we were growing the business at $70, $80 million a year? But retail was always an option in the planning process. It was on the table.

It's hard to identify all the factors at work in the mid-1980s that put L.L.Bean back on the growth track. An improving economy surely helped. The strategies we adopted—such as outdoors lifestyle merchandising— also played their roles.

> BILL HENRY: Much of it has to do with the aging of the baby boomers. First, the fact that they were there in huge numbers and they really were outdoors oriented as a group. Not hunting and

fishing so much, but they believed in the environment and nature and outdoors. We were tapping in to that, probably the only legitimate natural company in that area that also you could trust and had good service. Well, suddenly, as that baby boom generation reached a certain point, they decided they didn't want to wear suits and stuff to the workplace.

We began adding specialty catalogs to our circulation plan in 1984. Our specialty catalog strategy involved our traditional but special interest outdoors product lines. Each quarter we prepared and mailed an active specialty catalog of fly-fishing products, or hunting gear, or winter sports like cross-country skiing and snowshoeing, or hiking, camping, cycling, and canoeing equipment. Home and camp furnishings catalogs were also mailed seasonally. The more limited appeal of products featured in the specialty catalogs meant that we could not justify sending them to all our customers. We aimed each at an appropriate segment of customers and targeted prospects.

BILL END: The specialty titles were added for a couple of reasons. One was just to grow that individual merchandise category. For example, we added a Home Camp book, which just allowed us to show a much broader assortment in the home product areas, and were able to grow that business pretty aggressively as a result. The other major change that occurred during that period of time is we took, for example, a substantial number of the fishing pages out of the main book, because they weren't effective to the bulk of the customer file, and put them in a specialty catalog and made sure that anyone who had ever had an interest in fishing got that book. We did the same with other products, like hunting and winter sports. It was a much more effective way of distributing those pages to the people who were basically interested in those product categories. So all of those catalog changes had a fairly significant effect on the business and helped us grow at that point in time . . . It has made the brand be perceived by the customer as more casual, for sure, but that's, I think, part of the penalty if you want to grow to the size you are today.

Casual apparel got the most circulation of all our products; yet that same strategy enabled us to subsidize the expansion of our specialty outdoors products. We were very conscious of the balance among casual apparel and soft active and active apparel, as well as active equipment versus home camp goods. There was a right balance we were constantly trying to achieve to support our broad, outdoors-oriented positioning.

Exposure in our main catalogs of active products specific to a particular activity like fly-fishing or hiking or cross-country skiing became more a sampling of each activity's most important products. The catalog photography of these products included a lot of outdoors backgrounds. We used a two-page outdoorsy spread in the full catalogs headlined "Experience the Outdoors" and asked our customers to call our 800 number to receive the various specialty catalogs. We put a lot of effort into developing products and keeping our active product lines up-to-date and competitive. To offset any positioning drift, we continued to add new outdoors categories, such as sea kayaking, cycling, and fitness in the early 1980s.

In 1975 we had mailed four different catalogs with a combined circulation of 5.9 million. By 1990 we were mailing twenty-eight different catalogs with a combined circulation of 113.7 million. Customer perceptions continued to be most influenced by our four traditional seasonal catalogs.

Our full quarterly catalogs evolved to a more contemporary, soft active and relaxed weekend positioning. Our covers continued to be Maine outdoors or wildlife subjects, but they became less representative of the catalog content over these years. In 1975, about two-thirds of our total main catalog pages were active or soft active, versus about one-third by 1990. Most of the shift in our balance of products occurred in the late 1980s as we relied increasingly on the specialty outdoors catalogs to carry the traditional L.L.Bean outdoors positioning.

BILL END: I think it was an appropriate evolution where we moved with small steps in the direction of casual, where the bigger opportunity was, and I would say small enough in increment that the customer didn't know we were doing it. We would evolve year by year. The increments were small enough that the next year customers wouldn't see major changes occur. Just to give you an example, if you're a men's business and you normally ran sixty-four pages of men and then you add women's. If you put the women's in the front, they're going to notice. If you're going to double the size of women's, they're going to notice. But if you continue with what you're doing, and we always did that, we never changed the basic format of the book. And even when we made the biggest changes, which is to pull, let's say, thirty-two pages of fishing out of the spring book and do a specialty book, we left four pages of fishing in and we talked about, "We now have a specialty book. If you want it, send for it." And we had a few pages of product in there so the change wasn't black-and-white, all or nothing. And the fishing customers still got a specialty fishing book, which made us look like we were even more in the fishing business rather than less because there was dramatically more product than would have been in the full catalog.

In the mid-eighties we reorganized by splitting the Product Development department into Active and Casual divisions, each with its own director. We wanted to make sure that active products got as much developmental attention as casual. Pages were allotted by product managers, and procedures were put in place for developing new products, including more product testing in lab and field and more attention to vendor selection and relationships. Part of the reorganization was a comprehensive update of our merchandising strategies so that everyone would understand our active and casual lifestyle approach. This strategy included updating the current demographics and lifestyles of our customers; ensuring the right assortment balance between active and casual products by category; and a variety of other merchandising issues. The product area was of obvious strategic importance to L.L.Bean, and of primary interest to me. Products were at the heart of who we were.

CHRIS MCCORMICK: This is where it's almost an art versus science. There're differing degrees of casual apparel. So, Chinos and these denim shirts were more acceptable because they were more what we called the soft active type of positioning. Then you could get into the updated traditional, which is going down the continuum a little bit. Dressier clothes and blazers and flannel trousers and penny loafers are more in that category. Some of the things Leon left in because, you know, back in L.L.'s days, L.L. had an Oxford dress shirt and that's what fishermen would wear when they'd go to the camps back in the twenties or thirties. I remember the arguments pretty clearly because there was a separate product development group for casual apparel and then a separate group for the active outdoors. I remember the man who ran the casual apparel around that time. He wanted to take it to the extreme. He wanted the pink Oxford shirts for men, some ties, sport jackets. He really wanted to go in that direction and I remember Leon keeping him on a tight leash on that one.

We continued to believe that our customers were people like us, with similar lifestyles and product preferences. That was the theory. But here was where you had to have a strong merchandising point of view. For example, people like us who enjoyed the outdoors wore oxford cloth shirts for a "casual evening with friends." This was a typical extrapolation of L.L.: whatever he liked, his customers would like. He was the original lifestyle merchant. We wouldn't wear fashiony clothes or designer labels, and we wouldn't expect our customers to, either. We had to have a coherent L.L.Bean point of view that our customers would find relevant to their recreational interests and lifestyles.

I had no desire to get out of the "relaxed weekend" category of product. But the dressier products simply did not belong at L.L.Bean. They went over that dividing line. Whether to carry pink shirts was a big debate. It was a serious issue because pink was a popular preppy color and the question was whether we should cater to that trend. It was hard to resist, but I did. Putting logos on clothing was also an issue that generated a lot of discussion. Product people wanted them, but I doubted it was a feature "people like us" would want.

HELEN STILKEY: Well, obviously, [Leon was] the controlling force and not always viewed kindly, of course, because you could work a long time [on a product] that was not going to fly. You could look not only for the garment or whatever the product might be, checking out your vendors and all of that sort of thing. There was a lot of time involved in all of that. Then maybe it wouldn't fly. That was hard for them.

For years I'd worked informally with the individual product managers in managing the various product lines. By the early 1980s, we developed a more systematic product review process called the "blue book" reviews, often called simply "blue books" (because advance information was put in blue three-ring binders). The amount and detail of the information we required was considerable, as was the work of putting it all together. Blue books were an A-to-Z look at all of our products for a particular product group: item sales and internal trends, new opportunities, competitive activity, market trends, inventory situations, and so on. We made the decisions—what we were going to continue, what we were going to delete, what we were going to add—twice a year.

Blue books gave me a chance to work with the product people. If I disapproved something, or if Bill did, it was dropped there. We went along with most recommendations, but there were inappropriate products we weeded out and we had a chance to express our opinions on directions we should be taking. The blue book meetings acquired great notoriety within the company for their reputedly confrontational quality and my detailed involvement. But they seemed to work and were critical in bringing a common point of view to our diverse array of product groups and product managers.

WES DEVRIES: It's very intimidating for most people to be with Leon, because he's one of the few people I know who can sit quietly waiting for you to say what you're going to say. That silence . . . seems like an eternity. And people have to fill it. Leon is a very respectful listener and he feels no need to speak. It's intimidating to most people. It's a difficult style, and it's part of who he is. So people always struggled with really knowing him in some easy way. He's a wonderful guy. It's easy for me to sit down with anybody. I come and go. But for the people who work within an organization, I can see it's difficult if the leader is not your usual person. You're living your whole life with typical people's reactions to things and so that's your style. And Leon's unique.

When the product decisions had been made and it was time to prepare the catalogs, we had a room set aside for laying them out, with racks for the pages. I'd go down there and spend hours with the merchants and the creative people going through each catalog, page by page—the products we were going to feature, the editorial themes we were going to hit, the ordering information, the cover. As we divided the pages among the various product groups (casual, active outdoors, home, men's, women's, joint) I controlled the balance of space. If somebody wanted to shift catalog pages from active equipment to women's casual, I had to OK it.

BILL END: And of all the accomplishments I believe Leon had as a CEO, probably the number one was his recognition of what the brand was and wasn't and holding everyone within the confines of that brand. I think he did a terrific job of not allowing it to go off in the directions it could easily have gone off in. So I think he policed that very carefully, and I think he did a great job in that regard.

The lifestyle strategy wasn't our only significant response to the slowdown in sales. We introduced what we called our "Best" strategy in 1984. This strategy was a mechanism for continuous improvement in our customer service strategies.

CHRIS MCCORMICK: Out of that slowdown emerged the Best strategy. Leon said, "We want to be the quantifiable best resource to our customers in the value that we add to their purchases from us, product, services, and communications." It was meant to be an overarching, broad strategy, as opposed to what a lot of people say—for example, "We want to double our size in ten years," or, "We want to do this, we want to do that." It's always been my belief that what Leon wanted to do here was to create a model company. The Best strategy, I think, embodied that.

The Best strategy affirmed our commitment to being demonstrably the best of all the competitors in the quality of products, services, and communications. "Demonstrably best" meant that our performance criteria were based on measurable data or informed consensus as to how we compared with our competitors in those attributes most valued by our customers. It meant not being the biggest or fastest growing or the lowest in price or the most profitable, but rather the quantifiably best resource for our customers in the sum of the quality and value attributes we were adding to their purchases from us.

Most of all, the Best strategy represented our intention to go back to basics following the distortions imposed on us by the preppy boom and our brief, unwanted experience with fashion.

> JOHN FINDLAY: It was clear to me that when growth slowed down, there was a period of time where it was a correct call on Leon's part to look back into the bowels of the company and try to do things better, to redouble our efforts to serve our customers better. We had probably gotten a little bit away from it in the sense that, during those growth years, the preppy boom, we got so much good press and we had to beat people off with a stick trying to come visit L.L.Bean. I think we'd gotten a little sloppy. Including me. All the adoration sort of got to our heads. And then at some point in time when sales went down and the profitability was reduced, we were out ahead and we had to, I think, go back and look at what we were doing and make sure that we still were as good as we thought we were, essentially. I think it did focus the company during a time of low sales. One of the reasons why nobody panicked is we were busy trying to make sure that we produced the best service we could. And I supported that.

The idea was not to win an award for being best but to identify opportunities for improvement from our customers' perspectives and, as a result, to drive continuous improvement in all of our customer relationships. The Best strategy, and the "Best" way of thinking, permeated all parts of L.L.Bean. At the same time, we focused our financial goals on meeting superior financial levels for our various stakeholders, including a strong balance sheet at all times. We called this element of the Best strategy "quality growth."

The idea for the "Best" concept came from the 1982 annual report of a *Fortune* 500 company that a customer sent to me. Each of that company's business units was to compare its products, services, and operating performance against its top competitors and to implement plans to close any quality gaps. It sounded more like sloganeering than a planning mechanism. But the notion of a Best strategy was appealing, even though I didn't understand how you could actually execute it.

It came together when I was at a direct marketing convention in Chicago in 1984 and heard Professor Louis W. Stern from Northwestern University describe something he called a "global utility index." It sounded like a tool we could use to implement a Best strategy. The matrix focused on those merchandising and service attributes that most influenced customer buying decisions.

> MARK FASOLD: We came up with the idea of a customer utility matrix, which was the initial core of the Best strategy. It was in customer service, one of the pillars of the company. We researched with customers what were the most important services in their minds, and they were rank ordered by the customers. We would weight those elements. So, if we had a 90 on this one and Lands' End got a 95 on this one and the weighting was 80 percent, 80 times 90, 80 times 95, and you weight them down, you multiply them out, you get a score. That was the first Best strategy that came out, and that was the birth of the Best strategy.

In the service area we identified and weighted our 100 percent guarantee, returns service, order phone service, time to fulfill orders, being in stock, shipping service, alterations/repairs, inquiry service, and gift service. This articulation was based on customer focus groups, surveys, and internal discussions with our customer service people.

We set up a matrix that listed our competitors across the horizontal dimension, and the various service attributes on the vertical. We had a team of people in the phone centers who did nothing but place orders with competitors—up to thirty-five or forty orders a year with each. They recorded how long it took to get the shipment, what the internal fulfillment time was, whether the product was in or out of stock. They evaluated the quality of the telephone exchange, including attitude, and then they returned products and tested the guarantee. It was a rigorous and honest process.

Each year we might find out we were overall number one but not number one in every dimension. Maybe we were third in in-stock orders, for example, or second in the quality of the phone conversation. So that told us where we had to improve the coming year.

Our ability to provide personal service had been good, but, driven by our Best strategy, we decided to take service to a higher, more comprehensive level. We wanted activist telephone reps and support staff who fully engaged with our customers' questions and complaints and who made sure we responded. We wanted absolutely the best and most consistent and most caring customer relations anywhere. Getting "close to the customer" was the slogan of the day, and L.L.Bean wanted to be closest.

It was the third time that we formally upgraded customer service and our customer satisfaction department. It wasn't due to a sense that things had slipped. Instead, it was a matter of taking service to the next level of performance. Excellence in customer service doesn't just happen by itself. You have to periodically revitalize the commitment. We didn't want to take it for granted that we were the best. We had gained recognition for customer service, but we knew it was something we always had to work on, continuously improving, year after year. The Best strategy, with its utility matrices, gave us a way to do that. What was most appealing about this approach was that every company says they're the best, or they intend to be the best. So prove it. Here was a way of demonstrating quantifiably and verifiably how we compared among the best.

Under John Findlay's leadership we achieved the preeminent position in customer service or customer satisfaction in the catalog industry, the quantifiable and verifiable best. Our time to get orders out the door was among the best in the industry, and our shipping accuracy was 99.89 percent—close to perfect. People from major companies like IBM, Xerox, and JC Penney visited our distribution operation to see how we were achieving such high levels of customer satisfaction. We knew we were the best in the industry, but I don't think we would have been the best if we hadn't gone through this exercise and every year measured and improved our performance.

BOB PEIXOTTO: Everybody kind of looked at the Best strategy and said, "Yeah, that's something I could sign up for." Because the Best strategy was really Leon saying, "We want to be a model company." I think it was [well received], at least with my peers, it

certainly was. I didn't hear people saying, "This isn't the way it
should go."

Chris McCormick and I, at one of our planning sessions, we
gave a presentation on controlling growth, because we thought
we were growing too fast. We were jeopardizing the Best concept.
If you grow too fast and outstrip your operations capability, then
you don't provide good service, even though you make a lot of
money. And that sort of typifies Leon and the way he thought about
Bean. Chris and I joked during a subsequent downturn that we sure
did a good job of controlling growth.

The Best strategy, I think, directly supported the perpetuation of
the L.L.Bean mystique through the 1980s. Almost every year saw us
getting feature stories in two or three national magazines or major city
newspapers. Stories appeared in *Reader's Digest,* the *Boston Globe,* the
New York Times, U.S. News and World Report, Sports Illustrated,
Forbes, People, and *Time.* One feature story that appeared in 1981 was
reproduced in twenty-two other major newspapers.

Another writer wrote, "The L.L.Bean catalog out of Freeport,
Maine has character, action, and atmosphere, tells one sunny tale after
another for seventy-plus pages, offers a unique imaginative experience.
Yet never gets a tumble from reviewers of Pulitzer stories. Is there no
literary justice?"[1] Another wrote, "A large part of the story is, after all
these years, still about old-fashioned words like 'reliability' and 'responsibility' and Bean's revolutionary idea of caring enough to treat a
customer as a human being."[2] This was heady stuff. I hoped we were
keeping it in perspective.

The stories invariably told L.L.'s founding story and talked about
our "durable high-quality" or "well-made" or "practical" products.
Our excellent customer service (our "homey efficiency") was usually
featured as well as individual stories of extraordinary responses by our
people to urgent individual customer needs. These happened to illustrate the company's core values, and they were reinforced with a lot of
credibility by real-life situations recounted by some excellent writers.

We had maintained the mystical appeal that resonated with a lot of
people who shared our values. I don't know of any other company in

any kind of business that attracted this kind of attention in the public media and for such an extended period. We were not an ordinary company. We were living the legend of L.L.

The first batch of editorial mystique, in the 1960s and 1970s, was focused on the L.L. story. It was all about L.L. in those days. But now the mystique was shifting to the company. We were institutionalizing L.L. and what he stood for—the outdoors heritage, our product quality and customer service, and our trust in people. Illustrations of these values were provided by current L.L.Bean people, our telephone service reps and our hand sewers in manufacturing. More than one reporter spent a night at the retail store taking notes on the nocturnal activities of L.L.Bean customers.

Our Freeport retail store shared our passion to be the best. Sales reps served three million customers in 1986. Compliments to our staff were measured in poundage. The reps were respectful and accommodating, and they knew their products from personal experience as well as training programs. Twenty were registered Maine Guides, and many were certified instructors in canoeing, cross-country skiing, fly-fishing, and other outdoor activities. One of our reps lent a customer his own trail stove when we were temporarily out of stock and the customer was on the way to Baxter State Park. Another drove four hundred miles to deliver a canoe in time for a customer's long-planned trip. Our midnight shift supervisor delivered a parka to the Portland airport for a customer waiting at LaGuardia in the morning. People on the floor were part of our first aid team. Their knowledge of CPR saved four customers' lives in 1987.

Freeport as Mecca remained a consistent theme, as did customers having a personal connection with L.L.Bean ("It is as if L.L.Bean were family"). They loved the new store (1984) with its ample use of wood, spacious atrium, and granite paving. One wedding was held by the trout pond the first year, and a Connecticut woman had the pond replicated for her new home.

We did not take our mystique for granted. In fact we worked very hard at being the best we could be, doing the things day in and day out that led to these kinds of stories. There was nothing forced or phony about it. We were aware that we were something special, and our people took great pride in being part of L.L.Bean.

One further major change at L.L.Bean to emerge from the early 1980s slowdown—after adoption of lifestyle merchandising, the Best strategy, and aggressive direct marketing—was a more effective planning process: the way we worked through and implemented major initiatives supporting our brand strategies.

> BOB PEIXOTTO: [In] 1983, Leon put out a memo that basically announced the Best strategy . . . And then through planning meetings and through work within the planning department, we created these utility matrices, we rewrote the strategy document, we rewrote the KRAs [key results areas] to incorporate it all. We held, during that period of time, off-site planning meetings once a year with the management staff. And those events were where Leon would announce and introduce concepts that we would bring into the business.

We had set up a planning committee of our senior managers in the late 1970s after I got planning religion at the AMA program mentioned in chapter 7. To kick off the process, our new planning director, with my encouragement, put together a learned fifteen-page document on the planning process, its various components, and the beneficial results to be achieved. It set our process back by a lot. We were awash in strengths, weaknesses, opportunities, and threats (SWOTs). We had KRAs (key results areas), CSFs (critical success factors), SIs (strategic initiatives)—a whole new language of planning acronyms. I compounded this pedantry with my own inclinations to develop the perfect process the first time out. As a result we had an elegant but complicated approach to planning.

In 1982 we brought in a consultant to try to address our senior managers' concerns about expediting things. He had worked with us several times before and was highly regarded by all. His recommendations to simplify the process got all of us to agree that the plan would provide a strategic context within which we could delegate authority and responsibility. It would also enable full understanding of and alignment with

L.L.Bean's purpose, values, and policies. Broad participation in setting goals for operating plans and budgets was a desired outcome.

We developed an eighteen-month planning agenda with monthly meetings, and we focused the process on the three-year marketing plan. The process became more transparent and open, including greater participation by managers and supervisors, and especially the senior managers. The planning director and I had previously been doing too much of it ourselves.

BOB PEIXOTTO: Think about the planning process as a pyramid. At the bottom of the pyramid the first layer would be the corporate purpose statement.

Sitting on top of this document are key results areas. Leon got the term KRA from Peter Drucker, and it just meant areas of the business, not departments. It was actually very nondepartmental. It was broken up by customers, products, and services—areas to pay attention to in the business. The KRAs take that whole strategy document and translate it into a whole system of measures that measure every aspect of every concept that's covered in the strategy document. Leon's idea was that we would track each of these key results areas and it would tell whether or not we were living out our strategy. It was a balanced scorecard before the folks down at Harvard ever came up with it.

And then, as a part of each year's planning process, you would look at the results by key results area, and you would assess, based on that data and based on information you'd brought in from outside the company, what the industry was doing. You'd assess strengths, weaknesses, opportunities, and threats—the SWOT analysis. SWOTs change every year.

Each area, each function, in the business would put together three- and one-year plans to achieve results in each of the key results areas. Your three- and one-year goal plans were really the actions you were going to take to address weaknesses and threats, or to capitalize on strengths and opportunities. And that became the annual plan for the year. The one-year plans were obviously done once a year and each year the three-year plans were updated.

The purpose statement changed very, very slowly. The KRAs themselves were timeless as well, though the strategies and measures within each would change. The SWOTs changed every year. In the prime of Leon's day, this was a tight system.

Our objectives for strategic planning were to give everyone an overview of L.L.Bean, what we stood for, and where we were going; to provide a means for aligning our functional areas to meet common corporate goals; and to involve as many L.L.Bean people as possible in the planning and goal setting to optimize our available talent and to build commitment.

MARK FASOLD: The planning process is how Leon managed the business. I think that's what got people. They saw it as constraining, as opposed to opening things up. You know what? They were partially right. He used it to stay focused on the business, the core strategy of the business. So if you wanted to penetrate it, you had to get within it, as opposed to work outside of it.

The planning process was my vehicle for leading the company strategically. The process allowed us to deal with a changing business environment while keeping values and overarching strategies constantly in front of us.

CHRIS MCCORMICK: It was such a disciplined process that it took a lot of time and the organization would try to find ways to get away from that because it's such a demanding time constraint. But there were a lot of good things that came out of it.

Although our planning process was highly structured and systematic, we were always fully aware that it was executed by people.

BOB PEIXOTTO: In the eighties it was a very paternalistic organization, and not in a bad way, in a good way. The company really cared about its employees. At that time, we were still completing putting in our benefits program and were very careful to put in programs that we thought would be right for employees, almost regardless of whether or not they were going to be important to

175

them. What they'd need. That's the way I mean paternalism. Make sure that even though we have a lot of young people, that they are going to be adequately provided for in retirement. Those kinds of things. It was a very caring company. It was also young and hungry. When you joined this company, it felt like you were joining a growth company.

Our compensation and benefits programs were more than competitive with local and national norms, and we all continued to share in the company's profitability. Each person's performance bonus was a percentage of his or her base compensation. In the 1980s it varied from a low of 5 percent to a high of 31.2 percent and averaged 22 percent over the ten-year period. The annual bonus was a very important part of working at L.L.Bean.

We also had an open job posting system, and the vast majority of promotions went to internal employee candidates. To facilitate promotions, we had a management development program (forty-one courses), microcomputer training, "after hours" courses in job-related skills, and a tuition reimbursement program applicable to local universities, colleges, and technical schools. There was no requirement that these studies be business related.

Everyone still got a 33⅓ percent discount on L.L.Bean products. We wanted to encourage usage, especially in the outdoors. We looked for outdoors interests in hiring people. In 1982 we bought a set of sporting camps on the western end of Rangeley Lake, a premier cold-water lake in an exceptionally pretty part of western Maine. The area is known for its hiking, camping, and winter sports as well as its quality trout and salmon fishing. Seven cabins and ten tent sites were available to L.L.Bean families. We used a companywide lottery to allocate usage, and the camps were full almost year-round. We also made available at no cost an equipment pool of tents, sleeping bags, and outdoors gear, which was used extensively by L.L.Bean people.

BOB PEIXOTTO: Actually, the big thing that happened in the eighties was the introduction of the health and fitness program, which Leon was a big advocate of and really made to work. We instituted exercise classes, put fitness rooms in our facilities, and built a walking course around our headquarters facilities. It made huge inroads in people's health. In 1986, 22½ percent of our people smoked. Today 12 percent. In 1986, about 14 percent had high blood pressure. With a significant aging of our employee population, the number hasn't changed. We're still at about 14 percent, which is incredible. High cholesterol levels have come down from 29 percent to 19 percent of our employees. We've got a whole lot of data that shows that we've made significant inroads.

We provided exercise facilities, along with a staff of fitness professionals, because we believed that regular exercise could improve health, increase energy levels, reduce stress, create a more positive mental outlook, and help us improve the quality of our lives at work and home. I was a regular user of our fitness facilities and can attest to all five benefits. In a 1986 article, *Better Health & Living* magazine called L.L.Bean one of the twenty-five healthiest companies to work for.[3]

> BOB PEIXOTTO: Our corporate strategy document also talked about whether or not people's job satisfaction should be a goal. It wasn't necessarily a contributor to success, but it was important in and of itself that people be satisfied with their jobs than not. So the attitude survey measured job satisfaction, and the climate survey measured the elements that make up a motivating environment.

In 1981 we did our first attitude survey to measure job satisfaction, separate from motivation (which the climate survey measured). Those attitude results showed that Bean people strongly identified with our products and our customers and shared a high commitment to quality and service and our outdoors heritage. By and large we liked our jobs, our wages and benefits, and our working conditions and relationships, and we were optimistic about the future. There were problems revealed by our survey, but our overall results in achieving positive attitudes ranked with the best companies anywhere. Our people were genuinely excited about working at L.L.Bean.

One reason for these surveys was that I believed in the ideas of participative management and decentralized decision making. These ideas required a lot of employee involvement. Engaging people in these surveys and subsequent discussion groups was central to their participation in the operations and decision making at L.L.Bean.

In 1983 we resurveyed our people to update our responses and see how we were doing. Old problems receded as we improved in some areas, and new issues emerged. It was a process without end, one of continuous employee involvement and continuous mitigation of adverse work conditions. It helped us stay as close as we could to our employees and to be as fair and responsive to their ideas and needs as we could.

In 1989 we had 3,000 employees for most of the year and we peaked at 5,500 with seasonals hired for the Christmas rush. Even though L.L.Bean people were dispersed in our various facilities around the Maine countryside, and despite the addition of thousands of new people over the decade, our score on the companywide attitude survey for commitment to L.L.Bean's goals was 4.5 on a 5-point scale, the highest we'd ever achieved.

> BOB PEIXOTTO: I think [the company's aspiration to be more than a traditional business] is at the root of why people, everybody—customers, employees—have such strong loyalty to this place. For me as an employee I've loved L.L.Bean because it hasn't been about making a buck. We made money and that was great. But it's been about creating a social institution that could be something you could be very proud to be associated with. And I think our customers have seen that, I think everybody has seen that. That all came tumbling out of Leon's head.

My thinking about our responsibilities to our communities (local, state, and national), and how we should fulfill them, evolved through the years. It began in the early 1970s, when a friend of mine solicited me for the L.L.Bean gift to Greater Portland's United Way campaign. We'd given very modestly over the previous several years, because I wasn't convinced that Freeport was part of Greater Portland, as well as the fact that I was pretty tight with company philanthropy. A noted economist of the time advocated that corporations not give to any social causes. It wasn't the business of business, he said, which nicely supported my own frugal leanings.

But my friend took me aback when he said his personal gift to United Way was significantly greater than corporate L.L.Bean's. Economic theory notwithstanding, this bothered me. The more I thought about it, the more I realized that there were many relevant local, state, and national issues that were clearly a part of our business. Public education, the homeless, our natural environment, the Freeport Fire Department—none of them could be ignored honestly by any economic rationalization. We lived with these issues every day. Our communities were stakeholders to whom we had many responsibilities. To begin with, we needed to be a stronger supporter of Greater Portland United Way and its many clients with real-life problems.

We funded the start-up of a local agency that brought access to United Way's basic health care and human services to Freeport, and over the years we became the top or next-to-top corporate and employee contributor to the three United Way communities in which we had facilities and people.

Somewhere along the line I read that the national average for corporate giving was a little more than 1 percent of pretax earnings. So we expanded our giving to the 2.5 percent level and developed an allocation formula. The bulk of our giving went to human service agencies and to outdoors recreation and conservation organizations and initiatives. Our first major gift was $500,000 to the Appalachian Mountain Club in 1984. The AMC, a longtime partner of L.L.Bean's, is the oldest outdoor recreation and conservation organization in the United States. It provides a multitude of outdoors opportunities for people in the Northeast, and it advances a variety of important environmental goals. Tom Deans, executive director of the AMC at the time, said of our gift, "It's incredibly important, a real shot in the arm. What's more important is that it came from Bean people, the same people who appreciate the outdoors and use AMC as a resource. It's like getting support from an extended family."

In the mid- to late 1970s our annual directors' trips took us canoeing on various stretches of the St. John River in northern Maine. The upper St. John was the remotest and wildest river in the state and the longest wild river east of the Mississippi. The 130-mile watershed was an invaluable recreation and ecological resource. Its surrounding forests were also a major source of pulp wood for Maine's paper industry. As a consequence of the 1973 oil embargo, the idea of building a hydroelectric dam on the river (to provide 1 percent of New England's power needs) was being seriously advanced by politicians and government officials. The dam would have flooded 86,000 acres of northern Maine in creating a man-made lake to be managed like a national park. It would have brought a lot of government money into the state and consequently was controversial between those who might benefit economically and those concerned about massive destruction of the state's natural environment.

Prior to our 1977 trip on the St. John, John McPhee had written a comprehensive and insightful piece in the *New Yorker* about the river and about the disastrous consequences of the proposed dam.[4] We had read the article and were much influenced by it as we watched an Army Corps of Engineers helicopter being used to study the river during our trip.

When we got back to Freeport we decided that L.L.Bean should help defeat the dam, and we offered our assistance to the Natural Resources Council of Maine, which was leading the opposition. We asked our customers for help and got 33,000 signatures opposing it—that was 57 percent of NRCM's total—and we raised 40 percent of the funds needed to run the campaign. Eventually our entire congressional delegation came out against the dam, and the U.S. Congress killed it in 1982.

In 1980, there was a statewide referendum to close Maine Yankee, Maine's one nuclear power plant. I was on Central Maine Power Company's board at the time and was convinced that a shutdown of the plant would seriously damage the state's economy and environment by eliminating this source of efficient and clean energy. I felt that the radioactive waste disposal and safety issues were manageable. L.L.Bean publicly opposed the referendum and contributed a modest amount of money to the campaign to save the plant. I knew this would be controversial but felt an ethical need to come forward.

My ethical persuasion was not shared by a great many members of our public. We were deluged with thousands of letters criticizing our support of the nuclear plant and advocating boycotts of our products. It was the hottest public relations potato we had ever dealt with, and we couldn't cool it down. Articles kept appearing in all kinds of media. We responded to all with a fairly rational explanation of our position, but it was to no avail. Nuclear power was not a rational issue.

Businesses are criticized at times for taking too few positions on public issues. But it's complicated when your stakeholders are spread across all sides of issues. In 1985, when a new dam was proposed for the West Branch of the Penobscot River, we simply gave each side equal space in our retail store to tell its story and let the public decide for itself.

Generally, we've supported advocacy by the various conservation and outdoors recreational organizations we belong to as well as our various trade associations. These groups possess the expertise and resources to be involved in a credible and effective manner.

Our employees have been actively involved with Red Cross bloodmobile drives, United Way agencies, Junior Achievement, town governments, conservation groups, Little Leagues, and a multitude of other worthy community activities. Since 1980, L.L.Bean employees have maintained 18.5 miles of the Appalachian Trail in northern Maine. Our Outdoor Discovery Clinics program in Freeport has exposed thousands of people to various outdoor opportunities and skills, as well as safe and environmentally responsible enjoyment of the outdoors. In 1987 the National Wildlife Federation, the nation's largest conservation organization, gave L.L.Bean its corporate leadership award for consistent support of conservation education and our "outstanding" outdoors seminar program.

JOHN OLIVER: The original conservationists were sportsmen and that's the roots from which L.L. came. Hunting and fishing were the ways people got outdoors when L.L founded the company. By the fifties, there was family camping and people taking to the road in their cars and then, by the sixties, there was a greater environmental ethic, with the cleanup of waterways and people beginning to worry about our forests and whether we would have outdoor recreational opportunities in the future. As Leon saw the way people engaged with the outdoors evolving, L.L.Bean evolved to serve outdoors people and our product line evolved to keep up with the interests of people in the outdoors. But along with that evolution came a growing recognition that we have an interest as an outdoors company in preserving our natural resources and the opportunity to enjoy them. Leon's environmental ethic has become only sharper and more focused over the years as the threats have mounted and grown.

In spite of turmoil following the slowdown in L.L.Bean's growth in 1983 and 1984, my senior managers and I felt confident. We believed we understood the major causes and knew how to respond. When double-digit growth returned, it felt as if the company had resumed its natural course. We'd gone back to the basics of the business and it had really worked. The company seemed well aligned around the Best strategy, the lifestyle strategy, and the future of the catalog business. We believed we were headed in the right direction, and we were pretty positive about the future of L.L.Bean. If you wanted to identify a time when this management group was operating at its peak, this was the time.

The first year of renewed growth, up 20 percent, was 1985. Our results led the industry. We averaged 23 percent growth each year from 1985 through 1988, growing 33 percent in 1987.

We continued to have a very talented group of advertising and direct marketing people, the best in the industry. Bill End had put together and continued to lead this bright and capable team. Our circulation plans were reaching more than 25 percent of the households in the United States. We were mailing our new hunting, fishing, camping, and winter sports specialty catalogs to their special interest audiences, and we were testing fitness, women's-only, and home furnishings catalogs.

In 1983, *Consumer Reports* published a study of forty leading catalogs based on what 100,000 of its members thought of them. The criteria were high-quality products, excellent service, and ease of problem resolution. L.L.Bean was the highest rated.[5]

In 1985, Tom Peters and Nancy Austin published *A Passion for Excellence*, a sequel to the best-selling *In Search of Excellence*.[6] It too was a best seller and gave many examples of how excellence was achieved by satisfying customers. L.L.Bean was mentioned eight times. A full page featured our "Golden Rule" advertisement.

Consumer Reports did another study in 1987, after our Best strategy was in place. This time companies were rated within the specific product categories in which they competed. We were in seven categories (sporting goods, men's sportswear, women's sportswear, etc.). The criterion, again, was quality of goods and services. We were number one in all seven of our categories.[7]

At the 1989 Catalog Conference in Chicago, L.L.Bean was named the "Catalog of the Decade." We were recognized for doing a consistently excellent job year after year. Dick Hodgson, a direct marketing industry expert, said, "What I like best about L.L.Bean is that they know who they are, who their customers are, and their position in the marketplace."

As part of L.L.Bean's seventy-fifth anniversary in 1987 we introduced a new "Spirit of 75" insignia. It showed the sun rising over Maine's Mt. Katahdin. This mountain is the first piece of U.S. geography to see the rising sun each morning, bringing on a new day with new energy, growth, and change. The message of the insignia was that even with daily change, the mountain—the enormous granite massif whose name means "Great One" in Abenaki—endures always the same.

At our anniversary celebration, I spoke of new energy at L.L.Bean and our expectation to double in size over the next five years. The biggest challenge, I said, would be to remain the same L.L.Bean with its traditional values.

10

End of an Era

WHEN WE RETURNED from our directors' canoe trip down the Allagash in 1984 we were just completing our first doubling in size of the Freeport store. Going to 50,000 square feet was a big change for us. To do it, we converted the entire original buildings to retail space. We added a fair amount of new construction in addition to refurbishing existing space. We changed the exterior to a Maine barn-board finish and a nice front entrance framed with bricks. The building's main door still stayed open all the time. I could find some remnants of the old building there, but the new store was more than an evolution; it was a transformation.

It was a much-needed one. The old store had been so crowded with products that one customer said shopping at L.L.Bean had been like looking for buried treasure, but "now everything's out in the open." The expansion included an atrium as well as a trout pond (with fifteen healthy Maine brookies). It also provided room for selling bicycles, sea kayaks, and saltwater fishing gear.

Even though I had been much involved in the planning and had approved all the fixtures and floor layouts, it was still a shock to see such a change from the store I had liked so much in the 1970s. This was a big step toward modernity, and almost a complete break from the past. But what most upset me was that it seemed to change the personality of the store from a comfortable and woodsy, uniquely L.L.Bean environment to one that was starting to feel like other stores.

Putting down green carpeting in the store years earlier, which old-timers talked about so much, marked the dividing line between L.L. and me. Now it was clear, though perhaps only to me, that L.L.Bean had entered yet another era. We had grown as a company from $30 million in 1975 to more than $250 million in 1984 and were on our way to more than doubling that in 1990. The retail store's dramatic physical growth and change (it would almost double again, to 96,000 square feet, in 1989) reflected those of L.L.Bean's.

With growth came larger size in all dimensions, and greater complexity. Size alone would have brought problems, but many of the strategies we adopted to deal with a more competitive world (for example, product line extensions and service enhancements) brought even more complexity. L.L.Bean was a far different company from the one it had been only ten years earlier. During the 1980s, a writer noted that we had grown more than 100 times the size we were when I joined the company. "That is a problem," he said. "There are very few things in the world that can grow a hundredfold and still be recognizable. And if L.L.Bean is ever unrecognizable, the jig is up."[1] We knew this.

We were experiencing a number of paradoxes. Our traditional Maine values required increasingly sophisticated management techniques. Our high growth rates were the result of complex direct marketing systems and merchandising rules. We had a paternalistic working environment yet rigorous performance standards and the latest in human resource practices. We had family ownership and publicly traded financial standards. We wanted to be good citizens in our various communities and good custodians of our natural environment, backed up by a lot of knowledge and technological expertise. It was an ongoing balancing act to keep L.L.Bean recognizable. Keeping things simple was getting more and more complicated.

From a business point of view, the greatest problem we faced in the 1980s was a precipitous decline in profitability. Our return on equity fell from about 30 percent in 1975 to about 15 percent in 1990, with most of the decline occurring in the latter part of the 1980s. Although sales increased significantly, our selling and operating costs increased at a greater rate.

Our high profitability levels of the late 1970s and early 1980s, when L.L.Bean was discovered by the "rugged outdoors" and "preppy boom" trends, were simply not sustainable in the more competitive retail world of the 1980s. Much of our uniqueness in products had at least superficially been taken away by other retailers following the outdoors and preppy trends. We depended on double-digit growth rates to sustain a satisfactory level of profit.

To a great extent we were all responsible for the profit decline because of our bias to sell more Bean products and grow out of cost problems. Our orientation was toward growth rather than cost control, and this was the inclination of virtually everyone in management. Our ongoing loss of productivity, however, wasn't because we weren't paying attention. We were.

We recognized the initial productivity problem as early as 1976, when we developed and installed L.L.Bean's first operating budget. Almost every new iteration of strategic initiatives since then had included a cost reduction or productivity project.

In 1982 we adopted the American Productivity Center's cost and productivity accounting theory and system in order to identify areas where we were losing productivity. It turned out to be almost everywhere, with no obvious or easy answers.

WES DEVRIES: Leon tried very hard to increase the awareness of profitability. He introduced this fairly complex profit management system in the product arena, but that didn't seem to heighten the awareness of "How do I manage profitability?" . . . You didn't get the impression when you worked with the people that, "OK, the most important thing is my bottom line, so let me see how do I get there." The emphasis was on the top line. I think within the corporate purpose statement it says that the bottom line will take care of itself if you do all these other things. I think that's a true statement. But I think that statement got misinterpreted.

L.L.'s theory (and ours) was to sell good merchandise and treat customers like human beings. The profits were supposed to take care of themselves. Unfortunately, the theory didn't work quite that well. Our Best strategy meant being best for our customers—exceeding their expectations—as well as being best competitively. It was not directly related to our cost structure. Our customer orientation may have forced us to think we didn't need the same budget discipline and profit requirements as everybody else. A lot of Bean people had disdain for the *P* word.

Many of the organizational challenges of growth and complexity showed up in our employee surveys. The hectic pace and day-to-day workload were obscuring our long-range aspirations. Where were we going? Why were we changing the locations or layouts of our work areas almost every year, along with our manufacturing and customer service spaces and catalog production and almost all of our various departments? Could we sustain our employee commitment amid this apparent chaos? To cut through the complexity, we needed to be more effective at communicating up and down and sideways in the organization. More feedback on individual performance was especially needed. Interdepartmental teamwork was also perceived to be lacking.

> BOB PEIXOTTO: [Employee surveys through the 1980s] did show things and things did change. For instance, I know that we always got low scores on recognition, that people didn't feel recognized in the workplace. And building on that, what always happened, the way that Leon did business was, if you had a weakness—lack of recognition would become a weakness in SWOT parlance—then you had to have a plan in place to fix it.

By the mid-1980s the surveys revealed a perception of increasing centralization of power and a decrease in feelings of autonomy. This was despite our emphasis (or talk, anyway) on responsible autonomy and participative decision making. The latter may actually have been part of the problem.

> JOHN FINDLAY: Part of the climate survey results forced us to look for ways to expand the decision-making groups, with subcommittees and that sort of thing. And it was basically a disaster in the sense that, for whatever reason, we had some real decision

makers in that tight group [of senior managers]. All of us were used to making [decisions], wanted to make them, thought we knew what we were doing . . . The more people came up through middle management ranks . . . the more that became an issue and the more we tried to diffuse the decision making. I look back on it now, it's sort of funny, but basically, there was an issue of autonomy. Basically decision making was even more closely held than the five guys [senior managers]. There was one guy. So, we had five guys fighting for autonomy from Leon, essentially, and then ten other guys fighting for autonomy from the five guys, and, you know, it was never going to be solved. There wasn't going to be a resolution of that. I looked at it almost as humorous. I mean, it wasn't, but I understood at the time the problem was partly me, partly Leon.

As a result of productivity and team activities we had more committees and task forces than you could count. Decision making was buried in a lot of meetings. Ultimately issues were referred to our senior managers to keep things moving, and that exacerbated the feeling that power and decision making were at too high a level.

CHRIS MCCORMICK: It's not fair to point at Leon for this because we were all doing it. It was a high-control environment where before I'd present my ad plan to Leon, I'm going to be very involved in what my people are recommending. So, there's that type of micro-management, if you will, all the way down the organization. There was a feeling where people even lower would say, "Why do you need me? Chris is the manager of advertising and he's doing my job. "Well, because I want to make sure, because Leon knows his stuff. Leon knows the rep and he knows the circulation of the *New Yorker*. He knows the renewal rate and you better have that stuff on the top of your head because when you present to Leon, it's like going into a final exam. So that went down the organization. Was that what drove it, that Leon was so knowledgeable and exacting? That was part of it, no question. But I think also it was the people we hired. I mean, I look to myself. I'm more of a controlling manager too. I want to know what's going on. Plus, I loved what I did. I still do. So, I got involved in some of the details because I wanted to know how the *New Yorker* was doing.

Our growth strategies of the 1980s succeeded on the demand side. But we were not able to integrate them into our operations and merchandising in a cost-effective manner. Without lifestyle merchandising we could not have enjoyed the kind of growth we saw in the 1980s. Yet it directly and indirectly led to complexity and proliferation in the number of catalogs. Each specialty catalog, which focused on a different category of specialized outdoors products, required a separate round of planning, design, product selection, picking of recipient names, mailing, and results tracking. We increased our catalog mailings from five per year (in 1975) to twenty-eight (in 1990), and our circulation (total catalogs mailed) from 6 million pieces to 114 million. Each catalog required all kinds of internal and external coordination (creative agencies, printers, U.S.P.S., and more).

Because of the lifestyle strategy, we expanded substantially into men's and women's casual weekend apparel. These are product lines with higher year-to-year product turnover, broader color and size assortments, and higher return rates. Stockkeeping units (SKUs)—perhaps the biggest cause of complexity in merchandising, warehousing, inventory management, and throughout the organization—quadrupled in the 1980s, from about 15,000 to 60,000.

CHRIS MCCORMICK: I think as a result of that split [between active and casual apparel], what happened was there was more tension in the organization. Because now you're vying for space in the catalog and you've got two merchants who want more pages and more SKUs . . . We were competing with ourselves more than competing with the competition.

The lifestyle strategy was intended to be a unifying concept, one L.L.Bean umbrella that would cover both traditional and contemporary outdoors customers, the active and the relaxed weekend parts of their lives. But consistent and coherent execution became complicated. We developed an array of strategic guidelines regarding appropriate L.L.Bean product assortments, quality standards, service standards, a communications persona, and so on. Still, I worried that we weren't communicating our L.L.Bean concept effectively. People who were active users of outdoors gear may well have seen us as a casual clothing company, and casual recreational users may have seen us as an active company. Were we giving the L.L.Bean brand a split personality? Our investment in mailings for active products was disproportionate to their sales revenues.

Women had become the gatekeepers to purchasing for their families, as well as being customers themselves. We still hadn't figured out how to deal with this. Our catalog was still communicating to a male audience as it always had, with lots of technical information on products, outdoors positioning, and a focus on consistent quality and functionality.

> BRAD KAUFFMAN: I always had responsibility for men's product categories. So my job was to appeal to the guy. And even if the woman was the gatekeeper she was only going to buy stuff that the man in her life wanted. So you still had to appeal to the guy. This issue tended to play itself out more in terms of assortment planning and balance of sales issues. So in the Christmas full [catalog], how many pages can be women's product, and where should they be in the book? Can you open the book with women's product? Well, if women are the gatekeepers, maybe you should, because you want to pull them into the book. On the other hand, the brand needs to be at least slightly more masculine than feminine. And if you open the book with women's product, are you in violation of that? So there was this basic tension between the notion that the brand should be more masculine than feminine, and the fact that most of our shoppers, and in increasing numbers, were women. How do you strike the appropriate balance?

Our product developers knew the men's and the active product business well, but defining and merchandising to the Bean woman was a big challenge. We hadn't found the right women's product mix that was representative of Bean's functional value positioning and yet was appealing in design and coloration.

The Best strategy, our second major growth initiative of the 1980s, was instrumental to our achieving the high levels of customer service for which we had become known. But, in spite of a good effort by our merchants and marketers, the utility matrix proved too complex to apply in products and in communications (catalogs, advertising, and other marketing efforts).

> WES DEVRIES: [Reading from a report he wrote in the 1980s] "The Best strategy was looking for the best quality for each skill level: entry, intermediate, and skilled. Best for intended use. We do not want to be everything to each skill level, but we do have to provide an assortment appropriate to each skill level. We don't necessarily merchandise every skill level item. We must offer enough assortment to be credible."
>
> There's a good example of the difficulty of [the Best strategy]. Here you have entry, intermediate, and skilled. Now talk about the complexity.
>
> I loved the customer utility matrix. I think more people should think that way. That's really how the consumer behaves, in trade-offs. On the other hand, I found a leap between that as a concept and its real impact in terms of somebody saying, "Let me see, how is this going to work on this decision I have to make on a widget?" There was a big disconnect, many misunderstandings about it. As a practical matter, [when] you moved down into hundreds of people trying to do something with it, maybe more got lost than necessarily got gained by it.

"Best" product attributes included assortment, aesthetics, pricing, uniqueness, innovation, and the physical quality attributes: reliability, durability, and performance. It was difficult, however, to objectively measure and compare our products on all these attributes with our competitors' in a timely and meaningful way. For the various copy, graphics, concept, and ease-of-shopping catalog communications attributes, we had to rely on customer research, which was helpful but not as definitive in telling us where we could improve.

BILL END: I think the Best strategy was a good strategy as long as you could be selective and be the best in a couple of things. I think where Bean perhaps took it to an extreme was we wanted to be the best in everything, and you can't afford to be the best in everything competitively. And I think if it had been more focused, I think they could have had the bottom line as well. I think Bean after that period in time [the start of the Best strategy] was overly staffed and expenses were way higher than they should have been.

The Best strategy was also intended to define what we aspired to on a strategic level, and I think it accomplished that. Our people in every part of the business wanted to be best. It reinforced a very customer-focused mind-set.

Given the critical lifestyle positioning issues, I felt a need to continue my involvement in product selection, merchandising, and marketing for L.L.Bean. There was a perception by some that I was overly involved.

BILL END: And where a lot of debate came was how far do you go with casual apparel? Is a pinpoint Oxford shirt a reasonable product addition, does that work? [Laughter] And that's a good example of one where Leon didn't feel it did. He basically felt it was not appropriate. Oxford cloth is, but pinpoint isn't because it's too fancy a fabric. Lands' End does significant volume on pinpoint dress shirts. You kind of want to say, well, I know a hell of a lot of guys who wear pinpoints during the week and they wear pinpoints as a casual shirt on the weekends. Yet Leon drew that distinction and gave up a chunk of the business. He may have been right, I don't know. You do have to draw a line somewhere. He may have drawn it one place and I might have drawn it somewhere else, but you have to draw the line. He drew it where he thought was appropriate, and it certainly didn't hurt the company.

It wasn't a matter of the entrepreneur not being able to let go. I was happy to delegate big parts of the business, such as direct marketing, order processing and fulfillment, inventory management, and manufacturing.

I couldn't keep up with it all. We also had very good people in those areas, people I trusted fully.

There were certainly some stressful meetings when we put our seasonal product lines together. But that to me was the nature of the retail or catalog game. And especially in maintaining the integrity of L.L.Bean. Many intuitive judgments based on lots of experience and a total immersion in the concept had to be made regularly. It was extremely difficult, at least for me, to delegate a focused L.L.Bean merchandising point of view, and yet such a point of view was requisite for success in our business. It was not like delegating objective operating or financial accountabilities, which were more readily measured and evaluated.

BRAD KAUFFMAN: The quality piece of Bean's mission has always been very clear and relatively easy to execute because of the clarity. Other elements, though, are more complex. Because we have such a wide-ranging product line and because the Bean brand is about an outdoors lifestyle—that is, in a sense it's sort of a potpourri with so many different ingredients—it's important to have all those ingredients in exactly the right proportion . . . It seemed to come naturally to Leon, in large part because it may have been a reflection of his worldview, and also because his perspective was always the holistic perspective, the big picture.

But if you're a product manager responsible for a small piece of this puzzle, understanding and achieving all of those equilibrium points was a harder thing to do. So knowing where to really push and where perhaps to step back a little bit was challenging. That potpourri aspect of the brand makes for a complexity that I think other organizations, other retailers, may not confront. For me, that's the persistent challenge. I think we've tried lots of different ways to get at that.

Achieving the best product assortment for L.L.Bean meant that thousands of things had to be right: the right fit and fabrications, full grain leather, solid brass, virgin wool, Bean colors and pattern assortments. You knew it when you saw it.

What was right and not right for the L.L.Bean persona could be communicated only by hands-on involvement and lots of discussion. I wasn't inclined to put the L.L.Bean concept at risk through excessive delegation. It may not have been "professional management," but hands-on involvement by the senior merchant (or president, in our case) was essential to success. This was especially so when the merchandising strategy was one like the lifestyle strategy we had chosen, which required a deep and thorough understanding of the concept of L.L.Bean and the knowledge of how to translate it into the right products and catalog presentations in a coherent and appealing way.

CHRIS MCCORMICK: During blue book . . . the chief merchants would always have someone on either side of Leon to check what he's writing. They would also read his body language. (Again, I'm hearing this in marketing, I didn't go to the blue books.) If he scratched his forehead, "Oh, he didn't like that product." It was like a baseball third-base coach. [Laughter] . . . I don't think Leon was aware that people were reading his body language or trying to read his—have you seen Leon's handwriting? Yeah, hieroglyphics. He had a number of secretaries, but he had one, Karen Shea, who stayed with him the longest, and people would bring Karen candy. "What did Leon think about the men's blue book? What do the notes say?" Because she would type up his notes for him. So there was this underground going on to try to figure out, "Did Leon like blue book, or did he not like blue book? And what did he really think of Joe Blow over here who ran the men's business?" I never could really understand, because I always felt that I could walk in. His door was always open, and he never grouched at me if I knocked on the door, with no appointment or whatever, and asked his opinion about something.

John Findlay told me once (in one of our "candor" sessions) that my biggest failure was not to have developed and empowered a senior merchant to succeed me in that role. That was true. Part of the problem, however, was the difficulty of finding the right kinds of merchants for L.L.Bean. We needed outdoors people who were also merchants to translate the L.L.Bean idea into relevant product assortments consistent with our brand—people who "got" L.L.Bean, the character part, and who were also top merchants. It was almost impossible to find experienced merchants who had an outdoors interest. And, ironically, some of the most avid outdoors people we recruited to develop as merchants migrated early on to the casual side of the business because that's where the volume was.

> WES DEVRIES: I come out of merchandising and have worked with everyone from Bloomingdale's to whatever, and I have to say that in the best merchandising businesses, no matter how big they get . . . [key leaders] put their imprint on it. Now it might not be where they look at every last new product, but they use various forums to say, "Is that us?" And, "Yes, that's us, more of that." Leon did a lot of it. That was my impression. "That's us, that's not us." I think it's critical to a business where you get into the fuzzy, "What do we mean by 'home camp'?" It's very hard to fully delegate. He couldn't abdicate in the merchandising process the authority and responsibility. He had to truly delegate with the ability to participate. And yes, I think Leon participated rather fully. And of course, that's a real problem in any merchandising business. Yeah, at $250 million he can do a lot of it. At $500 million, you can still do some of it. At $600 million is where it's starting—that's a difficult, complex business.

The role I was playing, or more accurately the role I was perceived to be playing, supposedly created a risk-averse group of merchants who were afraid to do anything that I might not approve. There were all kinds of conflicting opinions on my role. I communicated more than enough, or too little. People didn't feel involved enough, and others felt we were too participative. Some people wanted to stay the course we were on, and others felt there was no excitement and not enough change.

As we became more systematic in the 1980s with our planning process, it too generated more complaints that led to more complexity in our relationships. The process wasn't facilitating change; it wasn't looking into the future far enough; it wasn't looking at alternatives to our current business model; it was adding complexity. We were averaging 20 percent growth per annum. From my perspective, the brand and the process weren't broke.

JOHN FINDLAY: It was just too much, too detailed, too much writing and rewriting, strengths and weaknesses and opportunities and threats and on and on and on . . . We had 125 strengths and 130 weaknesses. Then for each strength and weakness, you had to put together a plan to make that at least into a neutral and hopefully a strength.

Some thought we lacked the "vision thing," as another president once said. Visions were popular at the time. People wanted a vision of the future, although there was little agreement on what form it should take, and I thought I had already given them one: the company's value-based business model built on our aspirations of meeting all of our responsibilities to all of our stakeholders, using the planning process to continuously improve our execution. Apparently the words lacked something, because people kept asking me, "Where's the vision?"

BOB PEIXOTTO: The planning process was very much of a continuous improvement model. So every year you were trying to get better on every aspect of the business. It was a build-one-year-to-the-next model. If someone were being critical, you might say it was a somewhat tactical approach to strategic planning versus the leapfrog kind of thinking. Several times in the time that I worked with Leon, people would ask him in large group meetings, "Leon, where do you see the company five years from now or ten years from now?" And a very standard answer he would give was, "I don't see the future of this company in terms of numbers or bricks and mortar. I see this company in terms of, are we continuing to live the values that we have assumed as a company and are we meeting our customers' needs in the fashion that they would like us to meet them?" It was about that. It wasn't about a billion dollars by 1997 or anything like that. We never had those kinds of rallying cries.

The difference was that I never saw the planning process as something a company did for a short while and then stopped, as it implemented the plan. To my mind, planning was an unending cycle of plan-implement-review-plan-implement-review, with no clearcut end or beginning, no big book you could put on your shelf and never open. We had operating plans and budgets and strategic initiatives, but they were periodic outputs of the ongoing process, spun off at various points.

> BILL END: I personally had a hard time with our planning process just because of the level of detail that we went into. It was more planning by the numbers, planning by a process, rather than planning with the specific goal of getting a plan in place and executing on it . . . We never were able to get from the planning process to, "What are we going to do tomorrow morning?"

As I said earlier, the process was the plan and some people couldn't or wouldn't accept that. Most did. I should have called it our management process. It was just the way we managed L.L.Bean. Maybe I should have said, "This is how we set up corporate strategies and goals and how we measure ourselves against our goals and how these translate down into individual responsibilities." It was the sort of work you'd expect a manager to do. Everything fit within the process. It wasn't part of the job. It was the job.

> MARK FASOLD: I think many times . . . you would hear people say that it was too process oriented . . . I think it was very conscious on Leon's part . . . That's how he managed the business. If you weren't willing to go along with that, you could object to some of it . . . [But] if you wanted to affect how things were going to happen, you had to learn to operate within that.

Any group of people, especially if they're ambitious and capable, will have differences and usually will find ways to work around them or to function in spite of them. For most of this period, from the mid-1970s through the 1980s, we in senior management at L.L.Bean managed to work together effectively—not perfectly, but a lot of good things happened and they didn't happen by chance.

> BOB PEIXOTTO: Leon used to talk a lot about Theory X and Theory Y management. He wanted to create a company that was high on Theory Y, that was a warm and inviting place for somebody

to come and have a career. He wanted to have a place that would develop superior shareholder returns, that would have an out-standing reputation in the community, would be modern, up-to-date, efficient, and would have an appeal that would give it a pathway of reasonable growth . . . There's a vignette that always made me believe that Leon was trying to create the model com-pany. In the mid-eighties we opened a new manufacturing facility in Brunswick, Maine. And it was unlike any kind of manufactur-ing facility that you would have seen in Maine in that era. It had windows, it had a fitness center and a locker room. It was really a very nice working area, bright, light, airy, lots of safety features, etc. And I remember walking through with Leon. Several of us went up there for a tour once it was first opened. And I remember him turning to me and saying, "Well, this will be interesting, to see if this works, to invest this kind of money in a manufacturing fa-cility and see if we get the response from employees that Theory Y management would say you ought to get." That comment says, here's a guy who's experimenting with, "How far can I push this thing and make it work?"

But the emerging leadership issue was whether or not you believed in the core values and the lifestyle concept and the idea of L.L.Bean adding value for all of its stakeholders, or you believed L.L.Bean was a business like any other whose sole purpose was to maximize the bottom line. It wasn't an either/or question but a matter of balance between the two points of view. Senior management and I were beginning to dis-agree on where the balance point was.

JOHN FINDLAY: Turns out that Bill would be telling his people to do things, either from a marketing or product perspective, that Leon would countermand or say, "What the hell! Where'd you get this from?" . . . It was enough times so that the next level down . . . those people would grouse about and observe daily that Bill would be telling them one thing and Leon would be telling them another. You know, what the hell are they supposed to be doing?

But as differences in approach to the business or its purpose emerged, there arose an issue that came to be called "divided leadership" by the next level of vice presidents, or at least by some of them.

CHRIS MCCORMICK: Part of the problem I remember back then was clarity of goals going down the organization. Here am I in the marketing department and I'm told, through Bill End, that I have to improve profitability of our catalogs. OK. I'm going to improve profitability, I'm going to cut pages out of these camping books, and I'm going to cut circ and no fly-fishing, blah, blah. Then I present the plan to Leon thinking, OK, everybody's on board, and he says, "Why are you cutting pages out of fly-fishing?" [Laughter] "Well, I'm trying to improve profitability, right?" "No, we're trying to grow fly-fishing." That would happen all the time, and there was that tension in the organization around "So what is the goal?" That's one area that I think caused a lot of frustration, because there were clearly two voices back then. Bill End had both marketing and merchandising reporting to him. But, really, Leon ran merchandising. My sense of what happened was Bill was giving the direction to the marketing people to go for profit and then Leon's trying to grow the sporting goods business because that's his love and he's thinking of the brand. You could go through your work process to a point where Leon approves the advertising plan. Boom. Brick wall. Plus, Bill End's in that meeting too. So if I'm presenting to Leon and Bill End's right there and Leon asks me, "So why did you cut the pages out of the fly-fishing book?" I can't say, "Bill told me to do it." So I said, "Okay, well, I'm just trying to improve profitability." It didn't take many times to decide I'm not going to run up that hill again . . . Eventually I got to the point where I would circle into Leon's office. Not that I'm circumventing Bill, but Leon liked to look at creative and didn't mind someone just knocking on his door and saying, "Here, what do you think of this new ad?" He'd give me his feedback. And then either I or he would use that opportunity to say, "So, you know, what's the fly-fishing ad plan look like this year?"

. . . So there was some of that going on, but I think Bill End was trying to do the right thing in pushing for profitability and trying to maintain a balance and please the shareholders and so forth. But, boy, was there tension between the two of them, and you could cut it with a knife, and it just got worse and worse over time.

The 1980s brought high growth to L.L.Bean and high levels of excitement. But we'd lost a lot of our productivity. Things had become too complex. Our market position was showing drift and ambiguity. Further divisions were emerging in our leadership group. Between 1985 and 1988 our annual growth rates had averaged 23 percent. But in 1989 our sales increase dropped to 3.5 percent and our ROE to 13 percent. The country was in a recession and so were we.

The falloff in sales and profitability created a great deal of anxiety in our management group, even more than the slowdown in the early 1980s. Not only were jobs and bonuses suddenly in jeopardy, but our confidence in L.L.Bean was shaken. Apart from the economy's downturn there was disagreement, especially in the marketing department, on the falloff's internal causes and in our ability to turn the situation around.

BILL END: I think the first slowdown [in the early eighties] was moving away from the fashion trends. That one was pretty clearly explained. The second one was more of a concern, because I don't think we were as clear on why. I also think we had played a lot of the cards . . . so we didn't have as many cards to play that were easy. And it was more challenging . . . Towards the end you're starting to really tweak this analysis and you're working like hell for every point of growth and it's not easy.

The marketing department was at odds internally, with different VPs blaming each other for the slowdown and not working together to get through it. We had Jim Mahoney do an intervention. One vice president wrote a three-page memo listing all the issues, plus a lot of doom and gloom. They'd gotten carried away with pessimism. Several key people left the company in that time frame. It lasted about three years. A lot of people saw Bill and me not pulling together during the slowdown.

MARK FASOLD: Back in the early eighties, it was a smaller, tighter group [of senior managers, and] it led to quicker, faster turnaround actions. In the late eighties [the slowdown] seemed to really push people apart as opposed to bring them together. There was not that sense of people taking accountability, responsibility, around this one . . . If a team's not a team and things like that go wrong, then they bust apart a lot faster.

We'd had that controlled growth notion in our heads—that simply through managing catalog circulation we could achieve whatever rate of growth we wanted. The realization that we couldn't was a big part of the pessimism this time around. I don't think we had lost any confidence in our direct marketing abilities in the previous slowdown. Our only problem then was getting back to basics by using the Best strategy and resolving our lifestyle merchandising approach and turning up the circulation. It was not so easy this time. We couldn't go back to basics again, and there were no more obvious new circulation opportunities. We weren't bringing in enough new customers. There were memos, meetings, and informal discussions, with all elements of our marketing and merchandising efforts in play.

CHRIS MCCORMICK: I was a director in 1989 and I'm looking at the vice president group and it was like a Chinese fire drill. They didn't know what was going on or how to respond to it. That was the time where the relationship between Bill and Leon got even worse and [vice presidents] may have been feeling like they weren't getting any direction. We could really feel it, the layer right below that. You would see it directly in meetings. You couldn't get a decision, and there would be debates within the VP group about, "Well, I don't know what to do," you know—sort of washing their hands of the whole thing.

We sensed that our marketplace had changed, along with its perceptions of L.L.Bean and of our relevance to their lives. Our creative presentations had become dated as competitors put a lot more effort into fancy layouts and clever copy. This seemed to appeal more to the maturing baby boomers, now ages thirty to forty-five. In 1987, *USA Today* observed, "L.L.Bean is like family—a mildly eccentric but amiable uncle who lives up in Maine and sends us packages."[2] Not exactly an exciting and up-to-date image in the super-competitive retail world of the 1990s. I feared that the L.L. story was losing its mystique.

I remember sitting down at the time and reviewing all our 1990 catalogs, page by page. I thought they were OK; they had a lot of color, an outdoors attitude, credible assortments of equipment, and strong editorial support of our product and service positioning. I liked them. Maybe that was indicative of the problem. Maybe I wasn't the great merchant I thought I was. Maybe my intuition wasn't as informed or up-to-date as it should have been. In any event our customers weren't buying from our catalogs. There was a disconnect that we needed to understand. According to our research, customers liked us but we didn't seem to have the products they wanted. The theory of our customers being people like us was no longer working.

As previously noted, our main problem was that we weren't merchandising effectively to our women customers. They had become the gatekeepers to family purchasing and we were not appealing to them. I don't think I fully understood the implications of this.

> RON CAMPO: I think one of the biggest struggles the company had was with the women's business . . . Bean was built as an outdoors company and the apparel position was primarily men's in its early years. It did offer women's sizing. . . [in] Chamois Shirts or Maine hunting boots, the core functional L.L.Bean items . . . The issue that was contested and where there were divergent points of view was to what degree should Bean grow a women's-only business.

Given our success in the 1970s and 1980s, I was reluctant to give up strategies and a business model that had worked so well. The idea of a continuously improving line of products, catalog displays, and customer services, supported by the most advanced direct marketing and circulation building techniques, was hard to change. We had a dilemma. We had to do something different, but as *U.S. News* had pointed out in a 1985 piece on L.L.Bean, "Change always has received mixed reviews from Bean customers, who worry that innovations will compromise the company's Down East simplicity."[3]

BILL END: Leon asked us to get together as a planning group, which we did, and we came back with a plan that had a lot of the things I articulated—the store, acquisition, be more aggressive on the kids' business, things like that, that I believed would have turned the business around, though not necessarily under the Bean brand. Some of them would have been outside the Bean brand and some would have been the retail approach.

Naturally, talk of going retail came up again as the answer to our sales slump. I was even more opposed than in the past. The old reasons for not going retail were still valid. We didn't have the retail merchandising skills or mind-set; nor the logistical systems and operating know-how; nor the confidence that our product assortments and rate of product turnover would translate to a retail environment; nor the financial capacity to invest in a major retail expansion. In addition it made no sense to me to make this kind of shift in our business model during a period of sales weakness. We had to solve that first, long before any retail strategy could come to supplement our catalog business.

MARK FASOLD: When the slowdown occurred, 1989, Bill End pulled his team together, which I was a member of. We came forth with a fairly big presentation on what to do next with the company. That didn't go well. It was in the old conference room here. You could just tell it wasn't something that Leon warmed up to.

I acknowledge the irony of not wanting to go retail previously, when we were in a position of strength. Then it was because we still saw plenty of growth opportunity in direct marketing. This time, in the 1989–1990 slowdown, I simply did not want to go retail. Every intuition I had told me it was the wrong thing to do.

JOHN FINDLAY: I think that was when all of us felt that the only way out was going to be retail . . . [and] that's when, essentially, Leon said, "No way" to retail. [In the past,] he'd said, "No way, until we slow down and there's no other way out." I think most of us felt, "Okay. Now we're here. This is the time we've all dreaded." And I think he put his head down and said, "Retail's not going to happen right now." It was a big disappointment. I remember thinking that

that was a betrayal. It was a betrayal of . . . betrayal is not quite the right word, but we had hung on that . . . Things slow down, the one way to grow is through retail. So that was a disappointment, for sure, I think, for all of us. Certainly Bill End, myself.

Those of us running the company had done well through the first slowdown in the early 1980s. The most pressing issue then had been whether we should become a casual apparel organization like our traditional competitors Lands' End and Eddie Bauer, or continue to be an outdoors lifestyle company. But among us senior managers it wasn't a divisive issue. Bill and I agreed, and I think John agreed as well, that the outdoors heritage was key. At least we needed to maintain that part of the heritage, and we needed to keep casual apparel under control and not let it dominate the company's brand and brand positioning. Our differences over retail expansion would go away with new growth in the 1980s.

But this time things were different. Maybe it was because we all were ten years older and looking for new directions. And we didn't have a shared aspiration. I still wanted to find ways to perpetuate the traditional L.L.Bean.

The idea of being more Bean with more relevant products, better execution in all areas, and finding a more unique and up-to-date positioning appealed to me. Bill and John favored retail expansion as our vehicle for growth and were less committed to the lifestyle concept. Perhaps it was the time in their careers to do something new. Bill was certainly ready to run his own company, and I had no thoughts of stepping down.

> JIM MAHONEY: Bill was brought in specifically to eventually take over from Leon. That never happened. Bill eventually got frustrated waiting around and decided to go off with something else. That was quite understandable . . . I think eventually it became too frustrating for Bill and he talked about when a guy gets to be mature enough to run his own business. Bill eventually got to that point.

I think our coming apart as a management team had less to do with what we should do than how we should do it. I was certainly less convinced of the retail objective than Bill or John and more inclined than ever to a planning process of evaluating all the options and bringing in some new ways of thinking. I still believed in the fundamental approaches that had brought us this far, but I sensed that L.L.Bean needed something more basic than expansion of our retail operation. I was inclined more than ever to adopt a process of bringing in new ways of thinking. Bill and John wanted retail, I think, and not what they considered just more process.

BILL END: In 1990 Leon and I agreed it was time for me to leave the company and I submitted my resignation. We had come to disagree more and more on the future growth direction for the business.

The three-year plan that our management/planning group submitted to Leon recommended that the company open flagship retail stores, acquire other catalog businesses, and develop new businesses. Leon was very uncomfortable with these growth directions and decided not to accept the three-year plan.

My frustration at the time was that I did not feel we were growing the business to its full potential. I felt we had the potential to be a $5 to $10 billion business. If you could take Bean's market penetration in the Northeast and replicate even half that level of penetration nationally, we could have been a $5 billion business. That is frustrating to me because there are not many businesses in the world that have the potential to grow to $5 to $10 billion.

I stayed at L.L.Bean, Inc. for fifteen years and saw the business grow from $24 million to $650 million. My years with the company were the most fun, exciting, and challenging years of my professional career. During those years I developed great respect for Leon's leadership and direction for the business. Leon did a hell of a job as CEO and as the top merchant in the business. He kept the business focused and maintained the integrity of the brand through the 1970s and 1980s and for that he deserves a lot of credit.

In my opinion L.L.Bean is a great brand; it is a very successful, highly ethical business; it has always maintained a customer focus and a clear focus on its employees; and it has always maintained a clear vision for the business. The company was a great business in the 1970s and 1980s and continues to be a great business today.

During our ten to fifteen years together we created without exaggeration one of the most successful and most admired companies in America. Bill became the most highly respected marketer in the direct marketing industry.

And John achieved the highest levels of customer service anywhere. He could be cantankerous at times but always had the highest respect of those who worked for him and with him.

JOHN FINDLAY: I was beginning to recognize, I said to myself that I wasn't getting the job done as well as I used to, in late eighty-eight, eighty-nine. And I gave Leon eight months' notice or something, to try and find someone else . . . because Bill End left and we were short. To this day it was my best business experience, and Bean as a company, I really respect it and cherish it, even though we had some tough conversations over the whole thing. I was unhappy and he knew it. So I left.

Norm Poole, who left a few years later, had been a steady source of advice and counsel to all of us. And he made sure our financial structure was as solid as our business reputation.

It was the most remarkable period in the history of L.L.Bean. But that era was ending. Our senior group had come together in the 1970s when the company was moving beyond $30 million in sales. Now at $600 million plus, a lot had changed. We'd been the right combination for the 1980s, but we weren't the right combination for the 1990s. We'd grown older in a stimulating and gratifying business environment, but that was changing. And we'd grown apart in our ideas on what a business was all about, and especially L.L.Bean.

PART FOUR

1991–2000

Continental Rucksack

11

TQ and Other Ventures

A S WE ENTERED the 1990s I knew there'd be some changes
made. I wouldn't call them transformational because I still saw lots
of promise in the traditional Bean business model. But they'd be substantial, and they'd change a lot of our ways of doing business. It wasn't a matter of survival. L.L.Bean was more durable and long-wearing than that.

We'd met the challenge of L.L.'s passing in the 1960s and had institutionalized his story. We'd met the challenge of growth in the 1970s
without spoiling L.L.Bean. And we'd met the challenge of professional
management and fashion and further growth in the 1980s. We'd figure
out how to deal with the 1990s.

We had taken up Total Quality (also called Total Quality Management, or TQM) in the late 1980s to prepare for the new decade. We saw
TQ as a change strategy. It would take us to more productive levels of
performance and yet allow us to retain the L.L.Bean core values and
persona. A new chapter in the L.L. story. It had the potential to revitalize our leadership and to engage everyone at L.L.Bean in an exciting and
successful future. We had high aspirations. We had a kick-off.

In 1990, L.L.Bean sponsored the Mt. Everest Peace Climb, led by
Jim Whittaker, who in 1963 had been the first American on Mt. Everest.

Jim was also a man of strong character, great courage, and magnetic personality. He made the peace climb a reality, from concept to logistics to training the climbers to ultimate success on the summit of Everest.

I had first met Jim at the Woolrich Outdoors Hall of Fame in 1980. In 1987 he invited me to join a small group he was leading on a climb of Mt. Rainier. At 14,300 feet, it was by far the biggest mountain I'd ever climbed, and it was everything I'd anticipated and more: massive glaciers and crevasses; huge seracs hanging overhead; high winds that blew down our tents; and step-by-step steepness heading to the summit, snow up to our thighs. It was a beautiful bright blue day, with Mt. St. Helens still smoking off in the distance.

Jim's idea for the peace climb was to have a team of the best climbers from the United States, Russia, and China climb Mt. Everest together as an example of cooperative teamwork among the cold war countries. In addition it was to celebrate the twentieth anniversary of Earth Day by having the climbers, on the way down, clean up a lot of the debris left by previous climbers. (It turned out to be three tons of trash.)

The peace climb seemed a natural fit with L.L.Bean. It was outdoors and active, and it added a little bit of excitement we needed in Freeport. As a major sponsor, we furnished financial support and most of the gear. The climb would illustrate the quality of our products as well as our commitment to a clean environment.

In March 1990 the climbers traveled to Beijing and on to base camp in Tibet. I joined a group of trekkers who would also go to base camp and observe the goings-on. My brother, Jim, was in the group, and he and I were two of six trekkers to huff and puff our way to Camp III at 22,000 feet. It was heavy going on the Rongbuk Glacier.

Severe weather (including winds of 100 miles per hour) delayed summit day for our peace climbers on Mt. Everest into May, and on the seventh, six members of our international team reached the summit. Within three days the rest of the team, another fourteen climbers, summited, for one of the most successful Mt. Everest expeditions ever. Jim Whittaker had made a dramatic statement on behalf of world peace. We were proud to be part of it.

Back home we had another mountain to climb. Our sales were stagnating, our productivity was declining, and our mailing list, the lifeblood of a catalog company, was not growing. And we had a new management group to break in.

The U.S. economy, which had slowed in the late 1980s, was going into a recession in the early 1990s. Gross domestic product (GDP) was more or less flat. Consumer confidence had fallen like a rock to its lowest level in years. In 1990, the Harris Bank of Chicago said that because of too many stores competing for consumer dollars, the next ten years would be among the toughest for retailers since the Great Depression. The recession lasted through late 1992. It was a dismal retailing environment, with 1990 being the worst year for retail and for L.L.Bean in a decade.

> BOB PEIXOTTO: A significant emotional event for the company happened in 1991 when we had our first reduction in force. We lost some good people who left the company. Bill Booth, who was the head of marketing, and Mark Fasold, who was the head of inventory management and one of the architects of our planning process, and others. It was the beginning of the changing of the guard, I guess. We went through a period actually where the senior management began to roll over in the organization and really didn't stabilize fully, I would say, for years.

The baby boomers were maturing and having their own families. The backpackers of the 1970s had become the family campers of the 1990s. In response to the baby boomlet, most, if not all, specialty retailers (Gap, Talbots, etc.) and catalogers (Lands' End, Eddie Bauer, and L.L.Bean) got into the kids' business. When the boomers showed their domestic side with an interest in enhancing their home lives (called "cocooning" by some), there was a similar mass migration to home furnishings. Rugged wear was now an established apparel category, one of a few that were showing signs of life. We had new friends joining us in our marketplace. People were desperately trying to find ways to grow. (We even tried selling dog food by mail.)

U.S. companies were perceived to be a little short on the quality side. It was symbolized by our automobiles, which didn't have the reliability of the Japanese cars. And consumers had increasingly higher expectations for product and service quality. As a result there was a lot of interest and effort by U.S. companies to improve the quality of whatever they did and an eagerness to find the best ways to do it. The quality movement emerged, along with the Malcolm Baldrige National Quality Award. Many of the leading U.S. companies got involved.

Many U.S. mail-order retailers with the requisite high quality standards (e.g., Talbots, J.Crew, Williams Sonoma, and REI) were launching their catalogs in Japan and often with the cooperative support of Japanese partners. There was a great and growing popularity among Japanese consumers for the "American look" and for strong American brands. They had a lot of disposable income and a very strong currency, the yen, to deal with.

In addition, in the early 1990s Home Shopping Network and QVC were selling lots of merchandise over TV. An interest in television shopping and other electronic media was beginning to build—not only direct TV but also interactive TV, CD-ROM catalogs, the PC-based Prodigy shopping service, kiosks, and something called the World Wide Web. Nobody knew where the "new media" might go and there was wild speculation. But something important was going on, and we stayed informed on all the major tests and participated in some.

President Reagan had announced the Malcolm Baldrige National Quality Award in 1988. I attended the White House ceremony. I was impressed with the presentation and with the idea itself. Total Quality (as the quality movement was called) promised that high quality and high productivity go together. There is no trade-off. This was the kind of productivity strategy we were looking for.

> BOB PEIXOTTO: The way Total Quality looks at cost is you have failure costs in an organization, you have prevention costs, and you have inspection costs. And the way the theory works, and we saw some of it here, is if avoiding a problem costs you $1, having a problem actually created, say, in a factory, and catching it through inspection costs you $10, and actually having it get into the hands of a customer costs you $100. They call it the 1, 10, 100 rule. What we came to learn is we had too much failure cost in the organization and were spending a lot of time on the 100 scale, and if we could move upstream we could save money.

We applied for a Baldrige Quality Award that first year. Win or lose, we would use the process as a learning experience on Total Quality and the results as a mandate for moving ahead.

Our Baldrige Award application contained 169 pages of narrative and data. I think the weight of the document as well as its content got us into the finals. Then there was a three-day site visit by Baldrige Award inspectors to validate our application claims and to develop firsthand insights into the core quality dimensions of L.L.Bean. There were awards for manufacturing companies and for service companies, including retail. We were the highest-ranked service company, so we were told, but we did not receive a National Quality Award. We were judged to be "world class" in our commitment and ability to achieve customer satisfaction in our products, services, and communications. But being best in these areas was not enough.

Baldrige said we were deficient because we had an inspection-oriented approach to quality. We were reactive and not proactive; we didn't focus on getting it right the first time. The inspection team concluded that our organization was not fully involved at all levels through appropriate delegation and interdepartmental teamwork. In addition, it found limited use of contemporary quality methods and techniques at L.L.Bean. As a consequence, we had not maximized our quality efforts and had not achieved productivity benefits by reducing the costs of poor quality.

It would have been nice to win the award, but I really needed the mandate to move ahead. The Baldrige process gave us this.

We considered Total Quality a way to address our basic problems without changing our basic character or our fundamental values, persona, and product mix. TQ was the logical way to take our Best strategy to the next level, while simultaneously improving productivity. We needed to find the synergies between productivity and quality in all of our activities and relationships. After many years of rapid growth, sales growth was now to be secondary to productivity improvements. (Achieving sales growth would have been very expensive, in any case, given the low-growth economy and increasingly competitive retail environment.)

I still had confidence in our business model and our positioning in the retail marketplace. I felt our overall strategies were still correct, but we just weren't executing properly. That included especially my concern that we weren't merchandising as well as we knew how. I felt we could correct this with new leaders, new energy, and a new Total Quality environment. I was starting to be more receptive to new ideas, and TQ was one avenue to open up the thought process throughout L.L.Bean.

With the turnover of many of our senior managers, we could deal with our command-and-control leadership style and the lack of empowerment of managers below the senior level. Our climate studies continued to show that there was frustration in the managerial ranks about not having decision-making power. To restore productivity and enhance quality, it was important that we change the management culture to make it truly more participative. TQ would make our management culture more inclusive and team-based while reversing operating expense trends and maintaining or improving product and service quality standards.

The new senior managers who joined L.L.Bean in the early 1990s were a mix of outsiders and people who had been promoted internally. They were experienced managers, and all professed the L.L.Bean values and support for TQ, although most had inherited the Total Quality strategy and had not been part of its design.

There were two basic approaches to a Total Quality environment. The traditional way was to apply industrial engineering techniques using lots of process measurement and statistics. There was also the behavioral way: changing a company's culture in the way it does things through lots of training and practice.

We thought that you had to change people's behavior first before you could really get into process improvement, that you'd be hitting a stone wall if people weren't sold on the principles of TQ in their efforts to improve work processes. So we started with empowerment, using a variety of approaches that sought improvements throughout the organization by empowering those actually doing the work. We trained 3,570 L.L.Bean people in Total Quality using 722 flip charts and lots of facilitation. Internal customer relationships were established companywide. Cooperation and confidence improved with participation.

Much of our initial TQ work was meant to break down functional barriers and teach people how to be good interdepartmental customers and suppliers. Employees throughout the company held customer-supplier meetings with whomever they dealt with in the organization, making sure they were doing their part well and getting critiqued in return. Quality Action Teams (QATs) were organized to solve specific problems in the members' own areas. We couldn't do our best for our external customers if we weren't doing our best for our internal customers.

> BOB PEIXOTTO: Quality Action Teams or QATs were teams of employees that we really unleashed throughout the organization to work on specific issues that needed to be worked on. In each area people picked some topics that they thought needed work and we put employees on trying to solve the problems . . . I would say the teams were loosely managed. You could do a Quality Action Team on, to use an absurd example, fixing the company picnic. It really wasn't driving business results.

Given our history of command and control, our managers hated to give up control and a familiar way of working to the Quality Action Teams or to delegate to lower levels. Turf battles flared up. Lower-level QATs lacked the empowerment, as well as the confidence, to make hard decisions. We had many prioritization problems because we resisted telling QATs what to do. People at organization levels and in functional areas pointed to each other as not behaving in a "Total Quality way" (including pointing at me, although I felt I was playing the complete Total Quality role). TQ threatened to become a behavioral game and a way to run meetings. Direct linkages to cost savings were few.

> CHRIS MCCORMICK: There was a lot of skepticism in the organization about, "Is this really what we need to turn the business around? Is this really going to help us be a leader in the industry or give us competitive advantage?"

Maybe we'd promised too much too soon. Our quality guru, David Garvin—Harvard Business School professor and author of the very helpful book *Managing Quality*—was saying it might take us five years to be a Total Quality company.[1] We were learning as an organization. But our people wanted to be the best now and earn their bonuses *this* year. There was a lot of skepticism in senior management, especially among the marketing people, who were less impacted than the operations managers.

> CHRIS MCCORMICK: I think, looking back, it really died for lack of support in the organization. I think if you were to ask a sample of managers from the early nineties, "How did TQ change the way you did business, how you did your jobs, and what impact did that have on the business?" I bet you 99 percent would say, "I have no clue. I didn't do anything with it."

We persevered. Things began coming into focus in 1991. David Garvin said we'd unfrozen the status quo and were in the middle step of reshaping the organization.

> BOB PEIXOTTO: As we approached the mid-nineties, we focused on business processes and business process improvement. We defined the key processes of the organization and looked at where the biggest issues were in our core processes. At that point teams evolved from being Quality Action Teams to being called Business Process Improvement, or BPI, teams whose goal was to make significant improvements in those business processes. This is phase two of TQ at Bean. We created a significant number of BPI teams and I think made some significant change to the organization. For example, we had one that focused on merchandising, and another that focused on moving goods from our vendors to here.

It was time to change from our initial approach of problem solving by Quality Action Teams and behavioral change to a longer-term, more fundamental systems engineering strategy built on business processes. Strategic Process Management (SPM) was more of a top-down approach. We tried to involve senior management more in overseeing the process improvement initiatives so that they could help with setting priorities and coming to conclusions.

> BOB PEIXOTTO: Strategic Process Management was really taking Business Process Improvement into a much more full strategic realm, since it was totally managed by the Executive Committee,

and everything had to be tied to a core business process, with the teams focusing on the highest priorities within each process.

We brought in some consultants to help us design an SPM program to reengineer (the term of the day) the various critical processes that constituted what we did as an enterprise. The processes always cut horizontally across the organization and involved more than one function or department. The idea was to standardize the horizontal processes, define accountabilities at the intersections with the vertical organization, and provide an opportunity to improve the way the process worked after an assessment of weak spots.

There were six overarching processes: finding and retaining customers, communicating to customers, developing products for customers, merchandising products for customers, serving customers, and guaranteeing satisfaction.

The major cost savings were in longer-term projects, but there were a fair number of near-term "early harvest" opportunities. Our pilot program was our catalog production process ("communicating to customers") and the critical path that was behind all of our other processes.

I really liked this productivity concept. Strategic Process Management had a lot of disciplined but practical techniques, was well structured, relied on hard numbers, and addressed the logic of the company's model and strategic goals. It was customer focused. SPM would take advantage of the positive TQ behaviors and principles we had learned. It promised to be the overall productivity strategy we were looking for and the culmination of our TQ concept.

As important as TQ was to us and our overall strategy, there was much more going on in the early 1990s: a variety of major product line extensions and new distribution channels, more than we had ever taken on before.

Japan. We began doing a lot of mail-order business overseas, particularly in Japan. Japanese consumers had discovered us and were willing to pay the shipping and put up with the long delivery times. And with the strong yen, Japanese tourists were also coming to Freeport by the busload to shop the store. It was no secret there was a lot of Japanese interest in American brands. Our products were fashionable and cheap to Japanese consumers—not exactly our desired positioning, but there it was. (We also met their high quality standards.) There was considerable interest in environmentalism and outdoor recreation in Japan, and that worked to our advantage.

Two large Japanese companies, one a major retailer, wanted to partner with us and open retail stores (approximately 10,000 square feet) in Japan. When we met with the Japanese they talked about how important the L.L. story, product quality, and superior service were to them. It sounded good to us. The partnership would also give us an opportunity to learn more about the retail business. (The Japanese are mainly retail shoppers.) We signed an agreement in 1992. The Japanese media made much of our product assortments, the outdoors, and the heritage of L.L.

The first store in Japan did 40 percent over plan, and by 1995 we had four Japanese stores, all nicely merchandised with core and "authentic" L.L.Bean products (the Bean Boot, Fleece Jackets, Boat and Tote Bags, etc.), including active sports gear. L.L.'s Golden Rule was displayed prominently near the entrance. These stores represented the L.L.Bean persona very well, and we trained all the store managers in L.L.Bean's customer service policies. We also opened a catalog customer service phone center and distribution center in Japan, and the catalog was printed in Japanese, all to support our growing mail-order business.

E-Commerce. In 1994 we named a director of "Media Technologies." His job was to keep abreast of what was going on in the world of "new media," as it was called. The emerging technologies included CD-ROM (catalogs on CDs) as well as online shopping by computer, conventional network shopping on television, and, potentially, interactive television shopping. We were doing what everybody else was doing to make sure we weren't caught napping. Postal rates were increasing markedly, and we were looking to supplement the catalog channel with any kind of alternative media that made sense.

The World Wide Web became available to us in 1995. We (along with thousands of other catalogers and retailers) were quick to launch our own Web site that fall, featuring information about L.L.Bean, new and core products, outdoor sports, and a special section on national parks. The ability to change content quickly was most welcome, given the lengthy seasonal commitments to the content of our printed catalogs. But we couldn't guarantee secure credit card transactions and could only refer Web users to our catalogs or call center.

Visitors to our site numbered 175,000 that first fall, and we got lots of positive feedback on the look and feel of our site. Creatively the design and content looked like L.L.Bean to our customers, and they endorsed our focus on making it easy to use and reminding them of Maine. In 1996 we installed a secure ordering system. The first order was from a woman in Alaska for a pair of Gore-Tex Day Hiker boots. We received 1.5 million visitors that year, 70 percent of them new to L.L.Bean.

By 1997 we were also on our third director of e-commerce, the first two (and most of their staffs) having joined the nomadic world of dotcom "experts." This one, however, was a committed Beaner and stayed with us. She made our site one of the most highly regarded by industry experts and most successfully regarded by our customers.

The reason for our success was a continuing commitment to making our Web site faster, easier to use, more informative, and 100 percent focused on customer needs. In 2000 we did $164 million in revenues on our site, or 15 percent of our total sales, and were still growing. The *New York Times* called us "an E-Commerce star" and attributed our success to "a stubborn adherence to customer service and a steadfast refusal to let excessive technological wizardry interfere with [our] shoppers' experience on the web site."[2]

Women's Products. On the product side, our women's apparel line and thinking were repositioned. Women were clearly the gatekeepers for household spending, and if we couldn't meet their own needs we'd handicap our relationship with the whole family. Much of the questionable women's product was in the "dressy casual" end of things—leftovers from the preppy boom, and frumpy in many people's eyes—and didn't fit the L.L.Bean outdoors positioning. (There was, however, still a lot of sales volume in this dressy casual area—sales we were determined to give up.)

The solution was to include more products for women's weekend and outdoor sports activities, including petite sizing. We were not the source for career apparel, and the tailored women's product confused a lot of people. But we did need more style in our casual product, and more up-to-date, coordinated, and wearable colors.

BRAD KAUFFMAN: I was in product development at a time when the woman's version of an item was tweaked ever so slightly. You designed the jacket for men and you resized it and maybe threw in pink for women. It looked like a man's garment fitted for a woman, but it still looked like a man's garment. So we got to the point where we realized, there's no part of our strategy or brand identity that requires that, for God's sake. If we're going to do a program for women, it should be right for women. And that doesn't mean you can just take the men's item and resize it. You need to think about the silhouette and the materials and where seams are. The notion of a woman's version of a man's item became a whole different concept.

We produced a women's-only catalog, as well as a catalog exclusively for outdoorswomen.

Most women customers in the mid-1990s liked the direction of our repositioning. They liked the changes in our assortment, the updated styling, and the better color selection. But they felt we had a ways to go to be fully relevant to their lifestyles and their need for more style as well as function in their apparel.

Active Sports. Our outdoors gear grew significantly in the mid-1990s. We put a special effort into developing new and extra-functional products for the intermediate-level participant as well as offering the best value possible for the entry-level outdoors person. These were the areas where Bean belonged, for "people like us" who enjoyed the outdoors and wanted equipment that worked for them at a reasonable price. Product introductions included our Mountain Guide Parka, Micro Light Tent, Gore-Tex Cresta Hiking Shoes, Burrito Sleeping Bag, New Englander Shot Gun, and Aqua Stealth Wading Shoes for fly fishing. We even redesigned the Bean Boot with a new injection-molded rubber bottom that was more abrasion resistant, slip resistant, and puncture-proof than the longtime vulcanized model, as well as lighter in weight and better fitting. The upper leather was from a more waterproof tannage. We were able to reduce the price by $6.

Kids' Apparel. We introduced our line of children's apparel in 1993. It had been talked about for several years, but this time we had a merchant with a vision, a lot of energy, and a lot of talent. We also had a company goal to serve the entire family, not just mom or dad. Initially we kid-sized our most popular adult products, such as our Flannel Lined Jeans, Rugby Shirts, and Bean Boots. We wanted to keep our kids warm and dry in the outdoors. And nothing cute. We did, however, evolve to an assortment that acquiesced to the ever-changing styling needs of kids but always remained functional and durable. L.L. Kids, as it became known, did $14 million in its first year, was up 137 percent the next year, and grew at healthy double-digit rates for the rest of the 1990s.

Home Products. For years L.L.Bean had sold woolen blankets, the most popular being the Hudson's Bay. We also sold snowshoe furniture, kitchen cutlery, horseshoe sets, and the like—products that an outdoors family might have at its camp on the lake or cottage on the seashore or maybe even use at home. The origins were L.L.'s lifestyle approach to selling whatever he liked and used, whether at home or camp or in the field. As he wrote in his Spring 1927 catalog, "Put a pair of horseshoe stakes out near your camp or cottage and note how quickly your place becomes popular."

This line of home products seemed a natural part of L.L.Bean and a category we could do more with. First our people set some Bean-ness guidelines as to what was appropriate for the L.L.Bean home or cottage, such as "friendly and comfortable," "outdoors oriented," "functional and problem solving," "durable," "for the whole family," and so on. This enabled us to go beyond our classic Boat and Tote Bags, flannel sheets, and dog beds to Mission Futons, bed and bath products, and a full range of outdoor living furniture, lawn games, and gardening accessories. Our home business doubled in the decade.

Customer Satisfaction. We continued to improve our customer service. When I first came to L.L.Bean in the 1960s, a customer who mailed in an order one week started thinking about receiving the package the following week, and only if it didn't show up the third week would they start to worry about its status. By the 1990s, with 800 numbers, warehousing technology, and a series of logistical miracles by the package-delivery people, when you phoned in an order you started thinking about receiving it in a matter of days (and now customers expect it tomorrow, or certainly by the day after).

Similar advances were being made in all the dimensions of customer service, including e-commerce. Having in-stock product when the order was received has always been a key to customer loyalty. During the 1980s our in-stock averages were about at the industry norm of 85 percent; of every 100 items ordered, 85 were in stock at the time ordered. In the 1990s we made it one of our major strategic initiatives ("world-class service level," or WCSL) to increase our in-stock status to the 95 percent level. This required extensive upgrading of our forecasting abilities, major investments in inventory systems (including long-range weather predictions), lots of training programs, and close partnerships with our major vendors. We achieved our WCSL goal in 1998.

Our 100 percent guarantee had been for many years a distinguishing feature of L.L.Bean's customer service. (*Money* magazine once called it one of the greatest values in America.) If you wanted to see how good our people really were, wait until we made a mistake (which, fortunately, we didn't do very often) or you had a special need. Beaners would go to any extreme (and were encouraged to do so) to make the customer happy. One of our product support phone reps received a call from a woman hiking the Appalachian Trail in the White Mountain National Forest section of New Hampshire. She was phoning from a motel, off the trail, and her Cresta Hiking Boots didn't fit comfortably. Our rep got her a new pair from stock, drove to the off-trail motel, made sure the new boots fit properly, and went on to fish some local rivers since he happened to be there.

Partnerships. We've not done very many marketing alliances over the years because we don't want the Bean name mixed up with other brands. So when we join up we make sure our partners also get high marks for product quality and customer service. Ideally they would share in our outdoors heritage or at least not be inconsistent with it.

Our cobranded Visa credit card program (Outdoor Advantage Program, or OAP) was instituted in 1996 with our banking partner MBNA, the second largest credit card lender in the world at the time. MBNA had a regional headquarters in Camden, Maine, and was a good neighbor of ours. We liked the fact that its representatives dealing with L.L.Bean customers were all good Maine people with real Down East accents.

The program enabled us to provide free shipping to customer OAP members. This was a highly valued, longtime service of L.L.Bean we'd had to discontinue in 1991 because of its high cost. Customer members also earned points toward future purchases, and the program was quite profitable for L.L.Bean. The first year we signed up 345,000 members. In 1999, our millionth member joined and by the end of 2000 we had 1.4 million members. It was one of the top ten Visa cobranded programs in the world.

We also signed an agreement with Subaru of America to introduce a unique, top-of-the-line L.L.Bean Edition Subaru Outback Wagon in the 2001 model year. The agreement included joint advertising, outdoors marketing projects, and sponsorships of outdoors organizations such as the Leave No Trace environmental group. Subaru customers were similar to L.L.Bean customers in demographics and in having active outdoors interests. Our Outback was the first with an improved-performance six-cylinder engine; it had unique color schemes and L.L.Bean insignia; and it was made in the United States. Like all Subarus it had all-wheel drive, an excellent safety record, and high reliability; it got excellent mileage and had a highly functional layout. Good Bean attributes. Sales of the L.L.Bean Outback exceeded budget for eleven of twelve months in its first year.

At our annual planning meeting in June 1991, when sales were $616 million, we had set a three-year sales goal of more than $800 million for 1994. We intended to achieve superior productivity by driving out the costs of poor quality and earn in 1994 a return on equity of 20 percent (or the 75th percentile for the Standard & Poor's 500), up from

14.6 percent in 1991. Our 1994 sales turned out to be $975 million, with a 25.4 percent ROE. We paid a 22.5 percent bonus that year.

Not a bad report card. Our average annual rate of growth in the first half of the 1990s, despite a slow start, was 7.5 percent through 1995, superior to the industry average.

Considering where we started, our early-1990s performance was in fact exceptional. We had entered the decade in a depressed economy, especially in our key New England region; we faced increased competition in our outdoors lifestyle niche and extraordinary increases in catalog mailing costs and parcel shipping charges. All these factors depressed demand and reduced margins. We had responded by adopting TQ and a wide array of other initiatives that seemed to be paying off. Our basic Bean model continued to work.

Looking ahead to the mid-1990s, we saw that the economy was generally strong and growing and that consumer confidence was back to the high and healthy levels of the 1980s. Most industries were enjoying the new economic prosperity. Retailing, however, continued to be challenged by a proliferation of new store openings and, in the catalog segment, an excess of new titles and increased circulation plans by all of us. Supply was continuing to grow well ahead of demand, and apparel prices continued to drop as the manufacturing base moved offshore.

A strong brand was critical to success, or even survival, in this demanding environment. With consumers' lifestyles becoming busier, reducing the time and inclination for shopping, a highly recognizable store name or brand was essential, especially one that was trusted to provide the product quality and guaranteed service consumers wanted. The L.L.Bean name, backed by our L.L. story and its durable values, continued to be our competitive advantage.

ANDY BEAHM: I recall XYZ company was flying high [around 1995]. They were just getting incredible profits. So my work was to take different retailers, look at their performance, and come up with a recommendation in terms of financial performance for L.L.Bean. And so I pointed out the performance of XYZ company and was making a pitch to Leon about increasing our goals. He looked at me and he said, "You know, Andy Beahm, L.L.Bean will be here another hundred years from now. XYZ won't be." And he went on to talk about how XYZ, their success really was based on somebody who was able to pick the current fashion trends, and he said, "Nobody has the capability of doing that forever. L.L.Bean, on the other hand, we have real roots. We have a brand that's much deeper than that. It's not just about who's got the greatest colors on the shelf for any given season."

12

A Loss of Relevance

IN SPITE OF ALL OUR GOOD EFFORTS and the multitude of initiatives we pursued in the early to mid-1990s, our business flattened out yet again in 1996 through 1998. In 1996, in fact, we saw negative growth—a decline in sales—for the first time in my years with L.L.Bean. Along with the slowdown came a decline in our profitability. In 1996 our board of directors was unable to vote an annual bonus. It was the first time anyone could remember our not paying it.

The bonus had become a unique L.L.Bean tradition (dating back to L.L.'s days) and an important contributor to our values, culture, and loyalty. During peak seasons when we needed extra effort from Bean people they were always willing to come forward. They knew they would share in the profits of our success. People used to tell me how they renovated their homes or took a special vacation or put their children through college with the bonus money. Having no annual bonus was very bad news.

The biggest factor in our slowdown was the sudden collapse of our business in Japan. By the mid-1990s, more than three hundred U.S. catalogers were mailing into the Japanese market. The bloom was off that rose, and the widely heralded boom in international retailing was fizzling out in Canada, Europe, and England, as well as Japan. Most U.S.

specialty retailers catered to unique national lifestyles and simply weren't relevant in other countries. Japan stood alone in its affinity with U.S. brands and culture and its understanding of L.L.Bean's merchandising concept. But there were monetary limits.

> FRAN PHILIP: I would always remember something told to me by a very astute gentleman on the board of this company out in San Francisco that I started with two partners. I was the CFO and he used to just chastise me. He said, "If you're over budget (which we would think was a good thing) and it's more than 5 or 10 percent, that's as big a problem as being under budget by 5 or 10 percent, because it means you don't know how to forecast your business and you don't know what's driving your business." When I saw the Japan numbers spike up dramatically over budget, I could just hear his voice in my head saying, "Danger! Danger!" Everybody was all happy because these sales were coming in and very excited, but I'm thinking, "Red flag here." If we don't know what's driving this and how to manage it, it's going to come back and bite us big, and it did.

The Japanese economy went downhill in 1995 along with the value of the yen. In 1990 our international division had done $22.7 million in revenue, mostly from Japanese mail-order buyers buying from the United States. In 1995 we did $209.7 million mostly in Japan (20 percent of our total 1995 revenues), an almost tenfold increase. Then, starting the next year, 1996, Japanese sales plummeted, falling to $37.4 million in 2000, a $172 million drop over the next five years (to 3 percent of our total 2000 revenues). The yen fell from 95 to the dollar (in 1995) to 135 to the dollar (in 2000), effectively increasing the price of our products to the Japanese consumer by 42 percent. It was almost all we could do to offset the $172 million loss in revenue with domestic business. As a result, our total revenues increased only marginally for the rest of the decade (to $1.168 billion in 2000).

The collapse of Japanese sales was one of the most abrupt changes in L.L.Bean's fortunes in my experience with the company. We had been riding a wave there and some of us in Freeport thought there would be no end to it. Then, in 1995, the window shut.

BILL HENRY: In eighty-nine Bill End brought me back to work on the international business plan. And in the early nineties, I remember looking at the P&Ls of the company, and the international part of the business was the only thing that was growing the profitability of L.L.Bean. I remember Leon wrote me a letter saying it was almost like international was masking problems in the domestic business.

After the boom years, we disagreed with the new people representing our partners in Japan about L.L.Bean's future positioning there and acquired the retail business from them. They wanted to make L.L.Bean a low-priced sportswear competitor. We combined the retail operation, our in-country catalog business, our new in-country Web site, and our very popular Japanese Outdoor Discovery Program, and began the slow process of rebuilding a sustainable long-term and multichannel Japanese business.

In response to the earlier slowdown at the turn of the 1990s, we had undertaken many initiatives. We had added an all new senior management team. We had launched several significant new-product programs, were growing a promising Web site, and had substantially enhanced our customer service. And we had fully embraced Total Quality Management.

BOB PEIXOTTO: People recognized, I think, that Leon was very committed to Total Quality. It pervaded a lot of what we did and people recognized that their success at L.L.Bean was going to be partially dependent on how well they supported the Total Quality efforts. So I think by and large people jumped in and supported TQ, although I'd have to say there were always people behind the scenes who questioned it.

As noted at the outset, TQ was to my mind an extension and refinement of our Best strategy, which we had undertaken successfully in the mid-1980s. Total Quality had the potential to enhance all of the Best dimensions of product, service, and communications. At the same time TQ would make us more productive and profitable.

However, by 1996 we had been at Total Quality nearly seven years, and, win or lose, it was time for a change. Did TQ bring about the changes we'd hoped it would? Last impressions tend to be the lasting ones. Some considered it a failed strategy because it didn't deliver the big changes they expected or it had just run its course, as most such endeavors do. By 1996 my own view of TQ was wearing, but overall I believed it had been worth doing.

Our work on business processes, which was at the core of TQ, improved the way we put together our catalog. It reduced rework on catalog pages by 85 percent and saved nearly a million dollars in that year and every subsequent year.

CHRIS MCCORMICK: One thing I will give TQ credit for is the thinking around business processes, understanding how the business worked from a profit standpoint. I think there was a way of thinking that still remains in the organization today around how to understand how the business works. Through that understanding you can, I think, come up with competitive advantage, either from a market standpoint or from a G&A [general and administrative] standpoint. One example could be the strategic process we have of communicating to customers, which includes how we prepare the catalog and then mail it to customers. When we looked at the different handoffs and the time line for that process, it was our feeling back then that we were at a strategic disadvantage because from point A, start date, to point B, the end date when the catalog is in home, it was about a year. And we felt we couldn't wait a year; the market was moving too rapidly. So we identified steps to shorten that and we felt that would give us a competitive advantage. Another example is that goals sometimes weren't aligned across departments. And TQ, in its process view of the organization, helped call that out. They called it customer supplier alignments, and it was developing an understanding of what people needed either upstream or downstream from you.

In 1996 we completed a total of 330,000 square feet of new construction for our fulfillment operations and inventory storage space. A project team of Bean people, contractors, architects, industrial engineers, siting engineers, and governmental services representatives worked together using Total Quality principles and techniques. It was completed on time and on budget, with superior-quality construction and no lost time injuries.

Manufacturing really jumped into the whole thing and did a nice job of executing Total Quality practices. In 1993 it won the state of Maine's Margaret Chase Smith quality award (named after Maine's legendary first woman senator). We would not be in manufacturing today without the benefit of Total Quality.

Our manufacturing people exemplified empowerment, total involvement, innovative practices, and continuous improvement in using the various TQ techniques. The division's financial return increased by more than 200 percent, costs related to poor quality were down more than 50 percent (including a tenfold decrease in defects), and work in progress cycle time shrank from more than three weeks to four days. Lost time injuries were down by 87 percent.

As a TQ example, our Camp Moccasin soles were glued on prior to stitching. Excess glue from the machine had to be wiped off, wasting time and glue. Our workers modified the machine to save glue, speed up the process, and reduce labor by four positions.

We made a major effort to empower all of our employees and generated companywide acceptance of TQ principles, which altered the L.L.Bean culture significantly. Along the way, we got a lot of feedback from Bean people. Maybe too much. We got feedback from our annual motivational and job satisfaction surveys, from presentations made at planning meetings and individual critiques, at the periodic "town meetings" we held in all departments, and from just walking around.

Most of the feedback was positive and helpful, but some not so. An unsigned planning meeting questionnaire came back criticizing "Leon's foot-dragging leadership." Not a bad metaphor, although I wouldn't have used it myself. Another time I got a letter from one of our warehouse workers. He said, "I think if you did not inherit L.L.Bean you would have been a farmer selling vegetables on the roadside. Don't get me wrong. I think you would have a swell farm." He offered to have a talk with me, and it was a nice conversation. Unfortunately I thought his grievance was not justified, and he probably still thinks I should be running a vegetable stand.

FRAN PHILIP: I think that TQ was overused as a reason to do things. Unless you got opinions from every single person, it was thrown up as, "You're not doing it in a TQ way." For example, it wasn't TQ to say no to your internal customers.

But people lost track of the original reasons we pursued TQ whole-heartedly. We did stabilize the G&A operating expenses as a percentage of sales through the 1990s. That percentage had been shooting up through the 1980s. Under TQ, in spite of slow growth in sales and high growth of such major costs as printing, paper, and postage, we brought our operating costs under control. I can't say TQ was the only reason for this accomplishment, but costs did stabilize and that's what we wanted to happen. By the mid-1990s, I believe, we had substantially changed from a conventional top-down command-and-control man-agement environment to a place where people felt more empowered to make decisions and do things differently. And we'd substantially changed from a functional organization to one that worked more coop-eratively across units. Our internal survey scores for being open and in-novative, rewarding and developing, and challenging and empowering showed significant improvement. The quality of what we did, our ser-vice levels, and our products' physical quality were never better than they were in the 1990s. People put a lot of thought into doing things right the first time. And we continued to do it all with a reinvigorated focus on customer satisfaction.

BRAD KAUFFMAN: Did behaviors change as a result of using those TQ principles? I would say absolutely they did, and I think they changed for the better, and I think those changes persist to this day. I think those principles had a real impact, a real influence on the way we did things, and they continue to have that sort of influence. I think there's a legacy of Total Quality that persists.

TQ succeeded in another way as well: it pulled me out of the details of the organization, and that had been one of our goals. I delegated big parts of the planning process—the mechanism through which I had been managing the company—and pulled out of the merchandising process, all in the spirit of empowerment and decentralization.

A Loss of Relevance

We delegated operating budgets and monthly reviews to a committee of department heads as well as operational planning and execution. The Executive Committee reviews were held quarterly and operated at a fairly high level. Blue book product planning sessions were much abbreviated and were used more for information than decision making. I was no longer involved in catalog pagination (there were simply too many to keep up with) or in page layouts, copy, and graphics.

Every decade or so there seemed to be a major shift in my role as president. It evolved as a result of the company's growth as well as my own evolution from novice to entrepreneur to professional manager to strategist to whatever was coming next. I was becoming a process leader, looking to the group for ideas on direction and consensus. I remember thinking at the time that TQ was putting me out of a job.

TQ ultimately failed to deliver all it promised, I believe, because many of our senior managers weren't engaged in the game. It required a tremendous commitment by our seniors to adapt to the TQ principles and to lead the cultural changes on a daily basis. The senior managers who had taken on their positions well after we'd begun our TQ initiative didn't fully—or in some cases, even partially—buy in to the concept. As Total Quality says, people support what they help create and vice versa.

> MARK FASOLD: I actually saw some of the leadership issues below Leon coming. And it was one of the reasons I left [in 1991]. I didn't leave because I didn't like the company. I love the outdoors. I love the brand. I have incredible respect and admiration for Leon and was very loyal to him. But I just saw things beginning to develop that were not inviting for someone who's thirty-nine years old and still has his best years ahead of him.

Things would occur that needed the intervention of these managers, and they weren't there—neither coordinating nor facilitating. I should have been more sensitive to the leadership issue. I guess I was still exhibiting a bit of L.L.'s hubris in that if I thought an idea like TQ was a good one, everyone else would think so too. The Executive Committee would agree on high-level goals and initiatives, but the individual senior managers needed to facilitate the execution too. That was a key part of their jobs. It wasn't happening. We weren't executing.

ANDY BEAHM: I think a lot of people took the perspective of, "If I just ignore it [TQ] long enough, it will go away." They were just waiting it out. People wouldn't necessarily do their homework, and so the meetings were arduous and very unproductive. It just died a slow death.

We knew we had business problems, but I didn't fully grasp the leadership situation until we got involved in a leadership study coming out of our annual climate study.

Once we adopted Total Quality Management, we changed our annual survey of everyone at L.L.Bean to measure how well we were providing a Total Quality environment. Our overall results were generally good, although some dimensions, such as commitment, rose and fell with the company's performance. But one dimension—efficiency and effectiveness—was always rated lower than the others. Given our emphasis on TQ and on improving productivity, this was particularly frustrating. So we called in some consultants to help us find out why we were not perceived to be efficient and effective by our own people.

Our problem had to do with the so-called Bean Way, said the consultants, the downside of living the values in all of our stakeholder relationships (trying to do "the right things right," in TQ jargon). This was a strength but taken to extremes had unintended consequences. For some, the "Bean Way" referred to a pervasive and persistent belief at Bean that acted to limit experimentation, benchmarking, and learning. We were seen to require extraordinary justification of new efforts and to be receptive only to perfect presentations and solutions. It supposedly created a high level of self-censorship and conflict avoidance, and hence a reluctance to try new things. Insular and out of touch. We were seen to be too focused on perfection and predictability in what we did and less open to doing new and riskier things.

This was the first I'd heard of the Bean Way. It's not surprising that I didn't agree with this interpretation of our company's culture. It sounded like the downside of me. And maybe it was. Maybe we were "Leon-centric," as the consultants said. Maybe it was problematic for L.L.Bean. I can't honestly say I wanted to learn more, but I felt, in good conscience, that I should go along with the follow-up investigation.

ANDY BEAHM: Leon is a pretty wise guy. I don't think any-body pulled the wool over his eyes. But in the planning role I ob-served a fair amount of dysfunctional behavior among some of those senior executives. They would anticipate exactly what Leon would like to hear, and they would say that, but behind his back, out in the hall, they'd be in a completely different place.

After spending six months off and on interviewing L.L.Bean people and asking them why we weren't efficient and effective, the consultants generated an indictment of virtually every management practice we en-gaged in. All that was missing were specific examples of how we were deficient in all of those areas. This omission was unfortunate. The cri-tique was too broad to be credible.

The consultants and I agreed that the organization had little confi-dence in our senior management. The seniors were perceived to be inef-fective and untrustworthy. But the reason for that apparently had little to do with the senior managers themselves. Because the organization was "Leon-centric," it meant everyone looked to me for leadership, and that undermined my seniors.

We formed a leadership task force led by three senior volunteers to deal with the consultants' report. Because my role was central to the lead-ership issue, I was more of a listener for the rest of this exercise. The task force had several meetings over the next year or so. From my viewpoint, not much happened except that I thought more deeply about my role at L.L.Bean, and this questionable initiative went away.

So did most of our senior managers. Some went to dot-coms, which were recruiting heavily. Others departed who knew it was time to go. And there were a couple of terminations. We had nine senior VPs in 1995, and seven had left by the end of 1998 following three years of low to no growth. We did not replace them. Their subordinates were a capa-ble group. They had for the most part grown up in the L.L.Bean envi-ronment and had been doing most of the work anyway. They took on the seniors' responsibilities.

BOB PEIXOTTO: I would say there was pretty constant shuffling in the executive offices. I don't think Leon was totally happy with the people he put in place, and I don't think they were necessarily happy in the organization. We weren't finding good matches during that period. Leon had very high standards. He wanted people who would support his direction. He was looking for strong values and people who really bought in to L.L.Bean's way of doing business. That's a tall order for somebody who didn't grow up here. What was so hard for so many executives to take was that Leon didn't follow the numbers. He followed his vision. They'd see Leon making decisions for long-term strategic good, and say, "That doesn't make sense. Why would we do that?" They'd struggle with it.

Our departed seniors did not lack talent. They simply had little emotional commitment to the L.L.Bean concept: the values, the outdoors, the stakeholder commitment, or TQ as a way of working together. Nor did they have much inclination to deal with my management idiosyncrasies or to complement them in leading the company, as our 1980s seniors had. Our last outdoors trip as a group had been in 1992, a three-day sea-kayaking excursion in Penobscot Bay. Lack of time and interest had ended a twenty-five-year tradition.

FRAN PHILIP: How Bean-like were [the senior managers]? There's the superficial—"Did they hunt? Did they fish?" Some of them were avid hunters and fishermen, and others were not at all subscribers to outdoor activities we supported. Then there were the values. I would say [they had] a pretty loose alignment with the values.

Retailing competition in the United States continued at an intense level. Our success in Japan had let us avoid confronting problems in our home market, where pressure on value had become central. There was great emphasis on lower prices. When the country came out of the recession in the mid-nineties, retailing never fully recovered because the supply side (more stores and catalogs) kept increasing versus the demand side (sales) and the price competition just became more so. Product proliferation and sameness among sellers was also a major consequence of the competition. It continued to be a changing world for us, and the traditional Bean outdoorsy functional value formula was not as popular as it had been in the past. Or perhaps we weren't projecting it credibly in our products and catalogs.

Across the country, participation in active sports was not growing, although of the top ten activities in numbers of participants, L.L.Bean was in six: exercise walking, swimming, camping, fishing, bicycle riding, and hiking. And we weren't likely to get into the other four: bowling, billiards, basketball, and exercising with equipment.

ANDY BEAHM: The marketing folks were saying, "The reason we're not more relevant is that Leon won't let us be. Who owns the L.L.Bean brand? Is it Leon, or the customer? Leon won't let us go where the customer wants to go." The customers were saying, "If you want to be more relevant, just give me more pink apparel," you know. But Leon wanted the outdoors business to grow.

Relevance had to do with having the products people wanted to buy. We'd begun our ongoing Selection for Me research among our customers and prospects in 1991, and tracked the findings in subsequent years. Our problems in this area involved aesthetics or styling, assortment, catalog presentation, and, I believe, firmly held perceptions of what L.L.Bean was now, based on the strength of what we had been. Our ability to change without appearing to change had begun to work against us. The public had a preconceived and dated view of us. We were identified with "practical" products and a collection of core items that never seemed to change. People interested in casual apparel saw us as an active sportswear company and didn't open their catalogs. At the same time, some of our longtime customers felt we were going away from our outdoors heritage, although our assortments of gear were greater than ever. Everybody still thought highly of L.L.Bean, but we weren't top of mind when it came to buying things.

There was a balancing act between being true to the L.L.Bean character and being relevant to today's consumer. It was a constant juggling act. Who owned the brand? That was the core of the tension. We wanted to be true to L.L.Bean, but we needed to be up-to-date as well.

WES DEVRIES: Here's an eighties catalog. Compare it with a current catalog. Look at how different it is. Read the copy. Here, for example [reading a description of a sailing boot in the catalog]:

> Engineered under the experienced eye of yachtsman Gary Johnson, world class sailor, author and tactician for Ted Turner's successful 1977 defense of the America's Cup. Made in Maine by Sebago for high performance under the most demanding offshore sail-racing conditions. New high-friction compound sole and full wedge design with a single non-interrupted surface provide the finest traction available. Sole is bonded to uppers for strength and durability. Slant rear "hiking heel" prevents catching on lines, docks, et cetera. Uppers are made from the most moisture-resistant leather available. Premium Norwegian cowhides are scientifically shrunken so that the grain swells and actually blocks water absorption. Offers increased toughness and water repellency. Full grain leather innersole wraps around insulation for comfort and warmth. Perforated and cushioned, three-quarter sock lining is sculptured to fill the arch, providing comfort and vital support needed for quick movement. Johnson leather. Convenient pull-on boot style for foul weather and rough seas. Excellent for when the protection and convenience of a high traction, pull-on boot is desired. Contrast stitched quarter seams are double-felled for water resistance. Handy pull-on tab at boot top. Height 10¼ inches.

That's eighty-five. Why did Bean do so well? They had a clear persona that was highly differentiated and extremely hard to create and to maintain. Try writing that copy on product after product after product, page after page. Now try to do it with all these additional people in the organization now. I think you had an optimum size at that point where you could have these standards of communication.

[Picking up current catalog] I got this the other day. [Reading]

> Waterproof pathfinder hikers for men and women. The most durable, comfortable, waterproof hikers you'll find at this price.

Our exclusive waterproof membrane keeps moisture out so your feet stay dry and comfortable when tromping through mud or rain. Waterproof suede upper is durable and supportive. Cushion mid-sole provides the lightweight comfort of an athletic shoe. Supportive nylon shank adds stability and lugged rubber out-sole improves traction. Imported. Fits best with mid-weight socks.

It's good copy in today's world of catalogs. But it does not have the persona or the particularity or the vocabulary or the style or the voice that you had before. Two different businesses. Why did it change? I don't know. I think fundamentally it's going to come back to the unintended consequences of things, like starting to sell dresses. You have no reason to write that kind of copy for dresses. So now you end up with the vast majority of products that don't have those kind of copy points. It wasn't decided one day to change that. It might have been, "We had a focus group and they said the copy's too long." Well, I've never been in a focus group that didn't say the copy's too long. But when you test copy, longer copy usually beats shorter copy.

Our position in the marketplace had lost its clarity. The idea of "people like us" as defining our target market was not enough. When your products aren't selling and you think you've got a pretty good product line, it's frustrating. There was a disconnect that I couldn't understand. I remember a friend in the retail business coming through Freeport, going through our retail store and saying he couldn't find anything that he wanted to buy. But when I asked, "Well, what are we missing?" he couldn't come up with anything. Or if somebody said, "My wife thinks the women's products are frumpy" and I asked for specifics, they couldn't give me any.

The repositioned women's business in the early 1990s had achieved some success, as had the increased innovation in sporting equipment. But both had ceased growing by the mid-1990s, and along with men's apparel and footwear our core business was stagnating. Our new kids' business and our greatly expanded home and camp furnishings continued to grow.

FRAN PHILIP: There was so much infighting between the three vice president merchants, over space in the catalog, over, "Is that product really an active piece of apparel or is it more casual so it belongs in my product area?" There was an awful lot of that going on, and when you have that going on, I don't know how you can be so world class at product development and merchandising.

We weren't doing good merchandising. The problem was not only in the products themselves but also in the creative: the catalog, the artwork, the copy, and everything else related to how we presented ourselves and our products. We had drifted toward a more generic approach to catalog graphics. We'd lost our personality. Our catalogs didn't look any different from a lot of others.

We needed a strong and contemporary L.L.Bean point of view that could interpret our core values and traditions into product lines and catalog presentations that were coherent and compelling for the outdoors-oriented consumer of the 1990s. That was easier to say than do, given the discipline and collaboration required among a diverse group of merchants, product developers, creative people, and marketers, each with their own point of view of what L.L.Bean should be. I think we had the right strategic parameters in place, but the devil was in the details. It was one thing for L.L. to execute his own point of view by himself, or for me to do it with a small and willing staff, but bringing a large group of bright, independent-minded people together in a cohesive and compelling L.L.Bean point of view was another challenge altogether.

Since the late 1980s and our last period of extraordinary growth, I had become less able to devote time to being general merchandise manager. It was a full-time job. You were either in merchandising or not. It required total immersion to keep up with all the detail and bits of information. With Total Quality and empowerment, I was even less involved. It wasn't TQ for me to be hands-on in merchandising.

We conducted a search for an experienced general merchandise manager. After a couple of years we still couldn't find one that understood both L.L.Bean and merchandising. So we went with a solid group of senior merchants but still lacked the single, focused point of view.

BOB PEIXOTTO: There was a lot of turnover in the merchandising leadership in the nineties, and I think it had to do with the fact that Leon couldn't find somebody who as holistically saw the Bean brand as he did. The money in this business is in the apparel. So you either have people who really want to drive the apparel to drive profitability, or people who love the outdoors and want to basically work with the gidgets and gadgets of the outdoors industry and aren't quite as focused on making money. Neither one works. Bean is a whole concept. You sell apparel because the outdoors products create an authenticity that no other company can emulate. Leon had a hard time finding a merchant who could operationalize that.

Our slowdown in the mid-1990s was not missed by the press or the industry experts. Just as the media were overly complimentary in their coverage of L.L.Bean in the 1970s and 1980s, they were overly critical in the 1990s. One business magazine writer was especially cynical. After disparaging virtually everything we'd done over the past thirty years he wrote, "In everything from management to fashion, privately held Bean in Freeport, Maine is a company firmly stuck in the past."[1] So much for mystique.

In spite of that opinion, and my own tale of woe in the preceding pages, we continued through the 1990s to earn a decent profit, enjoy a solid balance sheet, be the service leader in our industry, and maintain a reputation for quality products without equal, all in accord with the L.L. story.

Consumer Reports continued to conduct periodic surveys of mail-order companies in 1991, 1994, and 1999.[2] Rating factors included overall satisfaction, problem solving, stock availability, delivery time, shipping charges, clothing fit, value, and so on. Thirty to forty companies were included. L.L.Bean was rated the best catalog company in each survey and in every product category in which we competed. These results were a continuation of our leadership in the 1983 and 1987 surveys. I don't know of many companies in any industry that have achieved that record of excellence over so many years.

13

Time for Transformation

B EFORE THE 1990S, I had complete confidence in what we were
doing and what we stood for. I just wanted to keep doing more and
more of it. Then, as we got into the 1990s, things changed. Our business
model seemed to lose its effectiveness. We'd been through TQ. We'd
been through the rise and fall of our Japanese business. We'd been
through senior management turnover and a leadership catharsis. All our
initiatives in the early 1990s, such as e-commerce and new product lines,
were in place. All these initiatives had come out of our planning process,
but the process was no longer generating new and exciting ideas. The
L.L. story seemed to be losing its mystique. I was having doubts.

ANDY BEAHM: Leon would say to me, "Andy, I know that some
things have to change, and some things have to stay the same. I
just don't know which of the things are the ones that need to stay
the same, and which are the ones that need to change." He had a
very strong image in his mind as to what L.L.Bean was, and it had
been very successful up until that point in time. But once we got to
that year where we actually slid down the hill, he knew that something serious was going on, and that he needed some external un-
biased assistance to work that through. I think that dysfunctional

senior management group almost made it impossible to have the kinds of conversations needed to move ahead.

As we entered 1996, the general economy was recovering nicely but retailing was still problematic. "Value retailing" (factory outlets and off-price retailers) was the fastest-growing segment of the industry. It was not an environment that played to our strengths. Product sameness in the marketplace and the intense focus on lowest prices were among the biggest challenges we faced.

The baby boomers were wearing casual apparel to the workplace, and the "casualization of America" had become a lasting trend. L.L.Bean was not in the career apparel business, but many of our relaxed weekend products lent themselves to the casual workplace. At the same time, Internet retail sales were doubling each year. E-commerce nationally did $500 million in 1996, something of a disappointment given the great expectations of the time, but with the transaction security issue solved, it was expected to hit $7 billion by 2000 (another reliable source predicted $200 billion).

The planning process started losing its effectiveness when we got into Total Quality, and we delegated a lot of the planning. Now, the old way of planning (or managing) was gone. TQ had not been a growth process as such, although it could facilitate growth initiatives. We needed something new that was transformational, something that would engage the whole company and would reenergize L.L.Bean. The idea of stepping way back and taking a fundamental look at the business, a strategic review, had come up in the early 1990s. We were doing all right at the time, and because it was a huge, potentially disruptive undertaking, we put the review off. Now, with our 1996 sales going backward for my first time ever, not to mention the challenges of the retail industry, it was a good time to revisit the idea.

I was invited to a conference hosted by The Boston Consulting Group, Inc. (BCG) in New York in the spring of 1996. The theme was "Turning Around the Successful Company." It was about what to do when your company has hit the wall, and how to know when your current model is not working: "Growth has stalled," "Competition is in a stalemate," "Economics of scale are not working," "Business concept not evolving," and more. The symptoms seemed to fit our situation, and the theme of the conference struck a responsive chord in me. We seemed to be approaching the wall, if not hitting it, and needed some kind of turnaround.

We decided in 1996 to conduct a Strategic Review. We developed a request for proposal and sent it to several leading strategic consultancies, including BCG late that year. We wanted a rigorous assessment of L.L.Bean that would seriously challenge our business model with new knowledge, new insights, and new ideas. Our "model" included our stated purpose and basic assumptions, our brand personality and basic values, our target markets, our recreational product offerings and our distribution channels, our "Best" strategy, our operating competencies, and our financial strategies. We wanted to achieve quality growth that added value for all of our stakeholders and to head into the next century from a position of strength. We wanted a lot.

We selected BCG and began the review. Phase I, the assessment stage, began in March 1997 with a fully dedicated team of L.L.Bean and BCG people.

In July the team identified the strengths we could leverage in the future and the elements of our business model that were problematic and in need of reconsideration. Strengths included our brand; the size of our mailing list; our reputation for product quality and service reliability; and our operations capabilities.

Weaknesses that needed to be addressed included the increasing peak orientation of our business; our active sports business being disadvantaged versus more focused competitors; deteriorating catalog economics (response rates as well as increased postage and paper costs); deteriorating international performance; and the problematic overall growth potential of the current model.

I was impressed with the quality and the quantity of the research done. The consultants were on their PCs twenty-four hours a day, bringing together new information and new ways of looking at the business. What I especially liked about the overall process was its action orientation. It targeted weaknesses one by one and developed initiatives to deal with them. It wasn't looking for dramatic concepts and revolutionary ideas. Rather, the attitude was, "Get it done. Make things happen." It took a three-year outlook and no further. The consultants said not to worry about long-term strategic issues, such as the future of the U.S. Postal Service. Deal only with the most pressing issues, they told us. Eventually those other issues would either become short-term or go away.

ANDY BEAHM: The Strategic Review was an important forum to put these [basic] issues on the table and to deal with them in a more healthy manner. I think that [Leon] really bared his soul in that process because he was willing to make changes. I think he took that process as an opportunity to challenge his own thinking about what L.L.Bean stood for. I think he was very open-minded in that, and I know that that was a big struggle for him. I think it definitely was an earth-moving kind of event for him.

There was a feeling in the company that I opposed changing the L.L.Bean model in any way, even though I had adapted or changed it continuously over the years with product line extensions and channel additions and had personally initiated the current review. Sometimes I thought people were attributing their own risk adversity to me. In any event I was open to change and looked forward to the results of the review.

The consultants did an exceptional job of designing, informing, facilitating, and coaching the process. They earned great credibility and buy in by L.L.Bean people. The teams were composed of BCG and Bean people. We became committed to the insights and recommendations that emerged. We owned the outcomes. They had a lot of momentum, and it carried over into the implementation of the teams' recommendations. The BCG process was very results oriented.

LISA GORMAN: Leon was very excited about the review. I do remember he was quite enthusiastic about the different groups. I think when some of the concepts were endorsed he might not have believed in all of them. I remember asking him then, "Why do you let it happen?" He said, "Because you have to let your people have something to work towards to get them excited."

I did disagree with the last issue the team identified (the limited growth potential of our current model), because I felt we still had significant growth opportunities, particularly if we could do a better job of developing and merchandising our men's and women's apparel. We should have taken this issue head-on. At the same time I wanted to build momentum for change and new energy in the business. So I was supportive of the team in its proceedings and its outcomes and periodically met with the team leaders in an advisory role.

From that initial review, BCG consultants and L.L.Bean teams went on to look at a variety of ideas and issues that the Strategic Review had identified. The five principal initiatives that emerged were Freeport Studio, retailing, cost reduction, brand management, and reorganization.

Freeport Studio. In January 1998 we launched the "Women's Casual Apparel Affiliated Brand" catalog business, subsequently named Freeport Studio. The idea was to generate significant off-peak sales with a business that, being affiliated (not under the Bean name and not part of the brand), would not interfere with the L.L.Bean brand and its positioning. Freeport Studio was to be a semiautonomous business that would provide stylish and contemporary but easy-to-wear and easy-to-care-for apparel for active, busy women. Its off-peak volume would take advantage of our unused off-peak capacity. The first Freeport Studio catalog was to be mailed in January 1999.

CHRIS MCCORMICK: One other thing, a benefit that came out of the consulting work was we should be looking at brand architecture. The Bean brand is solid, it has all the positive attributes you want, but it also has product or brand liabilities too. It is seen more for an older customer than a younger customer, it is seen more male than female, it is seen more Maine and Northeast than West Coast. So the consultants said that if we wanted to get into brand architecture we should introduce a new brand and go after some market opportunities. The one we decided upon was Freeport Studio. The thinking behind that was if we want to grow the top line of the corporation, not necessarily the Bean brand but the corporation, we should leverage our expertise, which is mail order, catalog marketing, and we should leverage our database and fulfillment operations. So it led to the conclusion that we should be in the catalog channel, and we should be in apparel too, because that's part of our expertise, and vendor base. From a brand standpoint, having a women's catalog like Freeport Studio took pressure off the L.L.Bean brand to be in the very casual, almost dressy, women's apparel under the Bean name. So that provided an opportunity for us to develop product that would be high sellers in women's dresses but would preserve the integrity of the Bean brand by getting those products out of the Bean catalog and into the Freeport Studio catalog. Another positive was we would learn how to start a business. We had never done that before.

Obviously, we had always known we had an issue with underutilized capacity during the spring through fall, or off-peak, season. But BCG made a more compelling issue of it than we'd seen before. There would be dramatic profit opportunities if we could increase off-peak volume and not aggravate the peak any further. This had been a perennial issue in the company. We had just never come up with a good way to deal with it. Hence, Freeport Studio.

Retail Expansion. "L.L. Regional" (as our retail venture was named) was launched in April 1998. Its purpose was to determine the feasibility of a regional retail store strategy for L.L.Bean, including pilot stores outside Maine. Retail stores would work in conjunction with our catalogs to communicate L.L.Bean's outdoors lifestyle concept outside the Northeast. They were a key way to address our "active sports" issue by enhancing our ability to sell sporting goods, which was more a retail than a catalog business. Retail stores would also provide us with substantial growth opportunities. That's where more than 90 percent of consumer products were sold. Our first regional store was planned for 2000.

ANDY BEAHM: If you looked at a full catalog, because of the profitability, there was not nearly as much outdoors business in there as you would like. We did have these specialty catalogs for hunting and fishing. So we were in that business. But if you looked at their circulation, most customers never, ever saw [the full range of our outdoors products]. Retail stores were the solution to that

problem. If the economics of the catalogs didn't allow us to position ourselves as truly an outdoors company, then let's have more
stores like the Freeport store, where we can get prospective customers to see L.L.Bean in person and understand the brand and
its real outdoors heritage.

In all my prior years with L.L.Bean, I had rejected the idea of expanding the retail channel. Most of those years we were fully challenged
for human and financial resources to manage our growing catalog business. I also knew that retail stores were a very different business from
catalog. The merchandising cycle, the logistical competencies, the advertising and promotion, and even the working relationships differed between direct marketing and retail. As I kept pointing out, I'd never seen
a specialty cataloger or retailer do well in both channels. Catalogers that
opened retail stores eventually converted to a retail mind-set and opened
more stores, while letting their catalog competencies diminish.

However, multichannel retailing was just emerging as a concept as
e-commerce began to become a viable channel. Eighteen of the top one
hundred retailers had significant mail-order operations. There was lots
of merger and acquisition activity involving the direct marketing industry as e-commerce aspirants attempted to acquire mail-order fulfillment
expertise. Most major catalogers were adding retail stores to support their
multichannel strategies. If consumers truly wanted to interact with a
retailer in a variety of ways, as early evidence was suggesting they did,
we would have to respond.

By the mid-1990s, I had also been losing confidence in the catalog
channel, or even the catalog business combined with e-commerce, as the
only growth vehicle for L.L.Bean. We had a large majority of the relevant households on our mailing list but had been unable to get a bigger
share of the business they were giving retail stores. We could always do
what we did better, but we weren't and I was not optimistic. It was finally time to look hard at our retail options.

But the real reason I agreed to the retail initiative was due more to a
change in my leadership style. Either you lead a group to goals you see
very clearly (and just say, "Follow me"), or you lead a group through a
process of identifying goals when you don't see them clearly.

When the company was small and I was more of an entrepreneur, I saw everything very clearly, especially our goals, and I could lead in a straightforward way to achieve them. "Not always right but never in doubt," as an entrepreneurial friend once told me. As the company grew and my role changed from entrepreneur to manager and beyond, my leadership style changed more to one of leading the process.

Beginning with the planning process in the 1980s to Total Quality and Strategic Process Management in the early 1990s to the Strategic Review in the late 1990s, my role was shifting to that of process leader. As L.L.Bean grew larger and more complex our specific goals and growth initiatives were not always clear, and I needed help in identifying and defining them. At the same time we had increasing numbers of managers who wanted to participate in the process, and we needed their commitment to achieve our goals. The retail decision as well as the other Strategic Review outcomes came out of my leading the process rather than my old entrepreneurial way of doing things.

The process approach also led to the great diversity of initiatives in the 1990s, some successful and others not. But we needed to try a great many ideas to find the ones that would indeed transform L.L.Bean and update the L.L. story for the new millennium. I should add that there's no shortage of resistance to process leadership. It's too slow, takes too many meetings, requires a lot of compromise, and wastes a lot of time. Many people, including me, simply want to leap to the next most obvious goal and not go through all the process steps. But, as some wise person once said, "The solution to a complex problem is oftentimes simple and it's usually wrong." Process is important.

Cost Reduction. In early 1998 our Strategic Cost Reduction team identified three broad areas where we could reduce costs significantly: cost of goods sold (COGS), or what we paid our vendors for the products we sold to customers; complexity resulting from the great many items (SKUs) we stocked and merchandised for sale; and selling, general, and administrative costs. In short, virtually everything we did was fair game.

Sourcing and supply chain management, as a means of reducing COGS, emerged as the priority issue and opportunity. Our Strategic Review had concluded that our costs of goods were out of line with those of our competition. Driving down COGS, while getting better-quality product with better on-time delivery, was becoming critical, even a matter of survival in the new global economy. The mass migration of apparel and footwear manufacturing to the Far East and the Caribbean, accompanied by Web-based communication technologies, was changing the concept of "vendor partnership." Finding the best factories, establishing the best logistical relationships, and getting the best production at the best costs were the biggest game in town.

> CHRIS MCCORMICK: I don't want to overstate it but we were lagging in our sourcing competencies. I'm guessing 60 or 70 percent of our items were probably sourced in the [United States] then. Maybe a little bit less than that but not much. What the consultants pointed out is that the world had moved offshore. Yes, it would be nice if we could keep sourcing products in the [United States], but, realistically, all those jobs were going offshore anyway. The competencies were leaving this country and from a competitive standpoint we really had no choice. The quality, by the way, would be just as good, if not better than the [United States]. So we created the sourcing department and gave them marching orders to improve our margins and reduce our cost of goods sold.

Cost reduction initiatives weren't new to L.L.Bean. We had mounted several of them in the 1990s. All of them had some success, but none of them was sustainable in resisting the ever-increasing costs of operations and capital. It was a constant budget battle to hold expenses level as a percentage of sales. With the BCG approach we were hoping for some big, long-term successes.

The L.L.Bean Brand. Another issue that emerged from the study team was the L.L.Bean brand. Our name was our most valuable asset and there was no disagreement here. It was what we stood for in our products and our service, in treating people with respect, and in our outdoors heritage. But how would we express these overarching values in our various businesses?

Certainly there were product differences within L.L.Bean: men's, women's, active sports, and so on. But what level of quality and value and aesthetics did they have in common that made them L.L.Bean? Then there were sub-brands, not part of the core or traditional L.L.Bean concept: L.L. Kids, L.L. Home, and L.L.Bean Traveler. And we had partnerships with MBNA and Subaru and affiliated brands like Freeport Studio. How did they all fit under one umbrella?

We needed rules for managing the relationships among all those different brand elements and businesses. All had to share, reflect, and reinforce L.L.Bean's core values. We needed to leverage their commonalities and yet provide for differentiation, relevance, and clarity in the positioning of our individual businesses. Where could each piece of the brand differ in customer markets, products, and distribution channels?

Also, we needed to protect our brand's integrity and ensure its relevance as we developed new distribution channels and product lines. What were the limits of our name? How much latitude would our customers give us? We needed a system for managing the fit of new businesses with the logic of our system and our values.

Organization Structure. Our organization structure needed to change to support our brand system. The Executive Committee (including me) also felt we needed to do this to fully realize the potential of our Strategic Review initiatives. We needed to align our organization structure, processes, performance measures, and incentives with our emerging strategies. We launched an organization review team in April 1998.

CHRIS MCCORMICK: We had gotten too big basically, and it was difficult to react to the market in a quick way. So BCG recommended breaking the organization into a decentralized organization of the ex-Bean structure. And the theory behind that was it's not an org structure to improve the efficiency of our G&A, it was more of an org structure to go after market share. And the theory behind it was if you had separate business units focus on different market segments they will become the experts of that market segment and be more effective at grabbing sales. That was the principle behind that. So we broke the business up into, I think, seven SBUs. So it was men's, women's, sporting goods, home, kids, travel, and Freeport Studio.

We adopted a strategic business unit (SBU) structure, supplemented by shared service units (SSUs), such as human resources, finance, and information services. We created seven product SBUs and six channel SBUs (in addition to catalog, e-commerce, and retail, we treated international, corporate sales, and factory stores as channels). We set them up in a matrix format, with each product area intersecting with each channel. The SBUs would have P&L responsibility, including sales and marketing responsibility. An overall balanced scorecard of performance metrics for the company was developed and disaggregated to each SBU and SSU. Overseeing the action was the Office of the President (three senior vice presidents and me) providing strategic direction and periodic reviews.

We hoped and expected that a decentralized, entrepreneurial, multibusiness organization model would drive a major cultural change in the way we did things at L.L.Bean. Our SBUs would be more aggressive marketers, more customer focused, quicker and more responsive, more accountable, and more focused on results. My biggest hope was that we'd become better, more relevant merchants.

> BOB PEIXOTTO: I think through the middle nineties Leon started to lose some confidence in how in touch he was with the modern-day consumer and with how relevant our brand was going to be going forward. Part of, I think, what led him to accept the strategic business unit organization was a sense that he didn't have all the answers any more and he needed to feed some responsibility for innovation and ideas and decisions to seven really strong people, the SBU heads, and see what they could come up with. For Leon, it was the ultimate stepping back from the organization.

So the reorganization seemed to be an idea whose time had come, for all the reasons just cited, but also because company managers were eager for it. Pressure was building for the kind of autonomy it would allow. "Let us run our own businesses!" was what I kept hearing from managers. Here was the opportunity, the ultimate empowerment.

We didn't take this huge step blindly. We clearly saw the disadvantages as well as the advantages: the need for great coordination among all the business units; unavoidable duplication of marketing and inventory management efforts; a lessening of expertise at the corporate level; and the need for many, many meetings, along with "role clarity matrices" to resolve the endless ambiguities of this type of structure and highly sophisticated cost accounting systems. We thought it would be worth the pain.

The Strategic Review had led to fundamental changes at L.L.Bean, as we expected it would. It was intended to be transformational. Our previous strategy had always been continuous improvement, with an occasional stretch. But we'd reached the point where continuous improvement of the current model wasn't going to be enough. So we wanted to fundamentally change the model. The outcome was a new and different business (Freeport Studio), a new and very different channel (retail), a new approach to sourcing, and a whole new organizational structure, along with new ways of thinking about our brand and the way we merchandised.

I came out of the review thinking it had been well worth doing. I believe it generated useful new ways of looking at things at L.L.Bean. It was a great way of motivating people to come up with new concepts. Many of the Bean people involved in the teams were also involved in the execution of their recommendations. So it proved a good way to maintain the momentum and enthusiasm for change. We could do new and different things and in new ways. The company's culture changed as well.

Our five key strategies would constitute what I was beginning to call our "Platform for Growth" in the approaching new century (and millennium). We intended to reenergize and renew the strategies annually, with new-business development and cost management teams. We would evaluate current efforts and recommend new initiatives. We hoped to introduce one major new business initiative each year.

In 1998, when all this was well under way, I addressed company managers and tried to explain all of it to them. Here's part of what I said:

> It is my opinion what we have set in motion will change dramatically L.L.Bean as we know it. That a year from now we will say that this is a very different company. That we will see a dynamic,

competitive, contentious, energized, and growing enterprise. And this new enterprise will remain true to our basic beliefs of what an excellent company should be.

There is considerable business risk in advancing these strategies. We are not betting the franchise but we are betting a lot. We have many changes and major unknowns to deal with in the next twelve months. But there is considerably greater risk in not moving forward.

Our financial goals for L.L.Bean 2000 include a net sales increase in excess of $300 million and a threefold increase in our pre-tax income. One issue that has come up several times in our Strategic Review is that profit is not a cultural value at L.L.Bean. We have always felt in the past if we did well by our customers and our other stakeholders, a "reasonable profit" would take care of itself.

This attitude was naive, perhaps, on our part although it served us well for many years. In today's environment, however, we are going to have to focus much more intently on profitability. And this means a better understanding of the role of profitability in our enterprise.

Profit is, first of all, a clear measure of our contribution to society; of what our customers are willing to pay us for the value we add to their lives. Beyond that, the flow of profits enables us to reward L.L.Bean people for their good efforts; to pay appropriate dividends to our shareholders; to support our communities with taxes and charitable contributions; and to be environmentally responsible.

Finally, the flow of profits enables us to reinvest in the purpose of our company. In short, the "P" word is not a bad word. L.L.Bean will never regard profit as an end in itself. But the proactive achievement of a "reasonable profit" is fundamental to all that we want to accomplish.

And nobody ever told us that profit would be easy to earn; or that we were entitled to it or to a share in it. Earning a "reasonable profit" in today's retail environment is going to require the best efforts of everyone at L.L.Bean.

Our leadership goal is to renew our commitment to a value-based organization that sets an example for all to see of what an excellent company can be.

We will be relentlessly ethical in everything we do—no matter the cost. That means practicing the Golden Rule with an outdoors orientation. The others we do unto are our stakeholders: our customers, employees, owners, communities, and our natural environment.

Our stakeholders have invested their patronage, careers, finances, social services, and outdoor values in our enterprise. They trust us to tell the truth, to sell quality products, to guarantee satisfaction, to pay fair wages and provide opportunities for growth, to secure their investment, to participate in society, and to sustain our natural environment. They trust us to grow to the extent we can enhance our benefits to them. They trust us to go the extra mile in everything we do.

Our core value is trust. It goes to the essence of respect for people. It is what the Golden Rule and L.L.Bean is all about. It's something we never want to change. It's what truly sets us apart. Please let me know if you ever feel we are violating that trust.

14

Platform for Growth

W HEN YOU ASK PEOPLE AT BEAN who were there what
the 1990s were about, you hear things like this:

> "It was a real transition period for L.L.Bean. We had to figure
> out how to go from the eighties, which were high flying, to the
> next iteration of L.L.Bean."

> "We lost touch with our roots in the nineties . . . we struggled
> with our product; we struggled internally . . . we lost confidence
> in who we were."

> "We lost some key Bean people in the early nineties—some
> great people with a great sense of Bean history. The influx of
> new people 'from away' had a huge impact on the culture and
> employee morale."

> "It was a very, very difficult time."

The feeling was that in the 1990s we'd run out of all the good luck
and success we'd had in the previous decades. Many of the forces helping the company in the 1960s, 1970s, and 1980s, the coming together
of our character and positioning with broad social and technological

trends (like environmentalism and 800 numbers) had now become mainstream or business as usual. Function was no longer fashionable. The baby boomers were getting older, and they were less interested in performance, reliability, and durability and in the outdoors. Internally we had a lot of turnover in our management group and a lot of change in our business model. Much of it proved to be good.

The outside world enjoyed a strong economy through 2000 and then dipped into a mild recession to kick off the new millennium. Despite the threat of Y2K, which proved to be a bit of a hoax, consumer confidence remained strong, although in retailing, overstoring, overcataloging, and price deflation continued on their merry way.

The baby boomers (aged forty to fifty-four in 2000) would continue to be the dominant demographic for the next ten years. But the "echo-boomers," also called the boomlet (people aged six to twenty-three in 2000), were coming on strong. It would be a challenge worth thinking about how any one brand was going to deal with the changing of the marketplace over the next decade.

E-commerce continued on its high-growth curve in the national marketplace although never quite achieving the more extravagant projections of a few years earlier. Locally, at L.L.Bean, our e-commerce sales were $160 million. They could well surpass our catalog sales in the foreseeable future.

All this meant that the 1990s for L.L.Bean was a decade of great change and transition, even transformation. We had a lot of ups and downs in the process but overall we came out OK.

Our annual sales grew from $616.8 million in 1990 to $1.169 billion in 2000, an average annual growth rate of 6.8 percent. Our target had been 5–10 percent per annum. The majority of the growth came in the first five years, with the latter five being only a little better than flat. (If you net out the collapse of our international business, our domestic business grew by 4.8 percent per annum during the latter five years.) Our profitability ratios increased significantly and compared favorably with other retailers. In 2000 we paid a 10 percent companywide bonus.

When I joined L.L.Bean in 1960, our catalog business was 85 percent of our sales, with the balance being our retail store in Freeport. By the year 2000 our catalog's share of the business was down to 60 percent, with e-commerce contributing 15 percent and growing fast. Retail was about 12 percent, including the three new out-of-state stores; our business in Japan was 4 percent of our total (having been as high as 20 percent in 1995); and our factory stores (outlets for discontinued products) made up the balance (about 9 percent).

Much had been accomplished in the 1990s, more than the people at L.L.Bean realized. We seemed to be changing again without appearing to change, even to ourselves. We did international. We started corporate sales (our business-to-business division). We opened factory stores. We got into new media and e-commerce. We got into partnerships with MBNA and Subaru. We got into the kids' business. We repositioned the L.L.Bean women's business. We expanded our home furnishings and our travel businesses.

Plus, we took on all the transforming initiatives that emerged from the Strategic Review. In spite of feeling a bit chaotic, there's never been another period when the company did more things—more new things—and it was reasonably successful in most of them. We were building the foundation of L.L.Bean's future.

Freeport Studio had had a good start-up in 1999 but was soon struggling to achieve anticipated growth and profitability. It was more complex than we'd thought; for example, it needed its own phone reps and fulfillment facilities as well as merchandising and marketing staff. We were proving we could start a business. But we couldn't keep Freeport Studio separate from L.L.Bean if we wanted it to succeed, and that was a problem. Research revealed that customers felt it was inappropriate of Bean to be in dressy women's career apparel. It was confusing people about what we stood for.

We opened our first out-of-state retail store in Tysons Corner, McLean, Virginia (just outside Washington, D.C.), on July 28, 2000. We called it a "core store," and it had 75,000 square feet of selling space. Forty L.L.Bean sales reps traveled down to help start it up and inject some Bean character. Tysons was one of the ten largest shopping centers in the United States, and we wanted to be where the people were, especially L.L.Bean people, of which 1.5 million lived within a half-hour's drive. The internal décor was a blend of traditional L.L.Bean wood, stone, trout pond, and natural light. Set within the mall's modern ambience, however, it was a good try but didn't look much like Freeport, except for the people and the products, which were what counted most. The opening was a success, and our senator and good friend, Susan Collins, said that L.L.Bean represented Maine as "the way life should be."

CHRIS MCCORMICK: Leon knew that retail expansion was one way to fuel our future growth. L.L.Bean was already well developed in the catalog channel and growth was slowing in that segment. We were building our competencies in Web marketing and merchandising with great success. This became and continues to be Bean's fastest growing channel. But we needed to penetrate the retail channel where ninety percent of all sales occur. This was a competency we needed to develop quickly.

In addition, at the time Bean's infrastructure supported the catalog and Web channels but lacked the necessary systems, processes, and general retail knowledge required to be successful. We started to work on this in the late 1990s until today—and we're still working on it.

Leon also realized if we could execute our strategy well, there could be a synergistic benefit across all channels which would fuel additional growth and profits plus create a competitive advantage for Bean. Based on an analysis we completed for the retail markets we're in today, it turned out Leon was correct.

We planned to locate stores along the New York to Washington (D.C.) corridor, where a lot of L.L.Bean people live. We subsequently opened smaller "Discovery" stores (about 30,000 square feet) in Columbia, Maryland, and Marlton, New Jersey. All the stores showed a strong, active outdoors orientation, along with our casual product lines. After completing the first phase we had learned a lot about owning and operating new stores. We needed to digest the learning prior to commencing phase II, but the initial results showed we could make a success of retail.

E-commerce grew dramatically. On November 30, 2000, we set a one-day record of 188,851 visits to our Web site and $2 million in revenues (about the same as my first year with the company in 1960). The Web was growing, 69 percent greater than the prior year. We had put an entirely new site online in 1999 and we gave it a major facelift two years later. This included a simpler design to make navigation easier, faster, and more intuitive. The content was closely coordinated with our catalog mailings and retail displays. The site had a more efficient search engine to find products (with more information than before), and customer services such as "Explore the Outdoors" information. It also included a new "L.L.Bean Traveler" mini-site complete with travel products, information (for instance, good travel shoes), tour companies, packing and travel tips (e.g., packing a carry-on), and links to the Weather Channel, Centers for Disease Control, and the State Department's travel warnings.

Although it did not come out of our Strategic Review, the notion of e-commerce as being synergistic to our other channels did. E-commerce was seen as an integral part of our newly emerging multichannel strategy.

We had always had excellent vendor relationships, but we had too many vendors. Within two years after starting our cost of goods sold (COGS) initiative in 1998 we went from sixty knit vendors, for instance, to six. We were able to negotiate better costs by making longer-term commitments, better quality control by being in the factories more often, and more reliable delivery times by having much-improved communications. By 2000 our success with reducing COGS ($30 million in savings) more than justified the entire Strategic Review effort, and there was more to come.

We had fully staffed and hardworking sourcing offices in Hong Kong (fifty-four people) and in Costa Rica (twenty-nine people). They were all part of L.L.Bean and our way of doing things. Our Costa Rican staff used several of their team days in the spring of 2001 to climb Mt. Chirripo, Costa Rica's highest peak at 12,533 feet. Nearly 25 percent of Costa Rica is protected as national parks, and our staff subsequently volunteered their time to support their wonderful outdoor resources. They were proud to introduce L.L.Bean values to Costa Rica.

CHRIS MCCORMICK: To this day [sourcing] was probably the most successful thing that came out of the Strategic Review. Today maybe 20 percent of our items are made in the [United States], and the rest are offshore . . . We needed to really learn quickly about vendors located in different countries, the quotas and all those tariffs, and everything about bringing product in here and we did that very quickly. The cost of goods initiative was probably the single biggest reason the year 2000 was as successful as it was. That's when our business really turned around. It wasn't so much sales growth that drove the performance of that year, it was improving margins that improved profitability of that year.

Prior to our sourcing initiative we were overly committed to long-term vendor relationships and slow to confront vendor performance issues. Several vendors were nonperforming on human rights standards, and we terminated one. Then a second and a third. Soon we began receiving calls and letters from all of our vendors telling us the actions they were taking to comply with our standards. And we've never again had significant resistance. We also found that those who do meet our highest human rights standards are the same ones that meet our highest quality, reliability, and delivery standards.

JOHN OLIVER: Since the movement to offshore we've been out front in a leadership role on the human rights monitoring, ensuring that we're not just going into undeveloped countries, grabbing the cheapest producer of products, and ignoring the conditions under which the labor is treated that's producing those products. That's all part of the stakeholder concept. You can do a cost/benefit analysis of whether any of these programs make sense or not, but most companies have come belatedly to the concept that they are necessary and important to pay attention to. We didn't spend much time analyzing it, we just did it, and the stakeholder concept is what tells us that's the right thing to do.

We began implementing the new organizational structure in July 1998, and it was staffed and in place by January 1999. We allowed a transition period through August 1999 before fully changing over to the new SBUs.

Until you go through this kind of organizational change, it's hard to grasp the work and complexity involved. It was enormous—the changes in accountabilities, decision-making authority, and transfer of knowledge, the physical changes in offices and operating areas, and the need for new job descriptions, inventory policies, new incentive systems, feedback sessions, and systems support. While doing all of this, we still had to run the business. It was like retrofitting your car's engine while doing 70 MPH on the Maine Turnpike.

The SBU structure increased accountability at the unit level, something we wanted, and we developed an elaborate and focused balanced scorecard for each of the thirteen SBUs. Unfortunately accountability for profit margins encouraged our SBU leaders to be more like general managers—overly focused on profits—than like empowered merchants striving for growth.

As a result, demand increases were not sufficient to overcome the costs of increased complexity and anticipated redundancies. In addition, corporate competencies in direct marketing and inventory management were diminished, and we had been world-class in those critical areas.

We began recentralizing the organization in the fall of 2001. The SBU organization was an exercise the company had to go through. We tried it and everybody agreed it wasn't working. We had tested and exceeded the limits of empowerment to everyone's satisfaction. In the process, many people emerged as good businesspeople and leaders who otherwise wouldn't have had the opportunity to show their strengths. We didn't return the organization to where it was before the SBU experiment. Instead, it became more participative, with more real accountability and autonomy than before.

BRAD KAUFFMAN: In the SBU world, you had folks who could see all the way across processes to outcomes. That line of sight to outcomes, I think, helped create a sense of ownership, and with a sense of ownership came a sense of accountability. And I think that perspective stays with you, so when you move back into a functional organizational structure, you're still more oriented towards outcomes as opposed to process. You feel viscerally more connected to results. I think that endures. A lot of the folks who had that experience are now in positions to be influential, and so I think other folks, who have come to the company since then, watch and learn, and tend to emulate the sorts of behaviors they see.

An ongoing theme at L.L.Bean throughout the decade was the effort to communicate our brand values and unique positioning in a compelling and up-to-date manner. The theme at various times was called "Selection for Me," "Merchandising Leadership," "Be More Bean," and "Brand Positioning." These initiatives were all about communicating the relevance of L.L.Bean in our catalogs and advertising, in our products and services, and in our various business channels.

Chris McCormick, then our director of advertising and direct marketing, led our first initiative in the early 1990s to develop a new communications strategy to be consistently applied in our catalogs, magazine advertising, retail store, telephone contacts, and public relations. We began with a common positioning statement: "L.L.Bean provides durable, functional products that let you pursue your personal relationship with the outdoors." To add meaning, depth, and human characteristics we developed a personality profile ("honest, dependable and trustworthy; humble; wise, outdoorsy," etc.) to guide our channel leaders in executing our positioning in all of our customer contacts. The attributes reflected traditional L.L.Bean straight from the L.L. story and provided a common guide in our relationships with our customers and, for that matter, all of our stakeholders.

It was our feeling that a brand is more than a selling proposition or marketing device. It should be the embodiment of all that the company stands for. We set up a Communications Steering Committee to better align our communications of the L.L.Bean personality across our catalogs, our stores, and our Web site. We paid a lot of attention to how our customers perceived the consistency of our positioning as well as our service execution in all these channels. From the best that we could determine, all the channels felt like L.L.Bean and delivered comparable satisfaction.

In 1998 another major research effort was conducted to update and verify the key elements of our overall brand identity. The research was designed to give baseline results for the various brand attributes that we would track in subsequent years. We talked to current and prospective customers by conducting surveys and focus groups. We looked at our brand imagery versus the competition's to identify the relative importance of our brand attributes from our customers' perspective.

Positive associations with L.L.Bean were "Company I can trust"; "Excellent customer service"; "Cares about its customers"; "Sells high-quality items"; "Good value for the money"; and "Good for outdoor items." We were pleased to have validated what we considered our core values. But our old problems continued. We were not seen as "Exciting," "Modern and up-to-date," or "Innovative." Again, this was not news but clearly defined issues that required a response.

Our overall strategy, as you might expect, was to reinforce our reputation for excellent customer service; high-quality items; and products for people who enjoy the outdoors. We hoped to augment being exciting and up-to-date and having channels that are fun to shop from.

Our formal brand positioning statement, including L.L.'s Golden Rule and our core values as well as our aspirational attributes, was reprinted on salmon-colored poster paper, framed, and posted in every common area in the company. We wanted to reemphasize the importance of all of us living the L.L.Bean values every day.

The brand positioning exercise was an important contribution to our "L.L.Bean Corporate Strategy" document, which we updated in 2000–2001. It was an updated compendium of what I felt were significant company beliefs, policies, and practices that had evolved over the years since L.L.'s time. The tome (ninety-five pages in all) begins with the L.L. story and goes on to the purpose statement and corporate values (including our stakeholder concept), our strategic positioning (L.L.Bean persona and brand positioning, business model, target markets, and Best strategy), and our strategic directions.

The latter part, which I called our "Platform for Growth," consisted of four overarching strategies. They weren't initiatives in themselves but rather a framework for developing initiatives. The four categories would help us in prioritizing one initiative versus another and in making sure we weren't neglecting an area crucial to our continued growth and vitality.

- *Enhance the L.L.Bean brands.* This included leveraging our current product brands and developing new-product opportunities compatible with L.L.Bean values.

- *Achieve competence and scalability as a multichannel retailer.*
  We wanted to be easily accessible to our customers when,
  where, and how they wanted to shop.

- *Achieve predictable and sustainable sales and profit growth.*
  This was necessary in order to fulfill and satisfy the financial
  expectations of our stakeholders.

- *Reinforce our commitments to our stakeholders.* This meant being
  a great place to work, being a great partner with our vendors,
  and being a great corporate citizen in our various communities.

Somebody commented that our strategies after the update still
sounded a lot like the old model. They did. The senior team continued
to believe that the essence of the model was still right. And we had
many initiatives in place, including those that had emerged from our
Strategic Review. What was going to be different was that this new and
improved model was going to have to work without me. It had to be a
viable business model, not Leon-centric, driven by an organization staffed
with new people, new energy, and new ideas.

The Platform for Growth provided me the exit opportunity to step
down from day-to-day management of the business. I'd been with Bean
nearly forty years, and it was time to think about retirement. I had not
reached the point, as L.L. did, of getting three meals a day and not wanting four, and I had no intention of hanging on that long.

I'd started as a novice in the 1960s, learning everything I could, and
had become an entrepreneur in the late 1960s and 1970s. It had been
great being a committee of one—a hands-on merchant—and enjoying
the excitement of rapid growth. The 1980s continued the rapid growth
but with professional management and lots of delegation. My role became more strategic although still close to the merchandising. A lot of
ups and downs came with the 1990s, and complexity with all the new
initiatives. With Total Quality I empowered myself out of any hands-on
activity, and I focused on the next generation of L.L.Bean.

The cumulative effect of the stresses and strains was getting to me. I
didn't have the energy I used to, even though I still worked out daily.
I believed in the L.L.Bean concept as much as ever, but I wasn't leading

it as well as I knew how, and I knew it. It wasn't fair to L.L.Bean to have a president who wasn't fully energized and not doing his best every day for whatever reason.

The Strategic Review was a way to start the process of positioning the company to allow for my retirement. It allowed us not only to update the corporate strategies in relation to what we saw ahead but also to assess our management team members as they engaged in various parts of the review.

There was never any talk of selling the company, at that time or any prior time. I had long ago decided for myself that family ownership was the best ownership format for L.L.Bean. The family had pretty much left me alone to run the company, and I liked it that way. We'd had many opportunities to be acquired or suggestions to go public, but I saw more constraints and threats to our concept than opportunities in those ownership arrangements.

In the early 1990s we retained some consultants with expertise in family companies and their unique issues. We convened the family owners on a quarterly basis for several years to better understand the alternatives to family ownership. There was a lot of good discussion and family learnings about L.L.Bean and the responsibilities of ownership. The family ultimately adopted a resolution at the 1993 shareholders' meeting in which they concluded that the retention of private family ownership by the descendents of L.L.Bean offered the greatest benefits to the company and its shareholders. The primary motivations were to achieve sensible investment performance and to preserve company values. There was no family member qualified to succeed me, but it was clear my successor should be committed to the L.L.Bean culture and trusted by the family.

In the late 1990s, Lee Surace and I often talked about the succession process. (Lee was now our chief financial officer as well as a longtime and trusted colleague.) We both felt that the time was at hand. We talked about various internal candidates and ways to begin the process. We picked the May 2001 shareholders' meeting as the date to complete our search process and to announce our selection. We both agreed not to retire until we'd made a successful transition. (Lee was instrumental to the success of the transition but regrettably did not live to see its conclusion.)

We included in our discussions our attorney, George Isaacson, and a board member, Lin Bell, who had been for many years the managing partner of our auditing firm. This was our "Screening" Committee (to mask the exercise), and George was chairperson. George and Lin would make sure we did the job right and with no foot-dragging.

GEORGE ISAACSON: An obvious question, and one that all members of the committee were comfortable posing to Leon, was, "Are you really going to be able to step back? Are you going to allow a new president of the experience and stature that we're looking for to be able to run the company? Or are you going to find that difficult?" There are certainly many stories out in America where founders have not handled succession well and were not able to release the reins to a chief executive officer. I was impressed that Leon was not only very open in discussing that issue but even said, "I'm not sure. I believe I can." He said he was eager to continue to be involved in Bean and to have a mentoring responsibility and a role in continuing to represent the interests of the family. And he said there were other things he wanted to do in his retirement. But he also said, "I'll have to see."

In early 2000 we had a work plan that included governance issues to be dealt with. The company bylaws, for instance, did not provide for a chairman of the board, which was to be my post-transition role. We also needed an executive search firm to assist in our search for a candidate, whom we expected to come from within the company and to be comfortable in our environment. But we wanted the search firm to validate our selection compared to outside possibilities. The plan called for developing criteria for identifying potential candidates, compensation, the family's role and stakeholder communications, the timing of the transition steps, confidentiality needs, and publicity plans on completion.

We selected a search firm in the late spring, and it did a thorough and thoughtful study of our internal candidates as well as several possible outside candidates. We had a winner.

During the spring of 2001 we completed meetings with the Bean family members to discuss our succession proposal, to answer their questions, and to assure them of the future prosperity of L.L.Bean. We got their support for the May board meeting vote. Our committee's recommendations were subsequently well received and our board voted its approval in May.

The May 21, 2001, *Bean Bulletin* headline read, "Leon Becomes Chairman of the Board; Chris McCormick Named L.L.Bean's President." Our board of directors had voted this change two days earlier. The transition had been in the works by then for more than two years, but our usually all-knowing grapevine had failed to pick it up. It was a surprise to everyone.

Chris was the first non-family member to be president and run L.L.'s company. In his mid-forties, he'd started at L.L.Bean eighteen years earlier as assistant advertising manager, and subsequently had been promoted through a variety of advertising and direct marketing positions; in 1994 he'd become senior vice president of the marketing department. In the early 1990s Chris had been instrumental in launching our international business and, in the mid-1990s, our e-commerce channel, as well as our very successful credit card program.

Chris had always been highly regarded as a direct marketer both within L.L.Bean and throughout the catalog industry. As part of the SBU reorganization in 1998, he became general manager of our women's business and in 2001 our chief operating officer. To further broaden his management and leadership skills he attended Harvard's Advanced Management Program in 2000. Chris took full advantage of these growth opportunities, and by the time our succession committee got into action he was seen by everyone as one of the top company leaders.

Following the announcement, Chris told our leadership group, "Not a lot will change; we're on the right track and last year [2000] proved that, with a record year for sales and profit." Most important, Chris said, "L.L.Bean customers and the community will continue to see a company with a unique set of values, committed to quality products, excellent customer service, and our outdoor heritage. The company will also continue to provide a work environment that demonstrates respect for people. I am personally very committed to these values."

Chris was off to a good start. We weren't looking for a turnaround person. We wanted someone committed to L.L.Bean and our stakeholder model, someone who would bring new energy, new ideas, and new discipline to the execution of our overarching strategies.

The announcement was well received by L.L.Bean employees and our community. Uncertainty about L.L.Bean's future leadership was resolved, and people who knew Chris were especially pleased with his selection. My staying on as chairman was reassuring, I hoped. Over the next several weeks we held town meetings in all parts of the company to discuss the succession in detail, to discuss our future prospects and plans, and to respond to any related concerns. Maine Governor Angus King proclaimed June 5 and 6 Leon Gorman Days in the state of Maine. Later in June our employees put together a "grassroots" potluck party at our Fogg Farm facility outside Freeport. More than seven hundred people showed up to show their appreciation for my forty-year tenure at L.L.Bean. It was most gratifying. I had the chance to talk and shake hands with everyone who attended, the people who had supported me and the company so well and for so long.

Chris had a full agenda to deal with. We had completed a rigorous review of our business model over the past several years. An array of strategic initiatives had been undertaken to position L.L.Bean for the new century. We had the Platform for Growth and we had new leadership to grow it. In addition to Chris's emergence as our new company leader, we'd developed a whole new team of talented and energetic senior managers and unit leaders, all of them committed to L.L.Bean values and to moving L.L.Bean forward—especially Chris, who, following his succession, sent me a note saying, "I won't let you down."

BOB PEIXOTTO: If you look at the top group today it's me, Chris, who both started twenty-two and twenty-one years ago, Mark Fasold, who was the boss who hired me when I started at L.L.Bean. He spent about seventeen years here, went away for ten years, and then came back. Ed Howell, who ran half of merchandising here for about ten years, went away, ran another company, and then came back. And then Fran Philip, who's been here for twelve years or so. So Leon's own have come back to roost and it seems to be working, the people he brought up.

One of my theories about why people from the outside didn't work was that Leon was trying to do something different and very special here and without the background and the upbringing steeped in L.L.'s Golden Rule and everything in the corporate strategy document, the corporate purpose statement. Without having grown up in all of that, it's a little hard to get your mind around it. Most of American business—I got this when I went to Harvard's AMP program—is managed to maximize value to the shareholders. Fundamentally that's the role of American business that most business schools teach. That's not Leon's philosophy. Leon didn't just run this company to make a buck. Leon ran this company to deliver shared value to six different stakeholder groups and to create an institution respected in the state and in the nation. It's a whole different set of drivers and a whole different set of decision-making criteria there than it is just to try to maximize value for the shareholder. And I think that's the fundamental difference and one of the things people coming in from the outside have a hard time wrapping their mind around and having the right instincts with.

A professor at a well-known business school, studying L.L.Bean in the 1990s, stated in his classroom material, "L.L.Bean (the person and company) had strong convictions which were consistent and congruent across the board. These values were more than company [mottoes]; they were brought to life in the company through tangible actions and policies. The company has grown and prospered through maintaining these values over the decades and in the face of many changes to the company, economy and market place."[1] A good summation!

In November 1999, the *Wall Street Journal* wrote, "The greatest century in entrepreneurial history is at a close."[2] The article went on to discuss the unmatched innovation, technological advancement, and competitive zeal of the past 100 years. The *Journal* picked ten of the people they thought had the most influence on entrepreneurship in the twentieth century "and possibly for long after."

There, with the likes of Henry Ford, Sam Walton, and Bill Gates, stood L.L. He was recognized for helping to spearhead what is now the

$1.3 trillion direct marketing industry, for redefining customer service with his unprecedented 100 percent money-back guarantee, and for personalizing the catalog shopping experience. The L.L. story was alive and well.

I wouldn't argue with the *Journal*'s characterization of L.L.'s accomplishments, but its writers, I think, missed what the professor had seen: it was a commitment to values, and not the Bean Boot itself or anything else tangible, that was L.L.'s great idea and that earned him a place among those worthies.

> DAVID GARVIN: The best thing that Leon did, the first thing he did, was he stayed true to the vision, and there's a real vision in his company, and it's distinctive. The second is that he knew how to enact that brand of values in product service. There is a perfect alignment between what the company stands for and what it has historically delivered for this product and service. The third thing, and I don't think he was given enough credit for it, he built an extraordinary organization and management machinery. Whether it was the strategic planning, the metrics that they used, the customer service, and telephone systems, those are all systemic properties. While he didn't always build them personally, he had oversight responsibilities. That's an extraordinary achievement. And then he attracted some very talented people, many of whom stayed. So if you add those up, that's four really significant accomplishments, and they all happened on his watch. I give him enormous credit for that.

The values and the essence of the L.L.Bean brand have been talked about and debated over the years and have been formalized in more recent ones. The lessons L.L. learned from his experience we now express as the company's core values:

- *Outdoor heritage:* The enduring worth of our natural environment and the physical and spiritual value of the outdoors experience; the state of Maine.

- *Integrity:* The physical quality of our products; telling the truth; and guaranteeing satisfaction 100 percent; L.L.'s Golden Rule.

- *Service:* Treating customers like human beings with the best, personal service we would all like to receive; and meeting all of our responsibilities to our employees, owners, and communities.

- *Respect:* Respect for all people involved in our enterprise and trusting them to be honest and straightforward; valuing their talents and points of view.

- *Perseverance:* L.L.Bean is in it for the long term; in good times and bad we will not yield in our values.

Values are fine. But it's what you do with them that counts, to borrow from Robert Frost. And Bean people at all levels have always done a lot with them. Role models in the exercise of L.L.Bean values are found throughout the company. It's the kind of leadership we recognize at our annual Bean's Best celebration. Winners of this award (a dozen or so each year) represent the core values of our enterprise and exemplify the positive cultural momentum that continually reinforces and strengthens L.L.Bean by day-in, day-out execution. People truly are the source of vitality, of progress, and of goodness in this and any organization.

One of our service managers, a Bean's Best and a veteran of twenty-seven years, credits her commitment to her first supervisor, who, in turn, learned hers in L.L.'s era. A customer from Alabama wrote, "L.L.Bean has a wonderful culture—at least to me, your customer. I *trust* L.L.Bean. I am confident I will get value and quality. And if I'm not pleased, I trust you will make it right." And it's all part of the legacy that generations of Bean people have passed on to their successors.

People have asked me what I learned over the forty years of my tenure at Bean. Much of it's here. I don't know whether it's a lot or a little. If the latter, I also learned a lot about hiking and biking and fly-fishing and cross-country skiing and more. I believe in L.L.Bean.

People have also asked me what L.L. would think if he knew what we'd done with his company over the years. He's probably spinning in his grave about some things, but otherwise I think he'd be pleased that we made his name synonymous with good merchandise, the best service, and the outdoors; that we've treated all of our stakeholders with respect, like human beings; and that we kept the faith and lived the L.L. story.

Epilogue

ROADS NOT TAKEN. (Frost again.) In 1991, our longtime competitors, Lands' End and Eddie Bauer, surpassed L.L.Bean in net sales. Lands' End had stayed with the catalog business model and its focus on casual and dressy apparel. Eddie Bauer had dropped its outdoors products in favor of casual apparel and converted to a retail model, with several hundred stores in various shopping malls. L.L.Bean had stayed with its outdoors lifestyle mix of active and casual products and with its catalog business model. We opened our first retail store outside Maine in 2000. In 2002, Sears bought Lands' End and, in turn, was merged into Kmart. In 2003, Eddie Bauer and its parent, the Spiegel Company, filed for bankruptcy.

When I retired in 2001, L.L.Bean's sales were $1.2 billion and we achieved a return on equity of 18.5 percent. These good results were largely due to Chris McCormick, our new chief executive, and his exceptional team of talented and committed senior managers. They all had spent their formative leadership years with L.L.Bean and were very comfortable in our unique cultural environment. They liked the L.L.Bean concept and were proud to be part of it.

Among their early tasks following my retirement was the management of the various initiatives that had come out of our Strategic Review in the latter part of the 1990s.

The sourcing project was a success from its beginning and continued to account for substantial savings, while improving product quality and delivery. Chris and his team shut down Freeport Studio in 2002 for the reasons I've mentioned, primarily insufficient growth and problems with brand consistency. We did learn what's involved with starting up a new business, and a lot about the limits of the L.L.Bean brand. The retail expansion was temporarily halted after the third store was built in 2001. It was clear the company needed to learn more about retail logistics and to develop the necessary retail systems prior to further expansion. Two new retail sites are scheduled to open in 2006.

Chris and his team also began unwinding the SBU reorganization to a more centralized structure and strategy in late 2001. The company had learned the cons as well as the pros of entrepreneurial autonomy. It's an idiosyncratic approach that simply doesn't fit with the collaborative and disciplined approach an organization of any size requires. The reorganization did introduce a new element of accountability into the Bean culture and what it took to manage to a P&L. The SBU organization also brought our best merchandising talent to the fore and illustrated vividly the need for a more focused and coordinated approach to merchandising. Finally, many people emerged who otherwise wouldn't have had the opportunity to show their managerial strengths.

We gained sufficient experience and knowledge from all the initiatives, the successful and the less so, to more than justify the entire effort. In fact, I believe the initiatives, along with all our other efforts through the 1990s, including TQ, transformed the company. A new leadership group came forward. The company culture changed in important and beneficial ways. L.L.Bean emerged from the 1990s as no longer Leon-centric. It no longer depended on my daily leadership, my conception of "the L.L. story," or my acting as chief merchant.

After my retirement, I became a true chairman or, at least, my version of what a board chairman was supposed to be. I advise Chris and act as intermediary between him and the board of directors. I do Chris's performance assessment and I review overall strategies with him. I spend between a half day and a full day a week at the company, using a small corner office I took over after Chris moved into the president's office.

Of course, I see and chat with people informally when I come in and out of the office, but I play no management role in the operations of L.L.Bean. I continue to attend the blue book meetings where products are presented and discussed, but I don't play an active role at all in the merchandising. If I have anything to say, I pass it on to Chris. It's a very passive role.

Outside the company I'm on the governor's Land for Maine's Future board. We provide funding to various conservation land trusts to set aside areas of ecological and recreational importance. Every Wednesday morning I work in a soup kitchen, the Preble Street Resource Center in Portland, serving breakfast. Lisa and I recently played a role in defeating a statewide referendum that would have allowed casino gambling in Maine. We travel. We hike and bike and ski and fish and hunt, both in Maine and around the world. We have five grown children living throughout the United States, four very busy grandchildren, and one lovely springer spaniel who can smell a grouse at a hundred yards. No complaints.

Chris and his team have L.L.Bean back on a growth curve. In the current year (2006) they're anticipating sales of $1.45 billion and an ROE of 18.4 percent and a very strong balance sheet. Sourcing, e-commerce, and Bean's private label credit card continue to generate growth and profitability, along with superior management and merchandising and an increasingly relevant L.L.Bean assortment of products.

Using our 1998 research results as a baseline, the company periodically polls customers to find out how we're doing on key brand attributes. The latest results show that Chris and his team have maintained our 90 percent and 87 percent ratings in customer service and product quality. That is, 90 percent and 87 percent of customers "strongly agree" that Bean's customer service and product quality, respectively, are superior. You realistically can't get much higher. Chris and his team have also significantly improved our scores in the other brand attributes—product relevance, outdoor heritage, and price/value—from the low 60s to the low 70s, a very respectable performance. Our brand and our values are in good hands.

We first started collecting demographic and attitudinal information on our customers in the mid-1970s. About two-thirds were from the Northeast and Middle Atlantic states. In the late 1990s this proportion had diminished to about half our customer base. But we were still a Northeastern company with a Maine-based heritage, which has shaped our values and oriented our brand. Some felt it was limiting, but I liked the strong relationship people saw between L.L.Bean and Maine, as opposed to competitors that didn't have a strong sense of place.

One of our governors once said (actually, it was Governor John McKernan, and he said it on two occasions), "Is Maine Maine because of Bean, or is Bean Bean because of Maine?" Our character and values are the same, he added. We're "an incredible matched set." I am very proud of our strong identification with Maine.

At our annual planning event on June 19, 1991, I said this in regard to the three-year plan we were working on then:

> I hope in 1994, people will say that, in addition to renewing our competitive advantage, we had the courage to maintain our values and our integrity; that we have defined our own business and not been defined by others; that we have fulfilled our responsibilities to all of our stakeholders; and that we continue to care enough to treat our customers, and each other, as human beings.

I renew these hopes for Chris and his team and for all their years with L.L.Bean. And I wish them every success.

Voices

T HE FOLLOWING is an alphabetical listing of the people I have quoted in callouts throughout the book.

For the L.L.Bean employees, I have also included their approximate employment dates and last job titles.

Andy Beahm, 12/6/82–present, assistant treasurer

Jessie Beal, 2/1/43–6/15/77, Carl's assistant and office manager

Bucky Bucklin, 8/20/52–6/4/89, manager of maintenance

Ron Campo, 1/2/79–1/16/87, vice president of product development

Mel Collins, 1/1/44–4/1/74, assistant clothing buyer and company
   photographer

Idalyn Cummings, 10/10/44–6/15/80, mailroom supervisor

Wes DeVries, marketing consultant

Russ Dyer, Jr., 6/22/81–12/30/94, manager of security

Bill End, 7/1/75–9/14/90, executive vice president

Mark Fasold, 12/5/77–12/31/91, 3/19/01–present, senior vice president
   and chief financial officer

John Findlay, 11/22/76–2/28/92, senior vice president of operations

Sandy Fowler, owner of Dingley Press

David Garvin, professor and business consultant

Barbara Bean Gorman, L.L.'s daughter and Leon's mother

Lisa Gorman, Leon's wife

Voices

Tom Gorman (John), 6/28/50–5/29/92, Leon's brother and head of logistics

John Gould, Maine author and good friend of L.L.

Wid Griffin, 9/1/35–5/25/79, vice president of operations

Shailer Hayes, 5/14/56–12/31/74, chief accountant

Bill Henry, 8/18/75–5/20/83, vice president of advertising and direct marketing

George Isaacson, company attorney

Irving Isaacson, company attorney

Brad Kauffman, 4/18/88–present, senior vice president of strategic planning and new business development

Jim Mahoney, industrial psychologist

Nancy Marston, 8/4/69–7/4/97, manager of order processing

Chris McCormick, 6/20/83–present, president and CEO

Joe Murray, 6/15/66–7/1/92, manager of security and grounds

John Oliver, 11/23/92–present, vice president of public affairs

Bob Peixotto, 8/3/82–present, senior vice president and chief operations officer

Art Perry, 7/1/72–9/7/74, merchandising manager

Fran Philip, 11/21/94–present, senior vice president and chief merchandising officer

K. C. Putnam, 7/12/70–1/17/76, hard goods buyer

Tom Sidar, 10/27/75–3/1/04, chief merchandising officer

Toby Soule, 4/6/82–5/3/96, copywriter

Helen Stilkey, 9/1/60–1/11/85, Leon's administrative assistant

Lee Surace, 10/5/70–3/18/01, senior vice president and chief financial officer

Don Williams, 9/12/49–6/11/74, salesroom manager

Ethel Williams, 7/7/35–3/31/75, L.L.'s assistant and advertising manager

Notes

Chapter 1

1. Quoted in L.L. Bean, *My Story,* 1st ed. (Freeport, ME: Dingley Press, 1960), 9.
2. Tom Mahoney and Leonard Sloane, *The Great Merchants: American's Foremost Retail Institutions and the People Who Made Them Great* (New York: Harper & Row, 1966).
3. Ibid.
4. Sam E. Connor, "Outdoor Sports Are Both Business and Hobby to L.L. Bean, Freeport," *Lewiston Evening Journal,* May 19, 1945.
5. Arthur Bartlett, "The Discovery of L.L. Bean," *Saturday Evening Post,* December 14, 1946.
6. Ibid.
7. Ibid.
8. Dan Callanan, "Sportsmen Know L.L. Bean, Master Salesman by Mail," *Sales & Marketing Management,* September 1, 1955.

Chapter 2

1. "U.S. Business, Retail Trade, What No One Else Has As Good As," *Time,* December 7, 1962, 89.
2. L.L. Bean, *My Story,* 1st ed. (Freeport, ME: Dingley Press, 1960), 51.
3. John Gould, interview by Toby Soule, tape recording, Friendship, ME, August 19, 1981.

Chapter 3

1. Arthur Bartlett, "The Discovery of L.L. Bean," *Saturday Evening Post,* December 14, 1946.
2. Paul J. Bringe, *Direct Mail Briefs from Bringe,* 1966.
3. Charles Leighton and Frank Tucker, "L.L.Bean, Incorporated," Case 9-366-013 (Boston: Harvard Business School, 1965).
4. "U.S. Business, Salesman," *Time,* February 17, 1967, 90.

Chapter 4

1. Stanley J. Fenvessy, *Fenvessy on Fulfillment: The Catalog Executive's Guide* (Stamford, CT: Catalog Age Publishing Corporation, 1988).

Chapter 5

1. Nat Ross, *Fact Book on Direct Marketing* (New York: Publications Division, Direct Marketing Association, 1984).
2. Berkeley Rice, "The L.L. Bean Mystique," *Boston Magazine,* September 1973, 75.
3. J. D. Reed, "In a Happy Hunting Ground," *Sports Illustrated,* December 11, 1972, 48.
4. Berkeley Rice, "The L.L. Bean Mystique."
5. Thomas Ehrich, "Homey Hustlers, Down-East Look Helps Maine Outdoors-Store Build National Business," *Wall Street Journal,* December 5, 1973.
6. Richard Goldstein, "The Best Undershirts in Christendom," *Village Voice,* September 7, 1972.

Chapter 6

1. P. H. Thurston, "L.L.Bean, Inc. 1974 1," Case 9-676-014 (Boston: Harvard Business School, 1975).
2. Boy Scouts of America, *Boy Scouts of America: The Boy Scout Handbook,* 11th ed. (Boy Scouts of America, 1998).
3. Elaine Shannon, "Maine's L.L. Bean—Sports Good Supplier for the Whole World," *Boston Sunday Globe,* June 15, 1975, 25.
4. "10 Great Stores," *Daily News Record,* March 8, 1976.

Notes

Chapter 7

1. John F. Childs, *Corporate Finance and Capital Management for the Chief Executive Office and Directors* (Upper Saddle River, NJ: Prentice-Hall, 1979).

2. George A. Steiner, *Strategic Planning: What Every Manager Must Know* (New York: The Free Press, 1979); Peter F. Drucker, *Management: Tasks, Responsibilities, Practices* (New York: Harper and Row, 1973); and Peter F. Drucker, *The Practice of Management* (New York: Harper and Row, 1954).

Chapter 8

1. Laurence Shames, "The Maine Line, How L.L. Bean Sprouted From a Yankee's Ingenuity," *Gentlemen's Quarterly*, 1981, 212.

2. John Hughes, "L.L. Bean Comes Through," *Christian Science Monitor*, August 9, 1985.

3. Bill Riviere, *The L.L. Bean Guide to the Outdoors* (New York: Random House, 1981).

4. Horace Kephart, *Camping and Woodcraft: A Handbook for Vacation Campers and for Travelers in the Wilderness* (Chattanooga: University of Tennessee Press, 1917).

5. Angus Cameron and Judith Jones, *The L.L. Bean Game & Fish Cookbook* (New York: Random House, 1983).

6. Lisa Birnbach, *The Official Preppy Handbook* (New York: Workman Publishing, 1980).

7. Stephen Koepp, "Selling a Dream of Elegance and the Good Life," *Time*, September 1, 1986, 55–58.

Chapter 9

1. Benjamin DeMott, "Heavy Breathing in Beanland," *New England Monthly*, April 1984, 17.

2. Suzanne McNear, "Annals of Marketing, Part II: L.L. Bean: Putting the Great Outdoors in High Gear," *TWA Ambassador*, March 1990.

3. Michele Salcedo, "The 25 Healthiest Companies to Work For," *Bruce Jenner's Better Health & Living,* April 1986, 69.
4. John McPhee, "A Reporter at Large (The St. John River)," *New Yorker,* May 3, 1976, 43.
5. Consumers Union, Mail-Order Buying, *Consumer Reports,* 1983.
6. Tom Peters and Nancy Austin, *A Passion for Excellence: The Leadership Difference* (New York: Warner Books, Inc., 1985); and Thomas J. Peters and Robert H. Waterman, Jr., *In Search of Excellence: Lessons from America's Best-Run Companies* (New York: Harper & Row, 1982).
7. Consumers Union, Mail-Order Companies, *Consumer Reports,* 1987.

Chapter 10

1. M. R. Montgomery, "'In' from the Great Outdoors, Marketing the L.L. Bean Look," *Boston Globe Magazine,* December 27, 1981, 11.
2. Craig Wilson, "What Hooks 'Em? Service, Sensibility," *USA Today,* June 8, 1987.
3. Cindy Skrzycki, "The Rustic Pitch Pays Off in Catalog Sales for L.L. Bean," *U.S. News and World Report,* March 25, 1985, 61.

Chapter 11

1. David Garvin, *Managing Quality: The Strategic and Competitive Edge* (New York: The Free Press, 1988).
2. Bob Tedeschi, "L.L. Bean Beats the Current by Staying in Midstream," *New York Times,* September 20, 2000.

Chapter 12

1. William C. Symonds, "Paddling Harder at L.L. Bean," *Business Week,* December 7, 1998, 72.
2. Consumers Union, Mail-Order Companies, *Consumer Reports,* 1991; Consumers Union, Mail-Order Shopping, *Consumer Reports,* 1994; and Consumers Union, Mail-Order Shopping, *Consumer Reports,* 1999.

Chapter 14

1. From interviews with Richard Grant.
2. Jeffrey A. Stout, Hilary Stout, and Rodney Ho, "Ten Who Changed the World for Entrepreneurs: During the Past Century, Through Action or Thought, These Lives Have Had a Major Impact on Business," *Wall Street Journal*, November 29, 1999.

Bibliography

Aaker, David A. *Building Strong Brands*. New York: The Free Press, 1996.

Gorman, Leon. *L.L.Bean, Inc.: Outdoor Specialties by Mail from Maine*. Princeton, NJ: Princeton University Press, 1981.

Herzberg, Frederick. "One More Time: How Do You Motivate Employees?" *Harvard Business Review* (January–February 1968).

Kotter, John P. *John P. Kotter on What Leaders Really Do*. Boston: Harvard Business School Press, 1999.

Montgomery, M. R. "In from the Great Outdoors, Marketing the L.L. Bean Look," *Boston Globe Magazine*, December 1981, 11.

Montgomery, M. R. *In Search of L.L. Bean*. New York: New American Library, 1985.

Ogilvy, David. *Confessions of an Advertising Man*. New York: Dell Publishing Co., 1963.

Takeuchi, Hirotaka, and Penny Pittman Merliss. "L.L. Bean, Inc. (C)." Case 9-581-159. Boston: Harvard Business School Press, 1981.

Index

Index

Index

L.L.Bean
Fall 1981

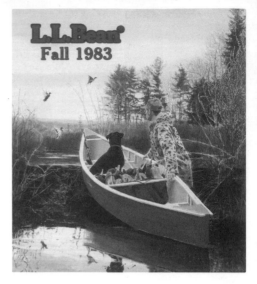

L.L.Bean
Fall 1983

L.L.Bean
Outdoor Sporting Specialties

Spring 1985

L.L.Bean
Outdoor Sporting Specialties

Summer 1987

L.L.Bean
Outdoor Specialties

Fall 1990

L.L.Bean
For the outdoors inside each of us

Christmas 1991